Goin' Down the Road

Mindy,

It has been great sharing a room with you. Between your love of music and Joe's love of the Boys, I hope this gets the pages turned. Good luck with everything and keep on keeping on

Love

Goin' Down

the Road

A Grateful Dead Traveling Companion

BLAIR JACKSON

Harmony Books
New York

This book is dedicated with love to my son, Kyle—may
your life be filled with magic, too

Published by Harmony Books, a division of Crown Publishers, Inc.,
201 East 50th Street, New York, New York 10022. Member of the
Crown Publishing Group.

Random House, Inc. New York, Toronto, London, Sydney, Auckland

HARMONY and colophon are trademarks of Crown Publishers, Inc.

Manufactured in the United States of America

Book design by Debbie Glasserman

Library of Congress Cataloging-in-Publication Data
Jackson, Blair.
     Goin' down the road: a Grateful Dead traveling companion / Blair
Jackson—1st ed.
       p. cm.
     The material in this book was previously published in the
magazine *Golden Road*.
     Includes index.
     1. Grateful Dead (Musical group). 2. Rock musicians—United
States—Biography. I. Title. II. Title: Goin' down the road.
ML421.G72J28 1992
782.42166'092'2—dc20
[B]   92-6714
                                        CIP
                                       MN

ISBN 0-517-58337-2

10 9 8 7 6 5 4 3

Contents

Acknowledgments

Putting out *The Golden Road* magazine has involved so many people through the years that to acknowledge them all here would be impossible. A few should be singled out, however.

My wife, Regan McMahon, has been my partner in crime every step of the way. Not only did she copy edit the entire contents of each magazine, she also participated in a number of the interviews in this book, wrote several articles of her own, and split the layout chores with me through the years. She buoyed my spirits when they were sagging and always managed to keep the chaos in perspective. It's safe to say the magazine (and this book) would not have existed without her.

Special thanks also to Mary Eisenhart, our indefatigable proofreader–circulation czar–cheerleader; Bennett Falk, for his invaluable computer assistance; Pat Jones, who helped us with the look of the magazine; Richard McCaffrey, our darkroom man; and Michelle Spahn and Steve Brown, the two people most responsible for keeping what was basically a loose, disorganized hippie business running efficiently day to day.

We are indebted to the Grateful Dead for putting up with us and even giving us their time; and to the Dead organization for their warm encouragement. Especially helpful were Dennis McNally, who acted as a liaison between the band and the magazine; Danny Rifkin, Jon McIntire, and Cameron Sears, all from the Dead's management; Len Dell'Amico; Eileen Law; Diane Geoppo; Maruska Nelson; Sue Stevens; and Annette Flowers.

At Harmony Books, eternal thanks to my editor, John Michel, for his patience and understanding in the face of the usual procrastination and flakiness; and to his crack staff, especially Laura Barnes.

Preface

From February of 1984 to March of 1991 my wife, Regan, and I put out twenty-five issues of our Grateful Dead fanzine, *The Golden Road*. Maybe you subscribed during that period; about 12,000 people did at one time or another. Or maybe you saw a dog-eared copy at a friend's house after a Dead show one night. Perhaps you heard the name but never saw the magazine. Or, just as likely, all this is news to you. We kept a pretty low profile. This book collects some of the most memorable interviews and stories from those seven years.

When we started *The Golden Road*, the Grateful Dead was still essentially a cult band, albeit one that could sell out a night or two in basketball arenas in most American cities. They hadn't put out a new album in a few years and they were all but ignored by the press, or dismissed as irrelevant Sixties relics. Yet their popularity ballooned with each tour in the mid-1980s, and the network of people trading Grateful Dead concert tapes grew larger.

Then came a fluke event: the Dead actually had a hit single in 1987—"Touch of Grey"—and the band received an unprecedented amount of attention from the media. The Grateful Dead had collided head-on with mainstream America. "We're sort of like the town whore that's become an institution," Jerry Garcia joked in a *Golden Road* interview that summer. "We've finally become respectable."

The Golden Road reported on the changes in Deadland and the problems that the band's increased popularity brought, but the scene was never our main focus. What interested us from the beginning was the music and the transformative quality of the whole Dead experience. Mythologist Joseph Campbell, who'd never been to a rock concert before attending, at the age of eighty, a 1986 Dead show, "got it" immediately—he saw the rapture in the faces of Deadhead dancers and knew that he had stumbled upon a modern-day Dionysian revel. This wasn't just rock 'n' roll—it was an unselfconscious celebration of life manifested in music and dance and community. He later declared that the spirit exemplified by the Dead and their fans represented, in human terms, "an antidote to the atom bomb."

What is it that draws doctors and lawyers and computer software designers and geologists and students and street people together to groove to the Dead? Is it the palpable sense of communion? Is the famous Grateful Dead "X Factor" describable? Where is this juggernaut headed, anyway? I'm not sure we answered any of those questions satisfactorily in the magazine, but with any luck we cast new light on many different aspects of the phenomenon and peeled away a few layers of mystery. In our interviews with the band members, we tried to steer clear of the usual Deadhead sociology questions, and concentrated instead on how each member experienced playing music. Our historical features were always written with an eye toward providing fresh slant on the old stories, as well as on digging up new tales. Ideally, you'll come away from this book with a better sense of who the Grateful Dead are (and have been) and how their unique chemistry has shaped their music.

Alas, what a book like this can't communicate is *The Golden Road*'s magazine-ness. For the first twenty-five issues, it served as an ongoing chronicle of the Grateful Dead world, featuring set lists and show reviews, photography by the best past and current GD photographers, news about the band and the scene, letters from readers, articles on the origins of the Dead's cover songs (most of which are included in this book), and a healthy dose of irreverent humor mocking the Dead and the Deadheads. At its best the magazine reflected some of the energy and unpredictability of a Dead show. And I like to think that it *always* had heart.

Because Regan and I were (and still are) professional journalists, putting out a magazine came fairly naturally to us. We did it because it was fun and because enough people dug it that we wanted to keep doing it for *them*. The magazine became our way of giving something back to the scene that had excited and enlightened us so much through the years. It was hard work, but the spiritual rewards were great. When, after issue number 25, we decided to take a hiatus, it wasn't because we'd lost the spark—we just needed a rest, plain and simple. (We resumed publishing, as an annual, in March 1992.)

We never aspired to be on every newsstand in the country; indeed, we purposely kept *The Golden Road* small in hopes of keeping it manageable. (It almost worked.) But that meant that a lot of Deadheads who might have loved the magazine never saw it, so I'm delighted that through this book the best of *The Golden Road*'s first incarnation can finally reach a wider audience.

"Let the words be yours, I'm done with mine."

For information about *The Golden Road* magazine and current/back-issue orders, send a SASE (Self-Addressed Stamped Envelope) to The Golden Road, 484 Lake Park, #82B, Oakland, CA 94610.

Goin' Down the Road

Garcia in 1988. *(Photo by Jay Blakesberg)*

Garcia

■ ■ ■ ■ ■ ■

Listen to the Music Play

An Interview: October 28, 1988

As Regan and I enter one of the downstairs offices at the Dead's Marin County headquarters to interview Jerry Garcia, someone hands him a copy of that morning's *San Francisco Chronicle*. There on the first page of the "People" section is a drawing of a make-believe postage stamp with his face on it; one of a supposed series of stamps commemorating famous Bay Area people and events. "Oh no!" Garcia says with a mixture of laughter and horror, shaking his head.

"Yeah, you never know where your face is gonna turn up," Regan remarks.

"It's bad enough it turns up on my head every morning!" Garcia replies without missing a beat, and he shakes his head again, chortles gruffly, and takes another sip of cappuccino.

Garcia's humility is real. He gives his "image" about as much thought

1

as he gives his wardrobe (boy, what a cheap shot!) and one senses that even though he is an open and gregarious interview subject, he'd probably be more comfortable talking about any subject other than himself. "I'm not really that interesting," he once told me, as if genuinely surprised that anyone would even want to know about him.

Garcia has been interviewed infrequently the past few years, and most of what he's talked about are specific projects—an album, a video, the rain forests, etc.—or the Grateful Dead phenomenon and all its sociological implications. So this time around we decided to avoid all that and talk instead about *music.* So much for introductory hoo-hah. Take a deep breath and dive in with us.

I'd like to find out a little bit about how you experience a show.
Okay. I see, this is the ultimate demystification process here, right?

Not really, no. But I'd like to sort of go through a show and find out what you're thinking—or not thinking—at various points along the way. What do you do before the show?
Lately I've gotten into hanging out onstage 'cause the back-room scene is too . . . distracting is not exactly the right word; I don't know what. There's something about it I don't like. I don't like to hang out too much backstage unless I'm feeling really sociable, and also feeling very confident.

So I like to go up onstage and play around with my guitar for a long time. Usually, Steve [Parish, his equipment specialist] changes the strings before every show—in fact he always does—and he puts it in approximate tune.

You change strings every show?
You have to. In fact, they don't even last a show. By the end of the night they're dead. They're gone. They're history. Remember, my top string is a ten-thousandth of an inch, which is not a whole lot of diameter. So by the end of the night, there's been so much chemical action on it that it's dull. The overtones are gone from it. You can almost not hear them. It's appalling how easily they just go to pieces. Also the intonation is greatly changed. By the end of the second set my guitar is not playing in tune. On top of all that I use a big, thick pick that deforms the strings.

So, Steve's put the guitar in approximate tune and I sit down with the guitar and stretch the strings out individually for a long time until it's really pretty stable. And that means I can bend strings, do multiple bending and that kind of stuff, and when it comes back it's still relatively in tune. The advent of the new tuning machines has really helped out this process a lot.

All this gives me a chance to warm up. I like to warm up onstage. I have warm-up routines that are purely mechanical; they're not musical at all. They're just "put this finger here, put this finger there," and they're designed to let your fingers relax and your hands loosen up so you have maximum muscle efficiency. That means releasing as much as applying. With the guitar it's articulation more than strength, so I have a whole bunch of little exercises that are designed to make it so my fingers work right. I like to do that for about a half-hour or forty-five minutes, min- imum.

Then I put the guitar down for a while and I just feel the place. Look around, talk a little with whoever is around. But it's quiet there where I am onstage.

This is sort of behind your amps?
Yeah. Steve's got a little cubbyhole for me.

I like to get to a show about two hours before showtime and spend most of my time onstage fooling with my guitar. So that's it for me as far as starting. I'm always experiencing stage fright until we actually start playing; that is to say, I'm nervous and kind of touchy. So I'd just as soon not be around a lot of people, because it's distracting.

Do you generally chat with the other band members during this time?
Sure, because they come up onstage at one time or another, and we all end up onstage, of course. If we're gonna talk, we generally talk right before we go on. Bob hangs out near where I do. We have the guitar corner. Everybody else has got their little quadrant. This has evolved over the years. It's sheltered just enough so that if we have to talk about what we're going to play or something like that, it's easy to do that: Usually, on the first set anyway, Weir and I try to remember which of us went first last show, so it's that ongoing thing. Eventually I hope we can dispense with some of the regular things about our show that have gotten to be so predictable. I don't know whether that'll ever happen or not. It would probably mean us being able to take a long time off.

Why?
Because there's a lot of special material we'd have to learn. It used to be we had material that went in more directions, but the nature of difficult

material is that it's easy to forget. So the things we used to have, which were difficult little passages and changes—like we used to have a jam at the end of "Eyes of the World" that featured some interesting dynamics and tonal things.

"Help on the Way" is another example.
Right. "Help on the Way" has a little complicated riff in there.

Yet you played it great when you brought it back from 1983 to 1985.
Yeah, we'll rehearse it again. [It was revived in the fall of 1989.] It just means we have to rehearse once in a while. But the Grateful Dead doesn't like to rehearse. Ideally, before each tour we'd go in and rehearse for a week or something like that, but sometimes that's hard to do. Everybody's got their own stuff that they're working on and we don't always get around to it. We're lazy, like everybody else.

If we don't do this quickly, by doing a radical change, it'll happen eventually and gradually change, just like the material gradually changes.

So the next thing is we go out onstage. It's time to start. Now you're out in the thing of your individual instrument. So now it's, "Does all my stuff work?" I go through all my effects and see if they're working, and if they're not I scream at Steve. [Laughs] I like for things to be predictable as far as the behavior of my guitar is concerned. I'm basically really conservative. So that's the first thing I do: Is my guitar in tune? Does everything about it work the way it's supposed to? If there's something wrong in there, sometimes I don't get past that, you know what I mean? I don't get out of that place. It's like a board game: DO NOT PASS EFFECTS! [Laughs] 'Cause if that stuff doesn't work I feel stymied.

Okay, once you get to the point where the effects and everything else are working, then it's a matter of how everything else sounds to me. Where I am, I have individual control over a monitor from Brent, so I can turn Brent to whatever level is audible to me and properly in balance. I'm close enough to the drums that I can hear them acoustically. Bob's right next to me, of course. I don't usually have a problem hearing him, but sometimes I do. And Phil is one of those things where I sort of have to build the whole band on how I hear Phil. My relationship has a lot to do with the way Phil and the drums sound to me, so this is subjective. Everyone in the band has similar problem-solving things they have to deal with.

Then there are the vocals, of course. If the vocals are not right for the first song, that usually throws me for three or four songs, because then what I intended to do and what really happened are two different things. I'm caught in this weird conflict and it takes me a while to recover.

About halfway through the first set, if everything is going smoothly, it's really like, "Oh! Okay, let's play some music!" Now I can hear everybody and it starts to be coherent. If not, it's going to be one of those nights—a bad night, a tough night. We can't hear very well, Phil is pissed off because his stuff doesn't work right—that kind of stuff. You're at the next level, which is if anyone is hung up in their world, that's as far as you can go—*their* hang-up.

Are the musical relationships reestablished quickly when you start playing? Do you instantly become the Grateful Dead again?
No, it's a process of rediscovery each time.

Sometimes, though, it seems like it's there from the first note.
That's when everybody feels right and everything sounds great.

Sometimes I'm not able to judge that. That's often a level of judgment I have to disqualify myself on. The nights I like are usually the nights everyone else thinks are boring. So, for me, the thing of playing is tactile and visceral. It has this element that fits into singing, the way it feels. And the way I like it to feel is *effortless*. It's like the times when you remember every joke anybody ever told you, and you're in a conversation and you're hot. [Laughs] It's something like that but more open-ended, obviously, because it's not tied to language or goals. But it has that thing of instant access. You can remember everything. It stops being memory at that point and starts being something else. It starts being synthesis. You're actually inventing, based on everything you know about music, about the guitar, about the Grateful Dead, about the song itself. Each of those things are hierarchies for me. Like I said, I'm really conservative. That means for me the song has the same importance as the band. Each one of these things has its own importance, and when they're all lined up just right then I feel like this is really happening. That's when it seems effortless. Like I say, though, these are the nights that most people find dull or predictable.

But that's because people don't hear me the way I hear myself. For me it's the details that count. It's not the big notes that count, it's the little ones. For me, it's the stuff that I play behind when someone else is singing. It's the way a phrase ends, whether it's graceful—whether it comes in for a landing. The stuff in between is always up for grabs, so

I don't ever judge it. But I do judge how I come out of a near miss. It has to do with grace.

Sometimes you'll come out of a solo and you almost have to chase the notes to catch up.
Right. Sometimes. There's a lot of room for me in the Grateful Dead, so I can go in just about any direction I can dream of, including things that throw everybody else completely off. [Laughs] It just depends on how I feel. So I'm not hung up on how I can move out, but I am concerned with how nice the landing is. To come back on the "one" and make sense to everyone musically—in the moment—is a trick. It's one of those things of being able to play into everybody's expectations, but if the whole band is on they'll hear it in two beats, three beats. I don't have to play like, "I'm circling to land" and it goes on for eight or nine bars. Sometimes it's "Coming in, you guys!" [Laughs]

As you go through a first set, to what degree are your song choices affected by what Weir has just played?
Only in that if he's just played a blues I try not to do one. If he does a song in E, I try not to do a tune in E. In other words, you don't want tunes in the same key after each other if you can avoid it. You try to make it so they're a different feeling. So if he does a slow shuffle in E, I'm not going to follow him with a slow shuffle in E.

Sometimes, though, you think of two or three songs as being sort of thematic, or they build on each other.

I've seen "Masterpiece" and "Bird Song" paired frequently and wondered if there's some connection.
No reason. It's random. I don't even have a song list, which is real stupid. It'd be real helpful for me because I just forget. If I was just a little bit more organized I'd have a printed copy of the songs we do on top of my amplifier so I could look at it. Sometimes Weir does, and sometimes he doesn't. We tend to be habitual. In other words, if there's a formula that works or worked one time, we tend to repeat it and do it to death. It depends on how many shows you go to—you start to think, "These guys sure love this transition. They're doing it *all* the fucking time!"

It used to be that a lot of what we were doing was going from one song into a wholly different kind of song where the transition itself would be a piece of music. Lately it's much less that. It's more that we're able to come up with transitions that are very graceful in a real short amount of time, because we've tried almost everything by now, in terms of going from one kind of thing into another. It's not that the transitional music doesn't exist anymore. It's just that we've worn the pathways.

I think it takes some of the spontaneity out of it if I can guess pretty easily that you're going to go from "I Need a Miracle" into "Dear Mr. Fantasy," for example.

But eventually you know all the music you have, you know what I mean? So even though we have 150 tunes, or 140, or 90, or whatever it is, we know those songs well enough to know the places between them— all the hypothetical places between them—because if we haven't gone from one song to another specifically, we've gone from one *like it* to a song like it. In that sense you start to know what you've got to the extent that there aren't many surprises left. So that's why you have to come up with new material or create new spaces out of which to build new things.

As a player, what is it that makes some of the modules work for you? Like "Goin' Down the Road"–"Miracle"–"Mr. Fantasy" is one you've done a lot recently.

Those work because of graceful key relationships. Those work well because we *picked* them to work well. To me, the interesting ones are the ones that have a lot of interim playing opportunities, like "Estimated Prophet" into "Eyes of the World"—even though that's one we do a lot. They have an interesting key relationship to each other. You can play an E-major seventh scale against the leading F-sharp minor in "Estimated Prophet" without changing a note. So it's the same intervals exactly; it's just in different places on the scale. That makes it so you can play through a lot of places. And while we're making that transition we go from, like, B-minor to C-sharp seventh, to a little E-minor, a little C-major. There are all these possible changes, so that by just changing one or two intervals, all of a sudden they'll work, but sometimes we have to discuss them because they're not all that obvious. It's not obvious what the leading tones are. Also, the rhythmic relationship is very "off." So I can find a pulse in there that'll be just a perfect tempo for "Eyes of the World" regardless of what tempo "Estimated Prophet" was at, and that makes it interesting for me 'cause it's wide open.

Bob tends to not design much in bridging material.

At the Greek Theater, 1986. *(Photo by Ron Delany)*

I was going to ask whether you feel that's your primary responsibility as the lead player.

No, it's just that when I choose to go from one song to another, I like a segue, I like the doorways. Bob doesn't seem to care about them one way or another. A lot of times we'll discuss an idea before the second set, like Weir will say, "Let's do 'Playin' in the Band' into 'Uncle John's Band' into something, something." "Okay, sounds good." And more often than not they tend to chop off, they tend to splice into each other.

You mean if you discuss the sequence in advance the transitions are truncated because the endings are foreseen?

Not necessarily, but if it's a Bob segue—if it's his design—he tends to like them to be like that. We've never really discussed it, but generally speaking I prefer the doorways and he prefers the splices. It just seems to work out that way.

Even so, what we need is a couple of new pieces of open material.

That's what I hear Deadheads saying, too.
But it's not that simple. It can't be anything like any of the stuff we've already got. We've already kind of used up what we've got. I mean when we stopped doing "St. Stephen" we *stopped doing it*—we used it up. We played it.

What makes something "used up"?
When we don't have any more ideas. When we do it and we have nothing new to say.

I guess that would probably be based on some sort of musical judgment most regular fans can't perceive. What makes a song like "Stella Blue" limitlessly interesting to play and "St. Stephen" not?
It's a better song. It's a more graceful song. "St. Stephen" has some real goofy shit in it. [Laughs] It's got little idiosyncrasies and verses that are different from each other, and if you don't remember every bit of it. . . . It's a piece of material that is unnecessarily difficult. It's been made tricky. It's got a bridge in the middle that doesn't really fit in. It's interesting and remains interesting historically because it has a couple of things that work *real* good. But finally, the stuff that doesn't work overpowers the stuff that does work, and the reason it does is just the thing of memory: "Let's see, what verse is this?" They're not interchangeable; you have to do them in order. So in that sense, a song like "St. Stephen" is a cop. It's our musical policeman: If we don't do it the way it wants to go it doesn't work at all. That means it's inflexible. When you get good enough at those kind of pieces, people think, "Wow, that's really far out and open," but that's an illusion. It's just written complicated, which is something you can always do. What we need is material that is authentically open.

"Dark Star" was successful because it was wide open. "The Eleven" was successful because it had a great groove.

It is a groove.
That's right, but you're really stuck in that chord pattern. It wasn't until you break out of the chord pattern . . . We used to go into E-minor out

of that A-D-E thing, which is like "La Bamba." "The Eleven" is like "La Bamba." It really is.

Well, there's a new segue right there!

[Laughs] No . . . well, it could be except that "La Bamba' is a trap too, just like "The Eleven" is, because you're trapped harmonically in this very fast-moving little chord pattern which is tough to play through. It's tough to play gracefully through except for the most obvious shit, which is what I did on "The Eleven." When we went into the E-minor, *then* it started to get weird. We used to do these revolving patterns against each other where we would play eleven against thirty-three. So one part of the band was playing a big thing that revolved in thirty-three beats, or sixty-six beats, and the other part of the band would be tying into that eleven figure. That's what made those things sound like, "Whoa— what the hell is going on?!" [Laughs] It was thrilling. But we used to *rehearse* a lot to get that effect. It sounded like chaos, but it was in reality hard rehearsal.

So the thing is, we need the stuff that lets us play at that edge of chaos, but doesn't require rehearsal, dig? [He chuckles] 'Cause we don't have the energy to rehearse like that. Then, we used to rehearse seven, eight hours a day—when we were youngsters. We needed to have our chops up because we were still all learning our instruments.

The next level of development was when we went to *Blues for Allah*. There, we came up with some very interesting, *other*, alternate ways to invent openness that would be developmental, as well.

Yet those songs were highly constructed, weren't they?

They were up to a certain point. Like I had this one idea that we actually did at the end of "Blues for Allah," the song. The original structural point of that "desert jam" there was that we could either play a single note or an interval of a fifth. You could play them for as long as you wanted to, but any time you heard a four-note chord vertically—see, the bass would be playing one note, Weir would be playing one note, then me and Keith—you could move your note so you'd change the harmonic structure of that chord. Nobody could hold a note more than two bars, or less than a whole note, so that would guarantee the harmonic shifting. It didn't quite work the way I wanted it to, but we did try it in some live jams and sometimes it worked.

My idea was to try to keep that going and then have it go faster and faster or slower and slower, and have the instruments play off the harmonies they would perceive at any given moment. So if Keith heard an E-minor seventh, we could play that until it disappeared. "Here's an E-minor seventh. I'll turn it into an F." It was almost a successful way to introduce the concept of almost no rules.

We still do this some. Mostly, Bob and I do it in the space jams now. With just the two of us it's easier to hear the harmonic content. Now Phil's been joining us lately.

When you hear your playing, say, from 1969—
It's embarrassing to me!

No! Really? Why?
I studied all that stuff to improve what I found embarrassing about my own playing. To me it's the thing of not being in tune a lot of the time.

We called it "endearing" in those days.
Yeah, it might be endearing, but I *meant* to be in tune. [Laughs] I hear what I meant, as opposed to what I actually played. Since then I've been able to pull the two things closer together and it's not as embarrassing for me to listen to myself now. But in ten years it probably will be. . . .

A few of your first-set songs—"Ramble On Rose," "When Push Comes to Shove," "Tennessee Jed"—seem linked somehow rhythmically. They're unlike any style I know of, and I'm curious to learn what their antecedents might be. Where in American music is that stuff coming from?
I haven't the slightest idea. It comes from *all* of American music, I guess. I don't know. They just come out of my mind. I don't know quite where I get them. Sometimes I think, "Yeah, this is kind of like a record I once heard somewhere," but I never find 'em. [Laughs] The rhythms come from my background in rhythm and blues music more than anything else. But they also come from a kind of rhythmically hip country and western style—like Jerry Reed and people like that. Memphis more than Nashville. Some of the old California country and western stuff—old Buck Owens—had some nifty rhythmic ideas in it, as opposed to the old 4/4 stuff, just plunking away. "Tennessee Jed" is a cop from that world, although not consciously and it's not from any specific tune. Just the feel.

Over the course of a set, are you consciously trying to explore a lot of different musical areas?

I like to think I can do that, but I've gotten to the point where I think I need a lot of new tunes. The long-lived ones—I've gotten to the point where I've done them too many times and I either have to get away from them for a while, or retire them and bring in some new ones, or I have to write a whole passel of new ones. I'd probably do that if I wasn't such a *lazy* fuck! [Laughs]

What do you do during the break?

Nothing. I sit onstage and hope it'll get better. I don't really do anything. What the break is for is really just to rest. Playing Grateful Dead music is not easy. It can be really hard. It's *physically* hard. We all need a rest. It used to be we could play all night long, but it's just not that way anymore. That's really time showing its . . . It's grim death gargling at you from every corner! [Laughs]

Do you ever discuss what's gone on in the previous set at the break?

Nah. What's the point? It's over. We never discuss the previous *anything*. We're not likely to do that set again, so what could we learn from discussing it? More often, if something bad happens or something everybody hates, we tend to all blame ourselves. And unless it's something like Weir getting totally upset at the drummers or me getting upset with Phil or any of those kind of things where you think somebody is fucking up *on purpose,* that's just our normal shit. But I can't remember the last time we even fought about anything. We don't *do* it to each other, you know what I mean? It's hard enough just to go out there every night. If we started bashing each other about things we imagine . . .

What happens more often is somebody'll say, "Hey man, that was really good," and you say, "Oh shit, it was horrible." Although the way it tends to be is either we *all* get off or we all *don't* get off. It's rare that one or two of us gets off like crazy and the rest of us hate it. If it's really good, we all usually feel good about it. And that has to do usually with the big picture—if the room sounds really good, whether it's a clear place we're playing in, and all that other stuff.

This last show we played at Shoreline, I felt like I'm just getting to where I'm playing just about as well as I was before my coma. That is to say, having access to everything I know about playing. I'm getting to that point where physically it's as comfortable. It's a special thing— and I can't really explain it—of feeling *there*. Before that, I've been trying

to come back, which is incremental and tiny and probably only percep-
tible to me. So now that I'm back to where I was, I'm looking to improve
from here.

But I'm also going through changes where I'm trying out other kinds
of gear and I'm trying new pickups and stuff. I'm sort of dissatisfied
with my sound right now. I'm not exactly sure why. It's some little
thing.

*You've said that you can point notes in certain directions indoors. What
happens outdoors?*
You don't get that outdoors. For one thing, you don't get the reflections—the reflective walls. You don't hear it the same way. Outdoors
is like a nonacoustic environment. There are no acoustics outdoors. That
makes the experience a lot different. The low end is clearer because there
aren't any huge low-end waves back and forth. Everything is drier sounding because you don't have the secondary and tertiary reflections going
on. That's the big difference.

Do you have a preference between day and night shows?
I prefer night shows.

*Because you don't want to see the audience? Hmmm, I don't mean that
negatively.*
No, I *like* to see the audience. I like day shows for that part of it, but I
like the night. I like the lights.

Do you think it changes the music significantly?
Not really. Maybe a little. I don't know.

*Well, is it easier to play trippy music if you're bathed in purple and
green light than if you're out in the blazing sun with the people in the
front row in your face?*
[Laughs] You know, I don't notice it that much. For me, if I want to
get to a place where it's just music, I close my eyes, whether it's outdoors
or nighttime or whatever. Sometimes visual stuff is distracting, but then
you have the option of closing your eyes and tuning it out. For me,
that's not much of a problem.

Really, each show is different. Sometimes I have a terrible time during
a daytime show and sometimes I have trouble at night. It's really hard

to generalize about it. Same with indoor and outdoor. Those things used to matter more than they do now.

I'd think the range would make it interesting.
It does. I see it more that way now. It used to be that each little change would represent more of a stumbling block. But now it's gotten to where that's no longer the case so much. Either my attitude has changed slightly or I'm ready to accept that things are different in each sort of place. It's one of those things I don't think about much.

For me, playing tends to be right in *here*. [He fingers the air in front of his eyes] It's like unraveling a whole bunch of little knots; it has that kind of quality to it. And then it jumps from that to the last row of the place. 'Cause once you get the knots untied, it's like, "Oh, too much! Now let's see what's going on!" Then your attention takes in everything else. But if you don't get the knots untied, you never get above that level. It's weird how that is. Some shows I never get past the knots. I spend the whole night trying to untie them, and my consciousness never breaks through to the first person out there.

Are there nights when you feel more like a singer than a guitarist?
Yeah, and that's something very recent, too. It's only in the last couple of years that I've started to feel like a singer at all.

Why is that?
I'm *not* a singer. It's as simple as that. [Laughs]

Okay, then why do you feel like one now?
I think I'm starting to *get* to be a singer. I'm learning it. I think it has to do with a feeling of emotional reality when I sing a song: Does it work for me emotionally? At its best, it's like standing there listening to somebody else sing; it's what I want to hear the song do when I hear somebody else sing it. That's the closest I can come to describing it. Again, it's one of those subjective things. I don't quite know what to say what it's like, because it's not like anything else. Singing is—you go out there and open your mouth and you try to hit the notes and you try to express something about the lyric. Sometimes for me it's also another thing, an X factor. It's *evocative;* it's what the song evokes. It's the context, somehow, of the song. But sometimes it doesn't have anything to do with reality. Sometimes it doesn't even have anything to do with the text. Sometimes it just has to do with something in my head, some little thing about the

way the chords work and the way the melody fits in—something graceful about the song that speaks to me. And it speaks to me emotionally. I don't have the language to say what it is—it's not a technical thing.

A lot of singing is technical. And I've definitely been getting more range.

You've been hitting notes in "Morning Dew" I've never heard you even attempt.
Yeah, the more I do it, the better I get, too. It's a race between cigarettes and improvement. [Laughs] If I could stop smoking I could probably bust through another four or five notes up on top!

But the point is, developing as a singer and learning how to sing is an ongoing process. But I don't know whether any of this means anything to anybody but me. I guess the way you would notice it out there [in the audience] is that my singing is more consistent, which is what I'm hoping for.

Sometimes if I can hear just right . . . like Shoreline is the best-sounding place we've played in quite a while. It has a great lower dynamic and a great upper dynamic, and the in-between is very smooth. It doesn't have bulges in it; it's very smooth. And so that helps that thing of being able to sing softly and articulately so you can close every line or every note really nicely. The sound of your voice, the tone of it, was something I could really get into there. But that's rarely the case that I can hear my voice well enough to be able to do that, except during acoustic shows. And at acoustic shows I'm almost *afraid* of my voice it's so big, and I still haven't learned to control it the way I'd like to. Also, the material is different; it's less openly emotional than Grateful Dead stuff is.

When you sing a song, to what degree do you feel you inhabit the characters in the song?
I don't feel like I'm inhabiting the characters, but I do feel like I'm inhabiting their *world*. I don't really very often relate to the characters in the song. I don't feel like, "Okay, now this is *me* singing this song." Occasionally Hunter writes me an autobiographical song, like "Mission in the Rain," which is a song that might be *about* me.

In what regard?
It's my life. It's like a little piece of my life. Hunter writes *me* once in a while. So when he does that, sometimes I feel like I can wear the song. But actually I relate better to Dylan songs more often than not. Some-

times I feel like I'm right *in* those songs. I mean, that is to say, that it's *me* speaking.

What spaces does he hit that Hunter doesn't?
I couldn't tell you precisely. You know that song called "Going, Going, Gone" on *Planet Waves*? And "Tough Mama," also on *Planet Waves*? Those are songs that I wear really well. When I sing them I feel like I might as well have written them. I relate to them that well. That rarely happens to me with Hunter's songs, but something *else* happens to me with Hunter's songs that I think is more special. And that's the thing of them coming from *a world*—some kind of mythos or alternate universe that's got a lot of interesting stuff in it. And I feel like I'm in that world and of it somehow; or at least I know it when I see it, and I feel like I have something to say about it and I'm participating in it, but in a different sort of way. It's participating in the mythos.

Does it change for you from night to night? In a song like "Wharf Rat," for example, there are nights when the line, "I'll get a new start, live the life I should," sounds ironic, and other nights it sounds downright serious.
Yeah. It depends on how good the song is. If the song is good enough, it has that ambiguous quality to it. Like sometimes I sing that song "Loser" and it's a self-congratulatory asshole. Sometimes it's an idiot. The lyrics have the guy an idiot, but the idiot's version of himself is, "Hey, I'm great!" I can ride that either way and there's lots of shading in between where it's both those things at the same time. I love it when a song is ambiguous like that.

Hunter is able to write that into just about everything—he's able to leave just enough *out,* so that you're not really sure whose side you're on, if it's a matter of taking sides. In "Wharf Rat" you don't know if you're the guy who's hearing the story or the guy who's telling it. It really doesn't matter in the long run.

He really likes to throw around the perspective, like in "Terrapin," where it switches back and forth from the story to the storyteller.
I encourage that, too. He actually writes more clearly than I let him. I mean he'll explain things if I let him. Like if you've ever heard his version of "Terrapin," he closes the door on the whole story; he brings it all the way back. I don't let him do that. He knows I like it [ambiguous] so he tends to juice that part of it up on the versions we do together. We're

manipulating there, but only insofar as we're not being precise when precision is *not* what's called for.

Songs are poetry, I guess, but it's how a song works that's most important, and that's not always a function of what the content is, but the whole thing—the texture of it, the sound of it, the way it trips off the tongue, all that stuff. Sometimes it doesn't have to mean anything and it can still evoke a great *something*.

Are there songs that have been hard for you to get a hold of?
Oh yeah, are you kidding?! There are all these songs that I feel like I'm *almost* on to it, but I don't have it.

That's how I feel about "Fire on the Mountain." I feel like I still don't quite get it, lyrically.
Yep, some of them are definitely that way. But that doesn't stop me from trying 'em.

So in other words you go through that same process.
Sure. Of course. It wouldn't be fun otherwise. That's part of *my* fun. [Laughs] If everything was black and white and written in stone it wouldn't be that interesting to me. Who needs it?

Have you found that how you feel about different songs changes through the years?
They evolve. Sometimes it takes the longest time before a song even really hits me.

What's an example?
Let's see. Let me think of a song I sang for a long time before I even realized what it meant. [Long pause] Let's see. It doesn't happen that often, but I remember it happened once and it surprised the shit out of me! [Long pause] Gee, I can't remember now. Maybe it's something I don't do anymore.

But it does happen, where I don't pay that much attention to the text of the song. I learn them by rote and sometimes I don't notice what they mean, but I like the sound of them and how the words fall together.

Maybe [it was] something around the time I was working on my first solo record—*Attics of My Life* or something like that.

Great song.
It *is* a great song. I want to bring that song back.

You've finally got the vocal blend for it.
Yeah, we could do it. [In fact, it was revived in the fall of 1989.]

Speaking of your first solo record, you once started to tell me the story of how you wrote "The Wheel," but you were interrupted.
Actually it was just one time through on the piano. I was playing the piano and I didn't even know what I was doing. Now the way I approached that side of the album [side two] is that I sat down at the piano—which I *don't* play—and Billy sat down at the drums, which he *does* play. So at least one of us knew what he was doing. [Laughs] And I just played. When I'd get an idea, I'd elaborate on it and then go back and overdub stuff on it. But that side was really almost all one continuous performance, pretty much. When a song would come up in there, or just a progression, we'd play with it and I'd work it through a few more times. And "The Wheel" came out of that. It wasn't written, I didn't have anything in mind, I hadn't sketched it out or anything.

That's interesting, because I've always felt that the opening sounds like we're entering a song that's already in progress.
Yeah, well, in a way it almost *is* like that.
  So then, after that, Hunter came in and wrote the lyrics.

I'm consistently amazed at how much wisdom there is in Hunter's writing; that he could turn out the stuff he did at twenty-five or thirty and have it seem so eternal.
Well, you don't have to be old to be wise. I always thought he was pretty wise. That's the reason I got together with him in the first place.

Do you find that the two of you are aging in similar ways, in the sense that what he wants to write are still things you want to sing?
Yeah. He just wrote a bunch of new lyrics for me for the Garcia Band that are not for the Grateful Dead. So he's making the distinction between me and the Grateful Dead, which I sort of like. I basically feel that a good song is a good song no matter where you put it, but he tends to think that there are Grateful Dead songs, me songs, him songs. It's useful for him to think that way. I feel like I'll take 'em wherever I can get 'em.
  I want to do things that are more personal, because I feel that the

personal expression stuff allows you to have even subtler layers of ambiguity. This is things that are about personal events in your life, or *one's* life, or *a* life. They're smaller, so they don't address a huge audience. They address one other person maybe. I feel a desire to do something like that. In the same sense that Brent's lullaby ["I Will Take You Home"] is like speaking to one person. That makes for a very moving experience sometimes. So that's an interesting direction.

Are any of the new Dead songs indicative of that—"Built to Last," "Foolish Heart"?
No, the new Grateful Dead songs are really a continuation of the last thrust, the "Touch of Grey" idea. In fact, I've had a little trouble with ... You know, Hunter doesn't mind addressing a big idea in a song. Sometimes for me it's like, "Can you really tell somebody something about life with any kind of integrity?" I have difficulty with that sometimes. Hunter says, "No, no. Sure you can! It's okay! This is good advice!" [Laughs] I say, "Okay, I'm gonna trust you, man. If you think it's good advice I'll *sing* it as though it were good advice—"

In Golden Gate Park, 1975. *(Photo by Richard McCaffrey)*

And then you get in it and you're not so sure?

Well, yeah. I'm not so sure. So then I sing it like maybe it's *not* such good advice. [Laughs]

Sabotage his intentions!

Not really, because it's not his intention to preach to the world. He wants to see the song work. I want to see it work, too, but I want it to work on lots of levels. I don't care if it succeeds in a face-value sort of way. It's more important to me that the song survives. Because for me, the songs that are useful are the ones that I can sing over and over and over again. So a song that I can wear out fast is not a good song for me. It has to have longevity.

When I talk about that thing of finding out what's in the song, I must've sung "Stella Blue" for three or four years before I started to really come out of it. Because originally I was taken with the construction of it, which is extremely clever, if I do say so myself. I was proud of it as a composer—"Hey this is a slick song! This sucker has a very slippery harmonic thing that works nicely." That's what I liked about it. It wasn't until later that I started to find other stuff in there. That's a good example of a song I sang before I understood it. I understood some sense of what the lyrics were about, but I didn't get into the pathos of it. It has a sort of brittle pathos in it that I didn't get until I'd been singing it for a while.

How do you feel out a new song? For instance, what is happening to "Foolish Heart" now that you've played it a dozen times live? What sort of processes are taking place in its evolution at this early stage?

It's one of those things, like trying on new clothes—"Oh shit, this doesn't quite fit!" If I'm being bright about it, I'll say something to the guys in the band—"Hey, in this part everybody's gotta play a little quieter." It'll start to develop what it needs.

It starts out, here are the chords, here are the words, here's the melody—*nominally*. Let's just play the sucker and see what happens. Then I'll figure out, "Well, obviously during this part it needs to build." Then some parts are not so obvious—"This part could build, or not. It could just hang there and go along and then take a quick drop in dynamics, or start up again." The sculpting of it, technically, is an evolutionary process.

But then there's another process that I find as a singer. I'll start to find alternate deliveries of lines. Sometimes I'll add a few notes to a line. It depends on how tightly constructed a song is. Like "Built to Last" has no air in it so far. It's real new and I'm still grappling with the lyrics. There are a lot of lyrics and I'm still trying to get them so I can spit 'em out. But "Foolish Heart" has a lot of air in it, so it has a lot of room for expression. I think "Built to Last" is going to be a powerful song when it gets going. It's just that it's still very new and the nature of the song is that it's going to take a little longer to wear it into something. In a way, though, it may be the more powerful song.

But you don't know. Like when we were rehearsing "Believe It or Not" it was like [he shrugs] "Eh. Big deal." But when we performed it the first time it had an amazing reception. It was an amazingly emotional moment. I had no idea that song would have that kind of effect; on me even. So now it's got its own place that it may go to, and I have no idea where that's going to be.

I was interested to see it turned up in the first set in Dallas. With "Black Muddy River," you moved it around a bit and then it became fixed as an encore. Is that because it didn't fit in, somehow, with the flow of a regular set?
No. "Black Muddy River" will eventually find its way to the first set, or some place like that. But with some tunes, there's really nothing to say after that song. After you've said this, there's really no place to go. Certain songs have that finality about them. But of course sometimes you can take that kind of song and change it entirely just by putting it in a place where it doesn't . . . become the parentheses.

Do you view the "Black Peter"/"Stella Blue" slot, as I call it, as your last statement in the show, knowing that Bob will probably close the show with a rocker of some sort?
Pretty much, though I don't think of it as *my* statement. I think of it as *a* statement. I think of it as a place where the energy goes down—*whooosh!*

How hard is it to make that shift?
With our audience it's not hard at all. But it's taken a long time to get that. Ideally there's a song in there that's so delicate that it's got a moment in it of pure silence.

We've all seen that in a great "Stella Blue" or "Morning Dew."
Yeah. When you get that you know that's a moment of alignment, and that's always nice. That doesn't come from anything other than the thing of being in an audience where you experience a moment like that. That

comes from my having been in audiences before. In a sense it's show-manship, but it's not overt showmanship.

I like for an experience to have a lot of range emotionally. I mean I like to get turned every way but loose.

In a way, you're entering into an agreement with the audience. You're pushing it on your end and seeing what they do with it. Some nights you get that quiet, and some nights somebody's screaming during the quietest parts of "Stella Blue."
Sure. Some nights it's just not happening on that level. Sometimes that's kind of funny.

At Madison Square Garden [in the fall of 1988] during "To Lay Me Down" the place sounded like a cocktail party.
Right. In New York, it's like Bill Graham used to say—they want the sword fighter, they want the juggler . . .

In New York they really want you to sock 'em with the rock 'n' roll. I mean they're tough! [Laughs] They're tough, and Madison Square Garden is not exactly the most intimate house in the world.

More often than not, though, you guys seem to rise to the occasion. You play great there.
We do okay. But you know, that was a tough run for us. It was ex-hausting. The simple truth of the matter is we're not as young as we once were and it's hard to do a long run like that. It's just hard.

Even when it doesn't involve traveling?
Being in New York is a sweat. Being in New York robs your energy—there's just no getting around that.

Can you detect it in the audience when you play a place like, say, Dallas, and there are obviously a lot of newcomers? Or is it not that different from your perspective?
It's not that different, but Dallas and Houston both had that thing where the audience sort of doesn't know what to do. Or the audience is not necessarily that involved. Usually there are enough Deadheads that they can swing it their way. But the vibes in Dallas and Houston were both a little strange. New Orleans was neat. That wasn't bad.

Well, that's a city that knows how to party.
In a certain kind of way, yeah. It didn't wear for me as well this time
as other times I've been there. But I'm not that much of a party person.
In New Orleans what that really means is go out and drink a lot. And
if that isn't your idea of a party you're pretty much fucked. [Laughs]
There's a lot of music there but not that much *good* music. The whole
zydeco-cajun music thing is so marginal, and it leans up against so many
other styles of music that allow greater proficiency, that while there are
a lot of great players, it seems to me sort of like a one-note thing. It's a
one-gesture kind of music, so it's a little flat. Players like the Neville
Brothers are rare—they have a definite thing they're going after, a definite
sound that's original.

*Did the experience of touring with Dylan have much of an impact on
you musically? Weir has obviously picked up a lot of his vocal mannerisms.*
It didn't change me in any specific way, except that it was enriching. It
was fun to do; I really enjoyed it. That's the most I look for in any
experience.

The most changing thing I've done lately is that thing with Ornette
Coleman. [Garcia is on three cuts of Ornette's *Virgin Beauty* LP.] Now
that really changed me. The changes are profound and I might not even
get around to them for a couple of years. I realize where it's going to take
me, but I know it's going to take me a while to get there. It's along the
lines of learning a different way to think. It's a paradigm change. I got the
flash and now I have to slowly put together the interior. And things start
to mutate ever so slightly in my playing. It'll be more noticeable in a year,
and in two years it'll be more noticeable, and in three years . . .

You'll be clearing arenas coast to coast, it'll be so weird.
Right! "What the fuck is he doing?" [Laughs]

*You've often said you like playing backup lines on other singers' songs.
What are some of your favorite Weir songs to play?*
He's burned me out on a lot of 'em. A lot of them have been fun but
they're not that fun anymore.

He's a little low on material right now.
A little skimpy, right. "Saint of Circumstance" is fun to play. "Estimated
Prophet" is *really* fun to play; it's very interesting and has a lot of places

that are surprising and challenging. "Throwing Stones" is fun. That one's probably more fun for the band than the audience. Same with "Victim or the Crime."

That one's pretty controversial so far.
Well, it's a hideous song. It's very angular and unattractive sounding. It's not an accessible song. It doesn't make itself easy to like. It just doesn't sound good, or rather, it sounds strange. And it *is* strange. It has strange steps in it, but that's part of what makes it interesting to play.

Bob's songs sometime don't make musical sense in a direct, traditional way. Sometimes he writes songs that are completely out of the mark and you have to really stretch yourself to find stuff to play in them. But I used to like to play on that tune he used to have—"Lazy Lightning." That was a fun tune to play, but pretty weird. "Black Throated Wind" was a really nice tune to play. "Looks Like Rain" is a nice tune to play.

What keeps "The Other One" so fresh?
It's wide open and it's got a great drive to it; those triplets. It's one of those things that you can still take anywhere. There's no way for it to get old.

Do you feel a historical link with it?
No, for me it's very much *right now*. It's felt that way all along. I don't really relate to the lyrics exactly; I relate to the way it sounds. And it sounds modern.

It seemed to me that you were never that comfortable with "Cryptical Envelopment" when you brought it back in 1985.
No, I wasn't. It's just not a very successful song. I find it uncomfortable.

Do you ever get to a point some nights where you're a little ways into a song and you realize it isn't what you want to be playing?
Yeah, that happens a lot. But I always feel like it's my failing, because I have the opportunity to call it, and I could've picked any other song. Sometimes I feel the whole night is a blowout. What would be great for the Grateful Dead is for us to have a run that would guarantee like four nights out of nine over a five-month period. We'd play some place like the Orpheum, in San Francisco, which sounds better than the Warfield. So we'd play there but you'd never know what night it was going to

be, so we could blow it out. "Hey, fuck it. I don't feel like playing. Do you?" "Nah." [Laughs]

Because just like any human endeavor, there are times when you should do it and times when you shouldn't. When you're making your decisions of where you're going to play a year in advance, spontaneity doesn't come into it. So no matter what state you're in, you have to play those gigs. And if we don't plan our tours well enough to allow us enough time to kick a mood, get out from a bummer—I mean everyone has bum days—it's pretty rough. Just in the course of human events you hit those nights when it's like, "God, I'd rather be *anywhere* but here right now." Oddly enough, the nights when any of us feel that way, we all feel that way, and then we're going out in weakness. And then that may be the only show we play in that part of the country for five years.

"Sorry, folks! Drive home safely!"
Yeah. [Laughs] Most of these shows we just did in the South were a little bit like that. Not quite us at our blinding best. And you *hope* to do a good show when you play a place you haven't been much, because it always improves the audience. Next time you go back, people are really hot to see you, because word-of-mouth works wonders.

The Midwest is like the East for us now, because we've played there enough and played well. But you have to play well, because you build an audience one member at a time.

Do Bay Area gigs feel different?
In a way. You know, it used to be that San Francisco gigs felt different than the rest of the Bay Area. But now we don't play in San Francisco specifically. So now the Bay Area is much more like, say, California, than the rest of the country. California is characterized by the Deadhead mall, and the loose, relaxed nature of the audience. They're more attentive. Maybe a little passive. While on the East Coast it's "*Aaaaaaaaah!!*" [Laughs]

It's getting more homogeneous, though. I think the ground-floor Deadheads are bringing their own version of Deadhead energy to enough shows in enough places that it's affecting it that way. And I think the thing of having the ticketing here might have something to do with that.

I don't know. It's hard enough for me to play music, let alone follow the sociology of the Grateful Dead. There's just too much there. It's nice that there are other people who are concerned about all this stuff. I'm concerned about it, but I don't have the drive to pay that much attention to it. I figure everybody wants me to play, really, so I'm working on that.

Through the years, the changes in the Dead's music have often been a function of changing personnel. The latest incarnation has now been together ten years—longer than any other lineup. What are the advantages of being together a long time?
Consistency is always an advantage. And the more you play together, the better you get at playing together. There's no question about that. So the more time you can spend with the same group of musicians, the better the music is going to be, the more personality it's going to have. The thrust of everybody's musical ambition is to keep getting better at it. My perception of it is that the Grateful Dead is still improving. It may be that age will run us off before we get to where we really *could* go, because of the energy involved.

Every time we do a tour now, the first two nights it's like just getting back to being able to finish a show! [Laughs] *Goddamn!* Even the guys who are really physically conscious, like Weir and Mickey, are exhausted. The nature of what we do is that it's difficult physically. So time itself is our greatest enemy.

You're a lot more physical onstage now than you were a few years ago. Are you really aware of that? Is it because you're healthier? Is it because you're having more fun?
It's all those things. I'm having a lot more fun.

Why?
Part of it is that I quit drugs. That certainly helped. The drugs that I was taking were escape drugs. It was like a long vacation. It worked good; I mean I got my "vacation."

For a long time there I sort of lost heart. "I don't know if I want to do this. I don't know what I want." It was that thing, "Fuck. Is this right? Is this good? Is this the thing I should be doing?" For a long time—about eight years—I felt like I wanted to get away from everything somehow. But I didn't want to just stop playing, or have the Grateful Dead stop because that's what *I* wanted to do. And I didn't even know consciously that that's what I wanted. I don't think I really realized that until lately. Looking back on it I see certain patterns.

Was it that you felt too much responsibility?
Well...
I don't really know. I haven't analyzed myself sufficiently. Part of my

nature is deeply pessimistic. And it's something I have to fight with a lot. Part of me is overconfident, too, so it's these two polar opposites.

I guess it's really a matter of luck that I survived my whole drug thing, because I certainly had enough drugs around to kill myself at any time and I was into them where I don't think I would've noticed, you know?

It's really only my friends' caring enough to let me know that they didn't want me to die that made me give up drugs. Giving up the drugs was really not that difficult. It took a long time. And then I got sick.

Stopping the drugs is not what made me sick. I stopped drugs and then three or four months later I got sick. Now, there may have been a relationship—undoubtedly there was—but it wasn't an obvious one. When I came out of the coma and asked the doctors about why it happened, they didn't really know, either. So I didn't really learn anything from the near-death experience in terms of what caused it.

There's still a large contingent of Deadheads who are into psychedelics. Do you feel farther away from that now than you used to?
No, no. I still feel as close as I ever did. Psychedelics are still the most important thing that ever happened to me. Psychedelics is a lot of why I'm here and doing what I'm doing. And a lot of the vision I have— such as it is—I owe to my psychedelic experience. Nothing has opened me up like psychedelics did. I mean, I was a different person.

Those experiences are like wellsprings, and I haven't even begun to exhaust what's there. Even if I never took any psychedelics again. I've already experienced hundreds of thousands of lifetimes' worth of experiences that are as valid to me and as real to me as anything. That's for keeps. That's mine forever. So there's no going back to before that— that would be like living in a little gray tube, compared to the psychedelic reality, which is like "Oh! *I* see!" [Laughs]

Of course the atmosphere now is considerably different from when you were taking your initial voyages.
Well, the world was really innocent then. Or at least innocent of those experiences. So you could go around and be completely crazy, and the most that people would suspect you of was being crazy. They didn't think it was *"DRRRRugs!"* [Laughs]

I was glad to be in on that. That was a remarkably lucky moment historically. That was fun.

Garcia on Haight Street, San Francisco, 1968. *(Photo by Steve Brown)*

This last question has nothing to do with all the other things we've been talking about. Most of our readers, and at this point, most Deadheads, never had the opportunity to see Pigpen perform. Tapes don't really capture his essence that well, yet he's this legendary figure. Can you shed a little light on him?

Well, Pigpen was the only guy in the band who had any talent when we were starting out. [Laughs] He was genuinely talented. He also had no discipline, but he had *reams* of talent. And he had that magical thing of being able to make stuff up as he went along. He also had great stage presence. The ironic thing was he hated it—it really meant nothing to him; it wasn't what he liked. We had to browbeat him into being a performer. His best performances were one-on-one, sitting in a room with an acoustic guitar. That's where he was really at home and at his best.

Out in front of the crowd he could work the band, and he'd really get the audience going. He always had more nerve than I could believe. He'd get the audience on his side, and he'd pick somebody out—like a heckler—and get on them.

"Hey, man—stop playin' pocket pool!"

Right! [Laughs] He'd crack us up, too. Sometimes he'd just kill me! And he was good with the blues, of course. He had great authority. It's hard for me to say what it was about him that people really loved. But they loved him a lot. I know *I* loved him a lot, and I couldn't begin to tell you why. He was a lovable person. Really, it hasn't felt quite right since Pigpen's been gone, but on the other hand he's always been around a little, too. He hasn't been entirely gone. He's right around.

I don't know . . .

You had to *be there* for Pigpen. He's a guy who's tough to talk about, like Neal [Cassady] or any other people who are not here, and what was special about them was themselves. He was special because he was special, you know? The way your friend is special. The way someone you love is special. Pigpen for me was a lot more than a performer. He was a very dear friend. Really a dear friend. We had a lot of crazy times together, and Pigpen was always on the side of the crazy times, although he and I were not always on the same side. But he could always be trusted.

Like I said, he was the guy who really sold the band, not me or Weir. Back then, Weir was almost completely spaced. He was just barely there. [Laughs] And I was aggressively crazy. I could talk to anybody till hell froze over but I wasn't really what made the band work. Pigpen is what made the band work.

Donna

The Greatest Story Never Told

An Interview: March 5, 1985

The long hair that once cascaded in a waterfall of brown down past her waist has been largely shorn now, and the name is different, too. Now it's Donna *MacKay,* and the trappings of what was once a hippie-ish rock and roll life have been replaced by what appears to be a very comfortable middle-class existence in a modern housing development in Petaluma, California (about an hour north of San Francisco). She hasn't sung rock and roll for quite a while now, preferring to sing the praises of the Lord in a trio called Zoe, which includes her husband, bassist David MacKay. Her afternoons no longer consist of sitting in some anonymous hotel room drinking and taking drugs, waiting to go onstage; no, there's her two year old, Kinsman, to care for, and Zion, her eleven year old by Keith Godchaux, finally gets the attention Donna wishes she could have given him during his infancy.

Wailing in the band, 1975. *(Photo by Bruce Polonsky)*

Donna MacKay is happy, happier than she's ever been, living a "normal" life out of the limelight after a long career in music—first as a background vocalist in Muscle Shoals, Alabama, where she grew up, and then with the Grateful Dead for nearly a decade. But she has no regrets. An intensely devoted Christian—her husband is even a pastor—her world is very different from the strange universe that the Dead and Deadheads inhabit. She looks back on her years with the Dead with some fondness, though certainly there was also much pain along the way. When she was at her best in the Dead, she was an electrifying presence who easily commanded center stage in a band of musical giants. Sometimes, though, her vocals seemed shrill, even off-key, and she detracted from the band's power. She's well aware of the problems she had in the group and is not defensive about it in the slightest. What many Deadheads don't realize is that before she moved to California in 1970, married Keith Godchaux and went on to join the band, Donna *Thatcher* had been a successful session singer, backing up the likes of Aretha Franklin, Joe Tex, Boz Scaggs, Elvis Presley, and scores of others.

Her odyssey from high school cheerleader to singer in the Dead to serene Christian mother of two has never really been adequately chronicled before. In early March, I drove up to Petaluma and talked with Donna for several hours about the ups and downs of her career. She is still a strikingly attractive woman, with a warm smile and a real sparkle in her eyes. She shows traces of an Alabama drawl, though fifteen years in California has taken much of the edge away. For many younger Deadheads, Donna Godchaux is just a voice on the tape; they really don't know much else about her. For them, and for the rest of us who *thought* we knew her (but didn't), here is her story.

Were either of your parents musical?
My dad and his sister played guitar and sang on a couple of radio stations in Texas, but I don't know of anyone in my family who was a professional musician. But I always knew I wanted to sing, and one of my mother's friends' cousins was running a recording studio in Muscle Shoals called Fame Recording, so when I was twelve, mother took me down to get his autograph. His name was Rick Hall, and he went on to produce a lot of hit records for people like Bobbie Gentry, Otis Redding, Aretha Franklin, and others. That was my first exposure to a recording studio.

Basically, I grew up in a situation where a new sound was originating. In the early Sixties, the whole Muscle Shoals scene was just beginning to get big. My first recording session was with Ray Stevens, right after he had a big hit with "Ahab the Arab." Felton Jarvis was producing, and one day one of the background singers couldn't make the session. I was fifteen, a cheerleader at Sheffield High and the whole bit. I remember I'd had cheerleader practice so I ran down to the studio in my little uniform, and that was the beginning. I still have the canceled check for $67.50.

Were you on call at the studio or something?
No, but I'd been down at the studio a lot by that point and I'd made little demos there. That's where I liked to hang out, which was considered a little weird. I guess I was a bit of a rebel in Muscle Shoals.

What kind of music did you like when you were growing up—country?
No, rhythm and blues. People like Otis Redding, Solomon Burke, Sam Cooke, Joe Tex. Amazingly, I ended up recording backgrounds with all of those except for Otis, because Muscle Shoals became such a popular place to record R&B. It had really started with Percy Sledge, who was an intern at the local hospital. He had a little band on the side, and my best friend, who sang with me in a vocal group called Southern Comfort, had a husband who produced Percy's first big hit, "When a Man Loves

a Woman." Us girls were the background singers for his first records.
I still remember the day it hit number one on the charts. Percy was in
the hospital with a kidney problem, and one of the other girls and I took
him the copy of *Billboard* to show him.

Was there any sort of stigma attached to being a young white girl into
R&B in the Deep South?
Oh yeah. Absolutely. After Percy's record, we were on other black records. The black artists who would hear us didn't know we weren't black.
Most of them, when they got down to the studio, would see four white
girls age eighteen to twenty-three, and they'd flat out lose it! [Laughs]
There were a few who refused to use us when they found out we were
white, but most of them were excited that there were white girls who sang
like them.

It must have been very exciting to be in on the ground floor of the whole
Muscle Shoals scene. So many of those artists were just beginning to take
off in the early and mid-Sixties.
It was incredible. People like Otis Redding already were starting to
become popular, but I remember seeing Aretha Franklin's name on the
calendar of people coming into the studio, and we all wondered who
this "*Aritha*" person was! [Laughs] Plus all the studio players were all
so good. It was the same crowd as today—Barry Beckett, Roger Hawkins, Johnny Sandlin, David Hood, Jimmy Johnson. I grew up with
them. They all played the local hops.

When you were singing in your teens, did you have any aspirations of
being a soloist someday, or were you happy singing backups with all
those great singers?
That's a good question. I was content to a certain extent in that I was
learning a lot. But you're around people who are successful when you
work in the studios. You're around people you adore or look up to and
read about. And after a while you begin to cop their attitude, for better
and worse. So I'd be lying if I said I didn't want to be a star.

After "When a Man Loves a Woman" became a big hit, that's when
the work really started to come for our group. It was really exciting.

How did you juggle studio work with being in high school?
Not very well. [Laughs] I was head cheerleader, and people would walk
around the corner where I couldn't see them and yell "STAR!!" and stuff

like that. It was real hard because people were very jealous and didn't
understand it all. Also, it was all so new, people didn't know what to
make of it. Socially, I started dropping out, and I didn't care if I was
head cheerleader anymore. In fact, after me, they voted to have two head
cheerleaders in case one of them flaked out. [Laughs] If we had a game
on Friday night and I was scheduled to go into the studio the next day,
I'd mouth my cheers so I wouldn't lose my voice. I was definitely going
through a lot of trauma for a sixteen year old.

*It seems as though in the very late Sixties there was a change in the sort
of artists who went to Muscle Shoals, with black music somewhat giving
way to white rock and rollers like Boz Scaggs and others.*
It did change a little, but there was still a lot of great black music being
made there. I remember when I saw the name "Boz Scaggs" on the calendar, I wondered, "Who *is* that turkey with the weird name?" That same
era I met Duane Allman, who worked with Wilson Pickett and some other
people there. I remember going to the studio and seeing Duane, lying next
to the bathroom door, on the floor, playing his guitar. I thought it was
very weird. I had never seen the California attitude—sort of laid back, and
the long hair. He totally blew me away. I couldn't really relate to his music
until I moved out here, but I knew that he was really, really good. The
whole hippie, trippy thing he represented was completely foreign to me. I
was really innocent. I had never even seen anyone smoke pot.

Were there sessions in the late Sixties that were particularly memorable?
Well, my greatest dream came true. Elvis was recording in Memphis,
and he heard a song called "Suspicious Minds" that our vocal group had
done the demo of. He loved it, and he brought us in to sing on that and
"In the Ghetto," which were part of his big comeback. It was a real big
thrill. I remember being thirteen years old and watching *Love Me Tender*
when it first came out in the movies. If I'd known I'd meet him and
make records with him some day, I couldn't have stood it. [Laughs]

It must have been intimidating.
It was. Elvis would be in the control room and he had them cue up our
vocal parts one at a time—that was really intimidating. But he loved us,
and that was so flattering. He was always really, really nice as far as I
could tell. Working with him is one of my fondest memories.
    A funny thing is that later, when Keith and I were in Jerry's band,
Elvis' drummer, Ron Tutt, was in the band too. I recall that we were

all working on a record one night—maybe it was *Cats Under the Stars*—and Ron had to leave the next day to go on the road with Elvis. And I said to him, "I don't know why I'm asking you this—because I've never asked you to say anything to Elvis before—but would you tell him I said hello?" The next day I was in the hospital because I had to have an operation. I woke up from surgery and the first telephone call I got was from Tutt, telling me that Elvis had died. Tutt told me, "Elvis says hello and he hopes to see you again sometime." That really tore me up.

Why did you come out to California?

I'd just always wanted to come here. The only thing that kept me in Muscle Shoals, Alabama, was the recording scene, but after a while it got to be like just working another job, like anything does. So I decided I was willing to give up music if I had to get out of there. A couple of months before I left, a friend of mine moved out here and got a job working at Union Oil, so through her I was able to get a job there too, processing credit cards and things like that.

A friend of mine named Carol Burns, who worked in the same department, had a friend named Keith Godchaux, who I met one day when a group of us took acid and went up in the mountains.

It sounds as though California corrupted you pretty fast!

[Laughs] It did. I smoked pot during the last year I was in Alabama, but I hadn't taken acid until that day on the mountain. Toward the end of the day, someone suggested we all go down to a Grateful Dead concert at Winterland—they all were really anxious for me to see the Dead. But I was the type who always needed to get a certain amount of sleep to be able to function at work, so I said, "I don't want to go when I have to work the next day." But they made me.

So they all took acid or mushrooms and I didn't take anything at all, so I'd be okay the next day. We were in the very back of the balcony of Winterland. The New Riders came on and I went, "Hmm—this is interesting." Then Quicksilver came on and I went, "HMMM!" Then the Jefferson Airplane came on and I said, "HMMMM!!" Then the Grateful Dead came on and I said, "What *is this?!* [Laughs] Whatever it is, this is where I'm at!" This is on no drugs in the balcony at Winterland. Well, as it turned out, I couldn't sleep that night anyway because I was so excited. I kept thinking, "What did they do? How did they do that?" They weave a spell. There's this whole mystical energy that happens when you see the Grateful Dead and you're ready to receive it. I was ready to receive it and I *got* it.

So every opportunity . . . every rumor that we heard that they might be playing, there we were.

I had no idea you were a Deadhead.

It was very short term, but very intense. As the weeks went on, we'd all go see the Dead together, or at the very least get together and listen to Dead records.

By this time I'd fallen in love with Keith, but I'd literally never spoken to him. We'd be places together in a group but we'd never actually talk to each other. I had said hi, but that was it. I didn't know it, but he was going through the same thing with me. Then one night my friend, Carol, invited me to spend the night at her house in Walnut Creek and ride with her in her carpool. We got to Carol's house and she called up Keith, who lived near her, and invited him over. So the four of us—Carol's old man Pete was there too—sat around and listened to the Grateful Dead. Keith and I still didn't talk to each other.

At the end of the night, Carol and Pete went to bed and Keith went to put on his coat to leave. I was standing on the other side of the room looking at him. Then, instead of leaving we started walking toward each other—it was just like you'd see on TV [Laughs]—and then we hugged. He said, "I love you!" I said, "I love you, too." And we sat down on the couch and decided when we were going to get married. It was really heavy. It was so heavy I wouldn't talk to the guy until I knew I wanted to marry him! I didn't even know that he played the piano, and he didn't know I sang, so it had nothing to do with music. I didn't really care about singing that much at that point. It was more like, "If I can't be in the Grateful Dead, why play music at all?" [Laughs]

The next Friday I went out to Walnut Creek to hear Keith play, and it completely blew me away. I couldn't believe that I was in love with this guy and he could play like that. He was a jazz player who was just starting to play rock and roll, and he was just incredible. At the break, we sat down and I told him that I sang. It was funny, because like every song that came on the jukebox during the break was something I'd sung on. And I remember Keith turned around to no one in particular after hearing a few of these records and saying, "She's a hauling ass singer!"

Pretty soon after that we got married and we lived in Walnut Creek. Keith would practice his rock and roll piano at home, and I was basically supporting the two of us. One day I came home from work and we went over to Pete's and he said, "Let's listen to some Grateful Dead." And Keith said, "I don't want to listen to it. I want to play it." And it was like, "YEAHHH! That's it!" We were just so high and in love! We said to Pete and Carol, "Hey, guys, we're going to play with the Grateful Dead," and we really believed it. We had no doubt.

We went home, looked in the paper and saw that Garcia's band was playing at the Keystone [Berkeley], so we went down, of course. At the break Garcia walked by going backstage, so I grabbed him and said, "Jerry, my husband and I have something very important to talk about." And he said, "Sure."

That couldn't happen today . . .

Are you kidding! Definitely not. [Laughs] I was totally ignorant about that sort of thing; I didn't realize that *everyone* does that to him.

So Garcia told us to come backstage, but we were both too scared, so we didn't. A few minutes later, Garcia came up and sat next to Keith, and I said, "Honey, I think Garcia's hinting that he wants to talk to you. He's sitting right next to you." [Laughs] He looked over at Jerry and looked back at me and he dropped his head on the table and said, "You're going to have to talk to my wife. I can't talk to you right now." He was just too shy. He was very strong, but he couldn't handle that sort of thing. So I said to Jerry, "Well, Keith's your piano player, so I want

Keith Godchaux playing electric piano, 1976. *(Photo by Bob Marks)*

your home telephone number so I can call you up and come to the next Grateful Dead practice." And he believed me! He gave me his number.

The coming Sunday the Dead were having a rehearsal and Jerry told us to come on down, so we did. But the band had forgotten to tell Jerry that the rehearsal had been called off, so Jerry was down there by himself. So Keith and Jerry played, and we played him some tapes of songs that I had written and was singing on. Then Jerry called Kreutzmann and got him to come down, and the three of them played some. Then the next day the Dead practiced, and by the end of that day Keith was on the payroll.

Where did you fit in to all this?
Well, they asked me to sing right away, but somewhere in my ignorant wisdom I said I wanted Keith to do it first, so he did two tours and I stayed home. I really wanted him to get to do it first. So Keith and I went into it as green and innocent as we could be. I'd never sung before an audience before, really, and Keith had only done very small gigs. We had no idea what joining a band of the magnitude of the Grateful Dead would mean. And the Dead is more than just a regular band, too. It's this whole . . . extended reality. It's not just a band, but a way of life. We were young and in love and just having the time of our lives, and we were really still in our own world at the beginning.

When Keith and I first got together, we wrote some music that we wanted to be meaningful and spiritual. We wanted to write music to the Lord, because it didn't seem like there was much out there that was spiritual. But when we heard the Grateful Dead we tied that in because it seemed to have such spiritual ties. It had a quality that was magical, ethereal, and spiritual, and that's part of what was so attractive about it.

The first time most of us heard you was on Ace *[released in early 1972], Weir's solo album. Did you already know before you made that record that you'd be in the band?*
Yes, it was pretty much just a question of when I decided it was time for me to do it.

The Grateful Dead has always seemed very male-oriented in some way to me. It's a very masculine scene, particularly with the roadies and all. Did being married to Keith make it easier to deal with that?
It *is* a masculine scene, but people were wonderful to me. Everybody always treated me like a queen. There was a lot of respect, a lot of love between us all. I never had any problem along those lines at all.

It must have been strange to tour when you basically had not been a live performer up until then.
It was strange, and I was kind of bashful about it. At that point I was in love and married and I wasn't particularly interested in looking nice or drawing attention to myself or having men look at me or anything. I didn't care about that. That was kind of a hang-up I had, in a way. Before I met Keith, when I was still in Alabama, I was the opposite—very flamboyant and loud. But by the time I'd joined the Dead I'd become more subdued. I was into the music, and into the scene, but as far as relating to the audience and relating to the band and myself as performers, I wasn't that into it.

Do you remember your first show?
My first show was at the Academy of Music in New York City [March, 22, 1972], for a Hell's Angels party. The first song I sang with them was "How Sweet It Is," which they quit singing right after that. It was so much fun, and it turned out it wasn't intimidating at all.

I remember at some of those early shows you'd come out onstage and there would be this huge roar from the crowd . . .
It was the long hair. [Laughs] Nobody had hair down to their thighs that didn't have one split end! [Laughs]

Who determined the vocal arrangements?
It would depend on whose song it was and whether that person had any specific ideas about it. If they didn't, whoever had an idea would pitch in. There was no set thing. It was pretty democratic, actually. People were always open to the best idea.

Was it difficult being a very good technical singer in a group of people with quirky voices? I don't think of Weir or Garcia as having great voices, though certainly Jerry is an excellent singer and interpreter.
Garcia's a really good singer, especially since he doesn't have a voice at all. He's nasally, his voice is thin. But he has this great sense of phrasing and he sings emotionally.

On a couple of occasions I read interviews with the band after I'd left and someone would ask, "Why isn't Donna singing with the band anymore?" and either Phil or Bobby would say something like, "Well, she sang off-key." And you know, I *would* be off-key pretty often. We used to go into a room after a concert and listen to tapes, and I would be singing flat. I'd say, "*What?* How is that possible?" Because I knew I could sing. I'd had Elvis Presley listening down my throat and had worked with great singers for years, but I *was* singing off-key.

The thing was, I don't have a real strong natural voice. Where you hear me singing strongly, it's because I'm pushing and it's not my natural voice. Onstage, I had to push my voice at all times because the sound onstage was so loud. So I couldn't really use my natural voice, and it would produce unnatural effects—screaming, off-key. I tried to compensate every way I could think of for the fact that I was singing with the loudest band on earth.

Or certainly the busiest . . .

The most *musical* band. Everybody's doing their own trip as hard as they can! [Laughs]

When you listen to a tape back and you're noticeably off-key, what do you do about it? What do you think of yourself as a singer? You're not a background singer in Memphis, Muscle Shoals, Nashville, and New York for seven years because you sing off-key, so what's going on here? It was horrible for me.

Was it something that you then became conscious of when you were onstage singing?

It took every bit of intuition, every bit of ability and concentration just to know what they were going to do next musically—when they were going into a new tune, how quickly. You had to know them individually and collectively and know their music to know when they were going to put it all together and go into a new song. So there was already so much to think about all the time. It's like all of my consciousness was needed all the time just to keep it together out there, plus I was moving to every beat. If I moved one of my hips wrong it could throw one of the drummers off, or something. It was really important that we all try to be conscious of the music on every level at all times. It's very subtle music, and it relies on the smooth interaction of everyone for it to really work, which meant we all had to be sensitive about what the others were doing. But if Bob's guitar was too loud, I couldn't hear myself, so I'd tend to shout above him, which is unnatural for me.

On the records, I never sang off-key, because that was my scene— that's where I'd come from. I had control of my audio environment to where I could hear everything.

From the audience's standpoint, we would see you come out for, say, "Playin' in the Band," you'd sing it, do your little wailing section, and then we might not see you again for twenty or thirty minutes. What would you do during that period?
I was listening to every microscopic beat to determine where the music was going. And it wasn't easy.

When you had your first real solo passage on a Dead record, on those two verses of "The Music Never Stopped," a lot of people assumed you had a heavy gospel background, since it had that flavor.
When I tried to sing in my Baptist church when I was young I'd get out in front with a sextet and just totally crack up. I would laugh so hard that I had to quit. [Laughs] So I never really got much of a chance to sing in church.

Did that solo passage come from your wanting to finally step out and sing a solo?
Not really, no. As I recall, originally Bobby and I were going to sing it as a duet on that part, and then I think he suggested I sing it alone.

Did you ever get dosed onstage?
I dosed myself a couple of times. I remember when we played the Olympia Theatre in Paris, I took a lot of acid and found myself at one point during the concert lying under Keith's piano, and I was just digging on the Grateful Dead. Then I had a revelation: "Hey, I sing in this band! How am I going to get up and sing?!" [Laughs]

Also, let me tell you this for all those people who saw the *The Grateful Dead* movie. The reason that Keith and I don't have a little interview segment in there like everyone else is that our interview took place on the last night of the Winterland shows [October 1974, before the "retirement"] and we were absolutely flying on acid. I was not in this world. I was out in the zone! The camera crew came with us back home to Stinson Beach and they were all loaded on acid, too. So none of the interview really turned out. All I remember was there was a lot of staring at the table. [Laughs] I went into the film editing room later and saw some of it and just said, "Oh *no!*" Nobody could relate to it, because we weren't on the planet. Later, they wanted to shoot some new stuff but we weren't into it. Keith was a very low-profile kind of guy. That wasn't his scene, and I wasn't into it either.

What kind of effect did being in the Grateful Dead have on you and Keith as a married couple?
Everything was so intense for both of us. Here we were catapulted into this immense world, and both of us were going through so many changes just trying to deal with the bigness of it all. It was awesome, and there was so much pressure. In other words, you couldn't be a mediocre musician and just blow your way into the scene. You had to really know what you were doing all the time to be one of them. For Keith, appearing in front of thousands of people and having your piano amplified a million times more than you'd ever imagined was a lot of pressure.

Plus you had the disadvantage of jumping into the middle of a work-in-progress, so to speak.
Right. It was the old thing of you're either "on the bus" or "off the bus," and it was going to keep going forward no matter what. There was never really an opportunity to "learn the part"—you had to *know* the part when you jumped in.

To digress for one second, I've seen it written that Keith memorized all the Grateful Dead's songs before he auditioned. The truth is he didn't know any of them. When he rehearsed with them that first time he had never played one of their songs. *Never.* He'd listen to them but never sat down and tried to play them, learn the chord changes. Bobby will tell you they tried every way they could to trip him up, but they couldn't do it.

The other part of the pressure we felt was the standard thing of having to suddenly spend your life in airports and hotels all the time.

What happened was that we started to take out our personal problems in dealing with all this pressure on each other. We were in love—we were newlyweds—and it became really hard on us. By the time we got to be making enough money to afford the drug of our choice, we *did* the drugs of our choice, and that made matters worse, and it was like everything we'd gotten married for and loved each other for was getting ripped off. There's no blame. It's just what happened. In a way, though, we did pretty well: ten years later we were still in love and still married.

I have to say, I got egotistical and selfish for a while there. There's a word the kids use in school today: "radical." Well, I was radical. I'm not saying that Keith was an angel—he wasn't—but I really acted badly quite a lot. There was one night we had Grateful Dead practice [1977], and it was during a time we were trying to stay separate from each other a little. And he just wouldn't leave me alone this night and let us be separated, so I took my new BMW and backed up and rammed into his new BMW; I backed up and rammed into it again, and then I did it *again*. I hit his car as hard as I could three times and completely totaled his car. Then I took mine and totaled it into a pole and took a taxi home.

Along the same lines, if the hotel we were staying at didn't get my silk blouses back in time so I could wear the one I wanted onstage, I would simply demolish the hotel room.

I don't think anyone would suspect that of you . . .
[Laughs] Ask Jerry. Ask Phil. I remember one time I did a spectacular job on a hotel room in Detroit, and Phil and Billy and the road manager came up because they'd heard it was the worst they'd ever seen. [Laughs] I was notorious for it.

Was there a certain point where the whole thing—being in the Grateful Dead—became more negative than positive?
Yeah, sure. It creeps in. Again, it's not the Grateful Dead. It's what success does to your self-image, what it does to the human spirit. It's destructive, and some people can handle it and some people can't. The point is, you're out there so long before people who adore you and start to believe their image of you—or, you realize you can't live up to that image, so you're in a very strange position. And, of course, I'm not even Jerry. I mean everywhere we'd go—especially on the East Coast, it was "Jerrr-y!! Jerrr-y!!" And I know the effect it had on him. For instance, I saw in your magazine that someone wrote in and said they have a "JERRY SAVES" bumper sticker. That would make him sick. The Dead fans put them up a lot higher than they want to be. They're just a band. They don't claim to be any more than that. They don't *want* to be any more than that.

Why didn't you just bow out?
Well, we did. But in a thing that intense, the inertia behind it is so strong that it's very difficult. I remember that two tours [fall 1978] before we finally left, Keith's and my personal life was so horrible, and in the band as a whole the feeling was that "the music stinks. Every concert stinks." It just got progressively worse. Things got to a point where on every conceivable level things were so bad that I went to the road manager and said, "I've gotta go home." And I did. I left and missed the last couple of dates. Then Keith and I did one more tour, discussing all along the way how we could get out of it. It was horrible, because we weren't quitters.

A question I've got to ask: I've seen it reported in some places that you quit, in others that you were fired. Which was it?

Donna at home with sons, Zion and Kinsman, 1985. *(Photo by Blair Jackson)*

It was both, really. What happened was, after I left that tour then Keith and I decided we wanted to get out and start our own group or do something else—*anything* else. So we played that benefit concert at the Oakland Coliseum [February 17, 1979], and then a few days later there was a meeting at our house and it was brought up whether we should stay in the band anymore. So we discussed it, as a band, and we mutually decided we'd leave. I'll tell you, I instantly felt like about a billion pounds had been lifted off me.

After that, we went to Alabama and stayed out at a place on the lake in Muscle Shoals for six months and water-skied every day. It was the first time Zion, Keith, and I had really been together as a family since Zion was born in 1974. Keith got healthy from being an absolute wreck, and then we came back here and joined The Ghosts, who were already in existence. They had already made a record and they asked us to be on it, which we did, and then they asked us to go up to Oregon and play a couple of concerts, so we did, just as a lark. That wasn't our idea of what the "Keith and Donna band" was going to be, but it was a lot of fun. There was nothing heavy about it, no trips.

As we played more we got more of an idea of the kind of music we eventually wanted to do, and as the personnel in The Ghosts started to change, we brought in new people, grouped around Greg Anton, Keith, and me, and it did become more our band. That's when the Heart of Gold band began. We brought Steve Kimock in, who is just an amazing guitar player. And we had a couple of different bass players. And that's right when Keith died. [Keith was in an automobile accident in Marin County on July 21, 1980, and died two days later.]

I handled Keith's death by throwing myself into that band. I didn't really face up to the fact that he was dead for about three months, and then I totally lost it for about a week and totally crumbled. For about three months I didn't eat any food. I drank beer for breakfast, wine for lunch, and Stolichnaya vodka for dinner. And I was smoking a lot of pot, of course.

Then one day I was sitting in my room. I wasn't drunk or stoned for the first time in I don't know how long and . . . well . . . the spirit of God came in my room. I had been in all kinds of spiritual energies through the years, but this was really different. I knew it was the Lord and he let me know that I'd be serving Him from then on. It wasn't like I was having "an experience" or was seeing "a vision." It was reality, so I said "All right, I'm ready." And it wasn't like it was some vague "I-am-everything" kind of god. It was Jesus Christ. It was real specific.

And he's led me every step of the way. I prayed that he would send some Christians into my life, some real ones, because I didn't know any. Three days later my piano player called me up and said, "There's this guy from L.A. who's a bass player, and he's going to audition tonight. I thought I ought to call you to let you know before you come down that he's a born-again Christian." Now, my band had no idea that my life had changed this way; I hadn't told them. I thought, "wow!!!"

So I went down and it was David MacKay, who's now my husband. He was a great bass player and I liked him right away. After one gig at the Sleeping Lady (a small club in the Marin County town of Fairfax) he told me he was going to church, and I said, "What? You're going to church?" I thought it was strange. I didn't connect what had happened to me with church in any way up to that point, but it sounded interesting, so I went. And I walked in and encountered the Holy Spirit again. It was wonderful. I wept and wept and all this bottled-up junk that had been inside of me came flowing out. I really became a different person. I had been in so many intellectually hip scenes over the years that if I went into a place and someone said [mockingly], "Oh Jesus loves you!" I would have said, "Who are you kidding?" But the pastor at this church, who had been a heavy Hindu for years before he became a Christian, was an intelligent man who had gone the spiritual gamut. He presented things about Christianity I'd never thought of before, so things really started to connect, not only in my mind, but in my spirit.

How did your experience change your music? The first two tracks on the Heart of Gold band album, both post-Keith, definitely have heavily religious overtones.

Immediately I started changing my whole direction and attitude. I knew I couldn't sing a certain kind of song. When I started singing this new music I realized that this was the kind of music I'd wanted to sing all along, which is actually praise and worship unto God. It was the direction that Keith and I were trying to get a hold of before we joined the Grateful Dead. I don't like all Christian music just because it has Christian lyrics. If it's not born of the spirit of God, it doesn't do much for me. What I want to be doing in music now is proclaiming what God is doing today.

This is the most incredible thing that's ever happened to me. I'm the most excited now that I've ever been about anything. I was never this excited about rock and roll. Or this committed. And the thing is it's not "Good today, not so good tomorrow, mediocre the next day." Your God is the same every day, and you're going to still have your ups and downs, but they won't be as extreme because you know who your God is and who you're serving. This is what I was looking for all along in my spiritual quest.

If I Told You All That Went Down . . .

■ ■ ■ ■ ■ ■

The Saga of Grateful Dead Records

By Steve Brown

In the land of rock, the discs
of sound are pushed by the
weasels of greed.
　　　—Anton Round

Fire! Fire on the mountain! My office was awash in a hellish umber glow as mountainous clouds of smoke draped across the sky. From our funky Victorian house in San Rafael, the Grateful Dead Record Company crew watched the nearby hills blazing wildly out of control.

It was hot and unseasonably weird on this spring day in 1976. Mickey *still* wasn't done mixing *Diga. Steal Your Face,* even after being rescued from bedlam, continued to suffer from a nasty curse put upon it by some obscure and mean old Pharaoh. Grateful Dead Records' president, Ron

The Dead's mid-1970s lineup. *(Photo by Bruce Polonsky)*

Rakow, who was in L.A. explaining delays while negotiating deals with United Artists, had become uncharacteristically quiet. Outside the GD Record Company eucalyptus trees were exploding in flames. There were ugly rumors of shitstorms on the horizon. It looked like my journey on this adventurous Grateful Dead trip was coming to the end of the road.

It was on the road—Highway 1 between the rural West Marin County towns of Bolinas and Olema—in March 1972 that Rakow had flashed on a whole independent record system that could work for the Dead. After six years with Warner Brothers, working with guys in suits who never quite understood them, the Dead had been considering declaring independence, and had asked Rakow to explore the possibilities. A slick financial appliance around the Dead's funky household (he had come to the band in the mid-Sixties by way of Wall Street, where he'd been a whiz-kid arbitrageur), Rakow proceeded to investigate, researching the financial statements, structure, and distribution systems of the major record companies.

On the Fourth of July 1972, Rakow's vision became a ninety-three-page report known as the "So What Papers" (probably derived from that awful cosmic revelation, "So what?"). The Dead didn't go for Rakow's initial proposal as submitted. Maybe some of the more conservative guys in the organization didn't like his idea of the Dead's records being distributed by Good Humor trucks. (Actually, it sounded pretty cool to me—"Here comes Uncle John's van, buy his vinyl sides.")

Some good Deadhead friends in the music scene (Hale Milgram, future president of Capitol Records, and Paul Nichols) tipped me off that the Dead needed additional input. Ah, my big chance! I contacted the Dead office and was invited by Rakow and the band's management to submit my own "What, How, Why Me" report. Inspired by my enthusiasm for the band, as a "dead-votee" from the Warlocks' Peninsula bar-gig days, I was psyched at the opportunity to communicate and perhaps participate with the Dead on their new venture.

For my report, I pulled deep from my heart and mind to relate my feelings and experiences. During the dozen years I'd spent in the music business up to that point, I had managed a band—The Friendly Stranger—produced concerts, been a music programmer at KSFO in L.A., a disc jockey at KPRI in San Diego and KSJO in San Jose. I'd also done record promotion, distribution, and wholesale buying in the Bay Area. As head buyer for the original Record Factory stores, it was with a missionary's zeal and joy that I had promoted and turned lots of folks on to some truly good old Grateful Dead in 1971 and 1972 (*American Beauty* through *Garcia* and *Europe '72*—hot stuff!).

In the beginning of 1973, I respectfully delivered to Rakow and the Dead my report outlining marketing, distribution, promotion, and advertising ideas for their independent record trip. Because of Pigpen's critical illness at that time, most business decisions were being forestalled. And after I had set a new world's record for breathholding, I finally got a call from Rakow to come meet with him and the Dead's management. We met, they liked me and stamped my hand okay. When it came up for the band's approval, the real acid test, I got that, too. All right! I was on the Golden Road, and the bus had stopped to let me on. A Deadhead's dream come true.

The Grateful Dead had firmly decided to have their own record label. In April of 1973 we put together a record company crew that would be administered by Rakow as president and general manager, with me responsible for recording production coordination and national promotion, Andy Leonard handling manufacturing and advertising, Greg Nelson covering distribution and sales, and Joshua Blardo doing national radio promotion. After taking over the Dead's old office, which looked like it had been transplanted from Haight-Ashbury to San Rafael, the new Grateful Dead Records office staff was rounded out with Jeanne Jones as accountant and Barbara Whitestone and Carol Miller managing the office.

Despite their reputation as a group of guys who liked to take risks, Rakow and the Dead decided that rather than jeopardize Grateful Dead Records, which was co-owned by all the voting members of the organization, they would create a second label to handle the more financially dubious solo projects members of the Dead were interested in pursuing. Thus was born Round Records, owned fifty-fifty by Garcia and Rakow.

Rakow financed the start-up of Grateful Dead Records and Round Records by selling foreign manufacturing and distribution rights to Atlantic Records for $300,000. He also set up a financial umbrella in which the First National Bank of Boston would approve and underwrite the eighteen independent record distributors we had chosen to use throughout the country.

In order to survey the retail and wholesale record scene and generally gauge the "Deadness" of the marketplace, I was sent back east in that summer of 1973. While there, I got to experience the awesome gathering at Watkins Glen and was treated to some memorable Dead–Allman Brothers jamming in a rehearsal trailer backstage.

Returning home after a summer of flexing their musical muscles, the Dead had a bunch of juicy new tunes ripe for their first offering on their own new label. And in August of 1973 the band, family, and crew moved into the Record Plant studios in Sausalito to start work on *Wake of the Flood*. Around this same time Robert Hunter was at Mickey's barn recording tracks on his and our first Round Records release, *Tales of the Great Rum Runners*.

From the beginning we were determined to make our albums of the highest-quality vinyl and apply our own personal quality control in all the phases of record production. Getting artists for album cover art was never a problem, as the Dead have been fortunate to have exceptionally talented artists around their scene for years. We commissioned one of my personal favorites, Rick Griffin, to do both initial releases of Grateful Dead and Round Records—*Wake* and *Rum Runners*. Rick knew from the biblical story of the Flood (Genesis 8:7) that Noah had sent forth a raven. But the raven he rendered on the back cover looked more like a crow to Rakow: He knew that either we'd make a good show of our first independent releases or we'd be eating that silly bird; better the skeptics in the record industry should eat it instead.

The *Wake* sessions went quite smoothly and pleasantly by Dead standards. When we finally had our first *Wake* album cassette copies fresh from mastering at the Lacquer Channel in Sausalito, I really felt that the Dead had recorded the sequel to *Abbey Road*. I loved it.

I was excited about making that October's album premiere tour, doing advance work for the band and turning on our distributors, radio stations, record stores, and Deadheads everywhere to some really good all-new stuff.

Shortly after our new album was released, after we'd spent lots of

Garcia's notes on different takes of "China Doll" during the *Mars Hotel* recording sessions.

overtime assuring product quality control, we discovered, much to our dismay, that sleazy counterfeit copies of *Wake of the Flood* were turning up on the East Coast. We'd been slimed! I had never imagined that the Grateful Dead would end up working with the FBI. By the time the counterfeiting subsided, we had been distracted long enough to lose valuable promotion and sales momentum. Still, despite the "evil twin" album, we were able to sell more than 400,000 copies of the real *Wake,* a healthy number in those days.

Around this time we decided to plug in more directly to all the Dead-heads. The Dead Freaks Unite campaign, introduced inside the "Skull and Roses" LP in 1971, had been a tremendous success—we'd built up a mailing list of 30,000 names—and we knew a direct mailing list and newsletter served as an effective communication link with the Deadheads. To reach even more people, we decided after *Wake* to send a Grateful Dead Records promotion booth on tour with the band. Our gambit worked: We signed up another 50,000 on the 1974 tours.

The booth was designed by Michael Gaspars of Bolinas and consisted of two pairs of 4 × 8-foot folding plywood panels, each with a custom Courtenay Pollack tie-dye representing one of the four seasons. A 12-foot table in front of the booth was also trimmed in Courtenay dyes. (Many Deadheads know Courtenay's work from the 1981, 1982, and 1983 Greek shows, for which he created the stage backdrops. He also made the Dead's famous early Seventies amp covers.) Signs over the booth were made by Kelley and Mouse that read: "FREE STUF" and "GRATEFUL DEAD COMMERCIAL MESSAGE." On the table for people who came to the booth already feeling a little strange, we had a mirrored infinity box containing a lovely two-headed skull-and-roses sculpture by David Best. It was a unique experience, to say the least, manning this kaleidoscopic wonder throughout the 1974 tours.

Giving out posters and postcards of all our records, signing up people on our "junk mail" list and getting direct feedback about the Dead and their records seemed an appropriate and friendly way of doing Grateful Dead business. Most rewarding to me was meeting all the wonderful people at Dead concerts all across North America and Europe. I was never in need of any booth handling help, setting up or taking down. Some Deadheads would follow along and help for a whole regional tour. Local Deadheads would turn me on to their scene and their town. I've often felt that the best "product" that the Dead have produced has been their fans. It was an amazing year of touring and expanding my reality.

Before the Dead went on the road in 1974, Garcia got into the studio and started his second solo album, titled *Garcia,* just like his first had been. Some tracks were cut at CBS and Wally Heider's in San Francisco, and others were done at Devonshire Studios in L.A. with session players like Michael Omartian (keyboards), Ron Tutt (drums), and Bobbye Hall (percussion). Backup vocals were added by Clydie King, Merry Clayton, and Maria Muldaur. It was a delightfully eclectic musical menu with vibrant cover art by psychedelic poster artist Victor Moscoso.

We had the *Garcia* promotional copies for radio stations, reviewers, and in-store playing printed with "Compliments of" over the title *Garcia,* instead of the usual "Promo Copy—Not for Sale" sticker. We thought it would be classier, but the disc jockeys and reviewers thought it was the title. Oh well, just so they spell your name correctly, right?

In March of 1974 the Dead started recording *Mars Hotel* at CBS Studios in San Francisco. It was the straight old corporate professional recording studio scene, complete with CBS company engineer—Uncle Roy (Seigel). The big advantage in Studio A was the capacity to sync-up two 16-track tape machines and record on up to thirty tracks. As the band's sound system seemed to be testing the mid-Seventies attitude of "more might be nice," it was not surprising to find them filling up almost all thirty tracks with something.

After making sure everybody had a pleasant supper at Cafe CBS, it was my job to keep a log sheet of all the tracks and each take on each track. Even with thirty tracks that wasn't too difficult. The real challenge was to accurately note the subtle, and sometimes not so subtle, differences in each take. Fortunately, my music tune-in factor was forever enriched by working next to Garcia during the playback of each take and adding his comments to the ones I'd noted during the recording of that take.

When it came time for naming this next Dead album, we had only to look a block away to the horribly seedy Mars Hotel just around the corner from the CBS Studios. Andy Leonard got up real early to photograph the morning's golden rays on that now-legendary and since-demolished landmark. For the album's back cover photo the whole band piled into my old Ford van and cruised over to the Cadillac Hotel in the heart of the City's Tenderloin district. Any hotel that *already* has a stuffed alligator on the wall of their lobby is our kind of zoo. From there, the creative geniuses of Kelley and Mouse were called upon to put these photos into the proper Grateful Dead perspective. While on a bad-pun jag late one night at CBS Studios, the phrase "ugly rumors" (from the Mars Hotel) snickeringly evolved. The line was passed along to Kelley and Mouse, who rendered it in pseudo-Aztec lettering. Holding these strange-looking words above the cover art one day at their studio, I was told by Mouse that I had the words upside down and backward. Perfect! This Grateful Dead release was going to be a lot of fun.

And fun it was. The free postcards and posters of *Mars Hotel,* the Heads' puzzling over the mysterious words on the cover, the comments and discussions of songs on the new Dead album kept the GD Records promo booth buzzin' that summer.

We lugged what had come to be known by the road crew as "Brown's box" across Europe that September of 1974. I had to learn how to translate the Americanese "junk mailing list" and "free stuff" into German, French, and British. We played first in London, and at the performances in the mammoth Alexandra Palace, Pink Floyd members came by to see the band. We spent at least a week or more in London, and I was able to check out lots of neat places like the Royal Albert Museum. There in the Egyptian exhibit, I stood in front of the *original* hieroglyphic inscriptions of the Egyptian *Book of the Dead.* There they were, those haunting words first heard proclaimed by the high priest of the Temple of Avalon, Chet Helms: "In the land of the dark, the ship of the sun is pulled by the Grateful Dead." Seeing the actual inscription allowed me to reach back and touch a reality from thousands of years past. And it *was* the Grateful Dead that had brought me to this very spot. It was a magic moment.

We flew to Munich next. During the performance at the Olympic Hall, Phil Lesh and Ned Lagin's "electronic" set actually began to start a massive mental riot in the Germans' minds.

When Germans get upset, they show their displeasure by whistling loud. The louder they whistled, the louder and more brutal Phil and Ned's electronic onslaught became. It was war! We were fighting the Jerries again. Well, they messed the hall up pretty good, but nobody got hurt and we made it out of Germany alive.

Since we couldn't nail down the planned Amsterdam gig, we decided to take the extra time and go to the next gigs in France by way of Switzerland. Phil, Ned, Dan Healy, and I rented a car in Zurich and went on an enhanced sightseeing tour through the Swiss Alps. After visits to Lucerne and Geneva, it was time to cross over into France. At the Swiss-French border check, we found ourselves shuffling the enhancement supply from person to person in a dance that could only be improvised by persons already greatly enhanced. Truly a classic performance. Everybody took their well-earned bows later, a little farther down the road.

The next concert was in Dijon, France, in the Burgundy region. Needless to say, we did sample the local wines, as well as breads and cheeses.

The last shows were in Paris, where we cruised the Louvre before heading home to do a run of last performances at Winterland. The band would then "retire" for a year of woodshedding and working on various projects.

It was going to be a busy year "off." About two weeks before the October Winterland "last shows," the Dead decided to film the performances and make their own feature-length Grateful Dead movie. Round Reels was formed to produce it. Crews were hired and shooting scripts were drawn up. I had an opportunity to take off my record-production hat and put on a film-production hat. It was a hectic scene for two weeks, but the shooting went well. Although the film soundtrack recorded all right, there were some major fuck-ups in the audio taping department, which later surfaced when it came time to put together the live album *Steal Your Face*.

I got a chance to script shot sheets (lists of things to film) and assist in production and post-production activities. My own mug even turns up in a segment of the film where we're onstage with Boots going over the logistics for his pyrotechnic effects to be used during the show. The scene shot backstage of Jerry noodling on his guitar and me continuously rolling joints and stacking them into his guitar case didn't make the final edit.

When I saw the animation work Gary Gutierrez was doing, I knew the opening segment would be really hot. To get the authentic chopper sound for the motorcycling skeleton in this segment, Dan Healy and crew went to Sears Point Raceway. There, from the back of Healy's Ranchero pickup, we miked a Harley chopper being audaciously commanded by Crazy Peter Sheridan. Jamming the throttle around the track, Crazy Peter was one of those amazing assholes that you love to hate. When I see that skeleton on his bike in the movie, I remember Crazy Peter—he's gone.

In January of 1975 the band was ready to hole up daily at Weir's studio and put together a new album more or less from scratch. They had given themselves the luxury of retiring from the road in 1975, and each band member seemed to be hungry to sink his creative teeth into this new recording, which would become *Blues for Allah*.

16 TRACK IDENTIFICATION CHART
CBS RECORDS
CR 8784   ARTIST: GRATEFUL DEAD | ORIG. JOB NO. SW:05594 | JOB NO. 105760 basic | PRODUCER Phil/band | ENGINEER Ray, Mike, Phil | DATE 4/17/74

CE NO. BASIC + ODs — TITLE: UNBROKEN CHAIN

1 (L)	2 (C)	3 (R)	4 (R)	5	6 (C)	7 (L)	8 (C)
DRUM	KICK	DRUM	HI-HAT	LEAD VOCAL Phil	BASS DIRECT Phil	GUITAR Jerry	GUITAR Bob

B —— D —— 3 PART 1ST HALF – J.

9	10	11	12	13	14	15	16
PIANO Mike Keith	PIANO DIRECT from pickup	ACCOUSTIC GUITAR Bob	CLAVINET EL. PIANO CELESTE Keith	BACKGROUND VOCALS Bob, Donna, Jerry	END VOCAL Donna	# SYNC TRACK	BACKGROUND VOCALS Bob, Donna, Jerry

CE NO. SYNC REEL

1 (L)	2 (R)	3	4 (L)	5	6 ARP	7 (L)	8 (R)
GUIDE	GUIDE	SYNTHESIZER #3 Ned	TIBETIAN BELLS Phil	SYNTH #2 Ned	KEYBOARD SYNTHESIZER DIRECT Ned	KEYBOARD SYNTH LESLIE MIKE	KEYBOARD SYNTH LESLIE MIKE

2nd Half — 1st half

9 (L)	10 (R)	11 (R)	12	13	14	15	16
Room	Room	TIBETIAN BELLS Phil	SHAKER Bill	ORGAN TUNING	LEAD VOCAL #2 Phil	# SYNC TRACK	DOUBLED LEAD VOCAL #2 Phil

Track sheet for the recording of "Unbroken Chain."

The long-run daily daytime drill of mining for tunes in Weir's studio ran up a healthy food and beverage bill at the Mill Valley Market... Lunch for Allah and a doggie treat for Otis, please.

The evolution of the songs for *Blues for Allah* was a fascinating and at times tedious process—working and reworking each segment of each musical piece over and over again. So it was with some dubious relief that the band took a busman's holiday to rehearse for a few days with other musician friends for the upcoming SNACK (Students Need Athletics, Culture and Kicks; it raised money for San Francisco public schools) benefit concert at Kezar Stadium in San Francisco. Working with some of their new material, they jammed with David Crosby, John Cipollina, Merl Saunders, Ned Lagin, and Mickey Hart. (It was during these "SNACK sessions" that Mickey began to rejoin the Grateful Dead.) Since none of the new pieces had lyrics yet, they were all rehearsed and performed at SNACK only instrumentally. As the *Allah* tracks became keeper takes, lyric sessions were held and the musical tunes emerged as songs. There was no doubting that this was going to be a strong album for the Dead.

Consequently we wanted strong cover art for the album. Phil Garris from San Diego was recommended to us by our surfer artist buddies in Southern California. As it turned out, Phil Garris had already completed a Grateful Dead painting. We flew him up to show us. It was of a robed skeleton playing a fiddle. Great! I took Garris and his paintings to the band's recording session that day and had him present it to the group.

They all generally liked it, but some sensed something unsettling about it. "Those green glasses and eyes, too insectoid," offered Lesh.

Well, Garris had to get back to San Diego and thought it might help if I hung on to the painting just in case they had a change of heart; he'd come back for it later. For safe keeping, I hung the painting on the wall at the foot of my bed that week. It was strong art, a good design. After some time had passed I called Phil and told him to get back up here and to bring his painting stuff. He repainted the glasses and eyes red, added a tiny tear running out from them, and integrated the words "Blues for Allah" into the design. Then we presented the new version to the band. "Ahh! That's it now" was the unanimous response. And *now* it had to be, because after seven months of recording, time was running out; our new distribution deal with United Artists was forcing the Grateful Dead to face again their most dreaded nemesis—the Deadline. Phil Garris' album art design, by the way, went on to be awarded first prize by the National Illustrators Association that year. My bedroom wall will never be the same.

The film was costing a bundle. We needed more money, so Rakow made a deal with United Artists for the manufacturing and distribution rights of Grateful Dead Records and Round Records. That helped us to continue to fund Round Reels, where Garcia was spending his time overseeing the film project—when he wasn't working on *Allah* or playing with the Garcia Band or producing albums with some of his bluegrass heroes. (Excuse me, folks, but this talented gentleman, Señor Jerome J. Garcia, *is* fucking amazing.) The Good Old Boys sessions at Mickey's studio were a special time for all concerned, as Garcia had a chance to produce artists he had long admired: Don Reno (banjo), Chubby Wise (fiddle), Frank Wakefield (mandolin), and David Nelson (guitar). Two days of pure bluegrass heaven for all of us, but especially for Garcia. Lotsa laughin' 'n' a pickin'. It was a good ol' time.

Sometime in the spring of 1975 I was approached by several of the local artists around the Dead scene to see about putting together a benefit for the family of one of their fellow artists who had died—Bob Fried. Since the Dead were "retired" at the time, I asked Garcia if he'd play and maybe invite some of his friends. I was able to get Winterland, Garcia was able to get some friends (all the members of the Grateful Dead), and with help from Uncle Bill the whole thing was a great success. We raised more than $7,000 for the Fried family.

There were two actual Grateful Dead gigs in this "year of retirement." One was Grateful Dead Records' album premiere party for *Blues for Allah*—a small by-invitation-only event at the Great American Music Hall in San Francisco (which was also broadcast on the radio)—and the other a free concert for 25,000 people in Golden Gate Park with the Starship. At the Park gig the Dead *and* the Hell's Angels decided to use my van for their backstage room. It smelled like a Heineken brewery for months. However, I did excavate about half a pound of some really good roaches from the deal.

It was time for another Garcia album, as per contract with United Artists. Songs for *Reflections* were drawn from material that the Dead had been performing live—"Might as Well," "Comes a Time," "They Love Each Other," and "Must've Been the Roses"—some of the basic tracks of which had already been recorded by GD band members at Weir's studio. The bulk of the recording and mixing was done at His Masters Wheels, Elliot Mazer's cozy studio on a little side street off Market in San Francisco. Garcia used his then–Garcia Band personnel— John Kahn, Ron Tutt, and Nicky Hopkins—to complete the other songs on this album. The HMW sessions contained some sensational jams, and the final songs on *Reflections* are well performed and include classic versions of familiar Grateful Dead concert tunes. "Mission in the Rain" is a nice hometown touch by Garcia.

I got to tour quite extensively with this particular version of the Garcia Band throughout the fall of 1975. You haven't really lived until you've had your limo escorted at high speed all the way from Central Park South to the Lower East Side by the Hell's Angels.

Mickey's barn cum studio, Rolling Thunder, was always a great place to work. It had the vibes of a place well lived-in with music making. It was like a secret clubhouse built out in the woods by boys who maybe didn't let girls join. The *Tiger Rose* sessions there with Robert Hunter gave me a chance to work with Pete Sears and David Freiberg from the Starship, David Grisman, and Dave Torbert. The *Tiger Rose* cover art design by Kelley and Mouse is exceptional and one of my favorites.

Another hot set of sessions at Mickey's were for his *Diga* album. There the Diga Rhythm Band—fourteen different players on a multitude of percussion instruments—cooked along, joined at times by Garcia, who wove in and out of the polyrhythms with dazzling guitar lines. Tasty stuff. Please make the effort to hear *Diga* someday; an exciting album produced by Mickey Hart.

By mid-1976 United Artists was due its next Dead album. Not being able to pull another *Blues for Allah* out of a hat just like that, the Dead opted to release a live double-album of the October 1974 concerts at Winterland. What no one apparently knew was that the original master recordings recorded by Bill Wolf were, partly due to his own fault, fucked up. It was like trying to get shit out of peanut butter. Nobody wanted to deal with it. At one point the whole stressed-out mess got to Wolf and he flipped out, holding the tapes hostage in his house in Stinson Beach. After the tapes were rescued, Phil and Bear (Owsley) bit the bullet and attempted to salvage what they could from these reels of magnetic kaka.

Rakow had promised United Artists the *Diga* album and was sweating it out in L.A., assuring them that it was coming.

The animation segment production for the Grateful Dead movie had turned into a black hole of funding (it had gotten too *good* to stop). The movie post-production expenses continued to mount up, as such projects are wont to do. And now Rakow was adding a new Hell's Angels movie into the stew. Jeez!

The Grateful Dead hadn't toured in nineteen months, and consequently there was no concert cash flow to help the situation.

Rakow just had this double live nightmare album to play as his main hand in negotiating more money out of United Artists. He'd been pushin' on Mickey too hard, and counter vibes were stirring in the artists' camp. Dead management was uneasy. There was talk of a revised corporate structuring. And worst of all, they were about to be humiliated by an album to which they were contractually committed.

Rakow went weird. The United Artists deal made, he cut himself a hefty unauthorized severance check and disappeared.

The Grateful Dead had been bitten by their own weasel gone rabid. It was then that Phil christened the album *Steal Your Face*.

Over a period of four years, Grateful Dead and Round Records had put out no fewer than fourteen albums, and Round Reels had produced a feature-length concert film. It had been an incredible flood of experiences goin' down the road with the Dead. But on that weird spring day in 1976, when the hills were blazing outside the office, the writing was on the wall. The GD Record Company's days were numbered. By the end of the year we were history, and before long the Dead would have the clammy handshake of Clive Davis to seal their new record deal with Arista Records.

Maybe the silver lightning–skull medallion, number 86 of a series, that I got from Bear augured the eighty-sixing of Grateful Dead Records ("then the lightning will!"). But in the sweet, sweet summertime of 1986, the Lovelight is on and them smilin' furry bears are dancing in the sunshine again. Especially this Brown bear, now with a touch of gray.

The Best Laid Plans . . .

Mars Bars

Prior to the release of the *Mars Hotel* album in 1975, I thought it would be a fun promotional idea to distribute to radio stations and record stores bunches of those tiny little bars of soap you find in hotels and motels, with a fantastic Kelly and Mouse–designed wrapper. To add to the fun, I suggested we use that joke soap that produces black suds when you lather up. The idea was shelved when we put our extra advertising dollars into a spiffy animated *Mars Hotel* TV commercial instead.

Holographic Cover Art

More than a couple of times, various holographic artists were invited to the GD Record Company's office to show us their prototypes of a three-dimensional holographic design for one of the upcoming Dead album covers. Due to the relative newness of this art form at the time, the cost per album was not economically feasible.

Ground Records

Early in 1976, we began to research the possibility of starting a new, third record label to handle GD and family "archive" album product, to be sold by mail order only, at a $4.98 list price. Called Ground Records, the label would release exceptionally good outtakes from various recording sessions (jams from *Blues for Allah, Reflections, Diga,* etc.) as well as some really hot live concert and rehearsal recordings. Financing, royalties, distribution, and product ideas had been all worked out on paper when plans ground to a halt with Rakow's sudden departure.

The Holographic Music Pyramid

One of the best hoaxes I've been proud to be associated with. Based on theoretical concepts of that time, the idea of encoding Dead music on a one-inch pyramid to be read by an optical fiber seemed to be plausible. In one of our junk mailing newsletters, we stated that the Dead would be attempting to come out with this new musical reproduction form, and actual scientists in the holographic field became more than curious about our heretofore unheard of efforts in this new medium. Of course Rakow had made a one-inch model of this wondrous little pyramid, which he didn't hesitate to grandly produce at the slightest provocation. Just about the time when we thought our cheeks could no longer stand the pressure from our tongues, some Deadhead scientist in New York working with holography reported back to us that he had made preliminary progress on a similar device and wished to speak with *our* researchers. We turned him over to Uncle Anton for further enlightenment.

A Short Break
with Bob Weir

An Interview: December 14, 1985

Despite many years on the periphery of the Grateful Dead scene in my capacity as a writer, fate and circumstance had conspired to keep me from meeting Bob Weir until mid-December of 1985. Of course I'd thought about what I'd ask when the fateful meeting finally arrived; what I didn't expect, though, was that the opportunity would come with no warning: "If you can get to the studio in the next half hour, you can interview Weir," the voice at the other end of the telephone said. I darted from my desk like Wile E. Coyote in pursuit of the elusive Roadrunner and managed to pull up to the Dead's Marin County studio in record time. Garcia was just leaving, all smiles and cheery salutations, as Weir, Hart, and Kreutzmann waved from the front door like some frontier family saying good-bye to Pa as he goes off to hunt bear.

Weir at the Greek Theater in Berkeley, 1984. *(Photo by Ron Delany)*

Inside, things were typically chaotic. Crew members clowned with the band members and each other. Mickey proudly showed off photos of his latest acquisition—huge Philippine drums that still lay in crates at the docks. A TV blared in a room adjoining the main studio, though no one seemed to be watching.

After a brief wait, I was ushered into a tiny utility closet that was cluttered with boxed reels of raw footage of the Dead movie. There, I finally met Weir, who was sitting on a metal folding chair waiting patiently for his inquisitor. I've seen prison interviews conducted in more appealing surroundings, but it *was* kind of cozy, and, predictably, I found Weir to be a friendly and cooperative subject. Not as verbose as some other band members, he is nonetheless very open and candid. Far from being "lost in space," as he is sometimes depicted, Weir struck me as a person with well-developed ideas and a crystal-clear vision of what he wants to get out of music and life. I had always imagined that I'd like him, and I did—very much.

On the way over to the studio today, I was listening to the version of "Throwing Stones" from the recent Rochester shows and it struck me that the song is now fully mature. It's arrived. Could you talk a little about the genesis of the song and what motivated it?
I don't know where all that stuff comes from. It rolls around in your head for years, maybe, and then finally there's a window and it finds its way out.

You'd been involved with antinuclear activities for some time—
But this is more or less just an anarchistic diatribe. It seems to me that the people who are running the show aren't doing such a great job of it on either side.

    I was watching the news one night and I was struck by the absurd posturing that the big governments take over issues, and the fact that governments lie so readily and so blatantly and then stand by it and expect people to—not to believe it, but try to distill from their lies some notion of what their position actually is. It occurred to me that governments are acting in the most inhumane and ludicrous manner, that got me pissed, and that rattled around in the back of my head for a while and a few lines emerged. I bounced those off of Barlow and a song eventually came out of it. It started out of nothing. I don't remember which part came first.

When you get the germ of an idea, how do you develop it? Do you then pick up a guitar and see what you can add with that?
Yeah, well, I work in any number of different fashions. Sometimes I'll start with the guitar, or start with the words, or they'll both come along in pretty close proximity. "Throwing Stones" is kind of weird because it starts on the dominant. I don't know how I arrived at that. I think pretty obviously the diatribe part of the song came first because for a song to start on the dominant is sort of a weird portent to begin with. Then I remember that it occurred to us that we were getting pretty thick pretty quick, and it was time to balance it a bit before the whole song became a full-blown diatribe and nothing but. The punks do that well enough. So it occurred to me that what I would do is temper all this by

lifting a melody and a couple of words from an old Bahamian folk carol called "Bye and Bye"—

Was that from the same Nonesuch record [The Real Bahamas] *you got "And We Bid You Goodnight" from?*
Right. So the second half of the first verse uses those chord changes, and it's meant to counterbalance things. It had that softness I wanted. It has the punch from starting off in the dominant mode. When it finally resolved in the tonic mode, I wanted to cool it out for the second half of the verse.

You cool it out lyrically, too, with some optimism.
Yeah. The world isn't all bad. But we wanted to paint a picture of the world as we both saw it that night. It took longer than a night, of course, but we had the form of it down in a night.

Were you physically together? I know you sometimes write by phone and exchange tapes and that sort of thing.
On this one we were out at his ranch in Wyoming.

I think the first time most people hear it they're struck by the "Ashes, ashes all fall down" refrain. It's something most of us grew up singing as children, though of course with a different context.
It's just the image that sooner or later, whether they know it or not, that's what they're saying—sooner or later it's all going to collapse; the whole house of cards is going to collapse. I guess the thrust of the song is what we will or won't do in the face of that: "We will leave this place an empty stone/Or that shiny ball of blue we call our home." Sooner or later we'll emerge triumphant as a race or we'll make our own graves.

The first couple of years after the song was introduced, the big jam about two-thirds of the way through the song was very dissonant, sometimes even angry sounding. Then, at the Greek in 1984, intentionally or not, the jam shifted to the bright progression of major chords that you still play. It seemed to change the tone of the entire piece from pessimism to optimism. Was that a conscious choice?
Well, we basically just got tired of playing it the other way. We got tired of the tension of that jam, partly because we have that kind of feeling in some of our other songs. So this new harmonic pattern came about over a tour or two, actually, and just kind of developed. . . .

You've described it as "anarchic." I initially thought of it as "political," but you obviously wouldn't agree with that word choice.
No, it's apolitical. It's antipolitics. I don't see politics as something that is doing much to serve humanity.

Was the song's connection to "Not Fade Away" something you discovered when you were writing it?
No, it just sort of happened that way, and as it developed it occurred to us that was one of the songs we could tie it to. There are others, of course, too.

What is it, from a musician's standpoint, that allows songs like "Playin' in the Band" and "The Other One" to remain totally fresh year after year?
We play for the moment. A lot of it is the structure of the band. None of us is playing by rote, and each of us is considering what we're doing afresh each time. If we were doing those songs every night, as opposed to once every three or four nights, I don't see how we could escape doing them by rote. The way we've got it arranged right now is in such a way that we do them often enough to keep the chord changes fresh in our minds so it doesn't just fall apart, but not often enough so we're doing it unimpassionedly.

Do certain songs have certain associations for you? When you play "The Other One," for example, is there any kind of flash of all the other versions of it, the lineage of it? I don't want to overdramatize this—
Well, yeah, it's a place I go when I sing that that's the same timeless place—or at least it seems that way to me.

Do you think the musical relationships within the band have changed much through the years?
They've changed *a lot,* and I assume they'll continue to do so. For instance, when I first joined the band, I wasn't a journeyman musician and I was barely able to hold down my position in the group. I've evolved through the years to be able to make quite a bit of noise. My role keeps evolving, and that takes the heat off some of the others—like Garcia, who had to make all the noise after Pigpen checked out. That gives Garcia a chance to sit back a little.

It's not really like he's "sitting back"—
No, no. It's like he has a foil to work off of. As Brent has become more

integrated into the band he's, in turn, become a foil for all the rest of us. As we get to know each other better each year, we get to interact musically in more interesting and meaningful manners. As I get older, too, playing and singing come a little more easily for me. I don't have to concentrate quite so hard at it, so I'm able to listen to more of what's going on around me, and I'm able to pay more attention to what's going on around me. But that's standard for any developing musician.

What are you listening for rhythmically in the band? Are you listening, say, to the drummers more than to Phil?
I'm listening to the whole. You have to, because it's all important. My position onstage these days is right in the middle, and I can hear discrepancies from stage left to stage right, so I have to listen to all of it and then try to come up with something that is more or less a common denominator.

Is it accurate to say that you're playing more pure rhythm today than in some years past? On a lot of old tapes, it sounds like you're playing more leadlike filigrees; your style was more ornamental. Do you think that's accurate?
Yeah. Part of it's the material, and part of it is the fact that we've got Brent now and he plays a lot of the color and does it real well. Over the years, too, I've just sort of developed a style where I like to provide a little more punch or block motion, or however you'd describe it, than I used to. I can still go up and play lines. Like in "West L.A. Fadeaway" I play almost no rhythm guitar—it's *all* lines.

Are the musical relationships among you ever articulated in rehearsals?
Sure. We'll try to define what we're doing. "What is that figure you've been playing?" [Laughs] "Is that a major third or a minor third?" "Do you actually mean to play that that way, or is that a mistake?" Because it can go either way. Sometimes what might sound like a mistake isn't a mistake, or a mistake can lead to modes that we pursue—especially during the jams, but then sometimes they also turn up later in songs.

You can see it clearly sometimes. It seems as though some of the ideas you tried in "Sage and Spirit," for example, were developed further in "Lost Sailor" a few years later.
That definitely is a case where that happened. There are other ones, too, but I can't think of them off the top of my head.

In certain ways, the Dead's music is less abstract now than it was in the past. Is it harder to get into the idea of playing "space music"?
In the early Seventies, there were fewer of us in the band, and during the space jams we were a little more mobile just because there were fewer of us. Now that we have more people and Brent's a relatively new member, it's taken a while to get back that kind of mobility again. When Garcia and I go out and play together, for instance (after the Rhythm Devils), it goes completely different places every night. That stuff is actually more mobile—in terms of the harmonic directions it takes— than any of the stuff we used to do. But the more people you have, the more everyone has to listen. I think it's starting to open up to where the space jams are getting looser and looser.

Also, for instance, with two drummers, it's almost impossible to do what we could with one drummer in terms of turning one rhythm into another. You can't get two guys to turn the same corner at once—though we're trying it anyway. [Laughs]

Do you and Garcia ever discuss the nature of the space jam before you return to the stage? In an interview with Paul Krassner that was aired during the Toronto SEVA [an organization that devotes much of its energy to fighting treatable blindness in the Third World] show in 1984, Garcia said you sometimes agree on a theme. To be honest, I couldn't tell if he was serious or pulling our legs. Certainly Krassner is a prankster...
For a while there a couple of years back we would discuss current events or something before we went out, and every now and again we'll still do it—come up with a motif for the jam. It's almost never anything really serious, though once or twice we did take it seriously. I think the night Bob Marley checked out we tried to do a little musical eulogy. Usually, though, we're just amusing ourselves back there during the drum solo, coming up with joke motifs for the jam: "Okay, you're the stewardess aboard this hijacked airliner," or something like that.

I want to ask you about your affinity for the blues. In the last year or so, it seems as though every show has a little blues spotlight in the first set, whether it's "Minglewood" or "C. C. Rider" or "Walkin' Blues" or whatever. What does that do for you as a player? You seem very comfortable with it at this point.
I like it a bunch. I've got a big collection of blues records and have always liked it. A few years ago, too, I took up playing slide guitar. It's just

one of the bases I like. Hardly anybody plays the blues anymore. We don't render classical renditions of blues. We don't sound like a Chicago blues band when we do those tunes. Nonetheless, those songs are part of the greater vocabulary from which we draw, and I think it's important for us and our audiences to bear that in mind. We do blues tunes, we do country tunes, we do stuff that harkens back to old folk music. I listen to Charles Ives, and every now and again you hear some of that in there. Or strains of Stephen Foster. We play American music and we try to keep all those colors on the palette.

I've read in different places that you either knew Reverend Gary Davis or took lessons from him or something. What's the story?
I went and visited him a couple of times in New York in this basement apartment he had. I learned "Samson and Delilah" the way he used to play it, which is not the way we play it onstage now—you can't play that style of guitar in a band, really. It would take a lot of work. I learned a few other tunes, too. . . .

A lot of Deadheads report that the life lessons they hear in Grateful Dead tunes are frequently adaptable to what they're personally going through at any given time—that different tunes speak to them at different times. As a singer of those songs, do you also get that sort of vicarious experience?
Well, inasmuch as the songs are little vignettes, or little pictures of life as it might be in someone else's life. When you write a song about somebody, and then you play the song, you're acting the part, you put on that mask and you're trying to speak from that person's point of view. I'm not thinking of myself as a performer performing that song. I'm thinking of myself as that guy telling a story.

Do you see yourself as a storyteller, in that tradition?
You mean as a balladeer? Yeah, that's part of it. Sometimes I feel like a balladeer, sometimes I feel like a crooner. Sometimes when I'm writing I'll just want to play with the melody, and what comes through my head in terms of lyrics isn't that important, and I don't put that much into it. Sometimes I really put a lot into developing the character in the story. It all depends. Sometimes I want to do both.

Barlow has said that what appeals to you lyrically are fairly specific ideas, as opposed to more general or open-ended themes.

That's not entirely true. [Laughs] He has his views. That's not entirely true in my estimation. It might have been more true a while back than it is now.

What sort of stuff are you working on now?
[Long pause] It would be very hard for me to describe. I have a song in the works about Trigger the Wonder Horse, for instance, as seen as a marvel of American mythos. I don't know—I have a lot of ideas. Having written "Throwing Stones," I don't think I'm going to get on a soapbox about anything else right quickly. "Throwing Stones" and "Esau," which is an allegory about what happened to members of our generation, where one brother went off and fought a war and one brother stayed home and more or less minded the store, and then the subsequent events and developments of that. There's a real specific biblical allegory in that story. I think Barlow and I might try to rework it so it's not quite so obscure. Without damaging the imagery, it might have a little more punch if it were a little bit easier to understand. I don't know—maybe it's better to let it roll around the subconscious and let it ring bells or not if people are open or not. [In fact, "My Brother Esau" was dropped from the repertoire in 1987.]

Was there ever a threat that you'd have to go into the military?
I got my induction notice twice, around the time I turned eighteen. I went down, but I refused to obey anything they told me. I'm not good soldiering material. [Laughs] They didn't want me. I'd show up—'cause if you didn't show up you went to jail—but that's *all* I did. I answered their questions with questions, and stuff like that. I was not into their way of life, I had no use for it, and I'd thought I'd be real direct and tell them that.

So you finally got off by being classified 4-S, "4-spaced"?
[Laughs] Last I heard I was still 1-A, but I think my file is probably stamped that I'm not a good soldiering prospect. [Laughs]

Has it been difficult at all for you to reintegrate Pigpen's material into the band? It's been a long, slow process.
No, it's only come up as it's come up. It hasn't been forced. It's happened on the moment. For instance, with "Smokestack Lightning," of course I knew the song, but I really hadn't considered doing it, but then we

were doing a jam and it fell right into that groove, so I sang it. That sort of broke the ice.

There are certain musical transitions that have become familiar, like "He's Gone" going into a blues like "Smokestack" or "Spoonful" or whatever. There, the link is fairly obvious, but what of a pairing like "Estimated Prophet" and "Eyes of the World"? What is the musical link that allows that pair to exist so comfortably together when, on the surface, they seem so dissimilar?
I don't know, really. There's a harmonic bridge between F-sharp minor and E-major seventh mode, and there's also a rhythmic bridge between the two, which is one reason Garcia likes to do it.

Are you generally predisposed to a certain direction during a song, or are you just listening intently to feel which way it might go?
Both. Sometimes people drop hints in a jam to indicate what direction they might want to take it. After the jam's gone wherever it's going to go, someone will introduce something that will suggest a direction, and then someone else will take a melody or theme or something and work that into something that we already know. We'll either pick up on it or we won't.

Or you'll battle over it. I've seen you drag a reluctant Garcia into a "Spoonful" or two.
[Laughs] It happens. It works both ways.

Is it harder to assert yourself some nights than others?
Yeah. Some nights you're hotter than others. When you're hot, it's not hard to assert yourself. On other nights, if I don't hear something coming, or if I have an idea that I think might work but I don't assert it with blazing authority, sometimes someone will pick up on it anyway, and sometimes it goes by unnoticed.

You in the band have always talked about experiencing the shows in "real time." You play it and that's it, basically. Do you have any of the Deadhead-level appreciation of, "Oh, yeah, the Cincinnati show was good. The first Richmond show was that great one where we ended with 'Gloria,'" that sort of thing?
Not really. If someone plays me a tape, I'll remember it. I'll remember everything about it. But having played literally thousands of shows, it

takes quite a show to . . . I liked this last run at Oakland [November 20–22, 1985] quite a lot. There were moments when it sagged, but for the most part there was a lot of energy and we hung together pretty well.

What are some of your favorite Hunter-Garcia songs?
I like a lot of the ballads. "Stella Blue" I like a lot. I like "Wharf Rat" a lot, "Black Peter." What else? [Pause] "Brown-Eyed Women" is a neat tune. That hangs together well. There are a lot of them. It depends on my mood.

From a player's perspective, which are the most interesting?
It's hard to single any of them out because they all have different feelings. "Eyes of the World," if it's happening really right, is a lot of fun to play. The ballads are a lot of fun to play. Maybe not "fun," but all-involving. The ballads are very all-engrossing; I tend to get very involved in those. Again, it totally depends on the night. Some tunes flat surprise me.

Do you find that with your own tunes as well—sometimes they're more involving than others?
Sure, they go hot and cold. We retire tunes and bring back other ones. From night to night anything can be flat and anything can be hot. You just don't know usually until you're in it.

Can you remember the last "bad" show you played?
I think there was one off night on the last [fall 1985] tour, but our percentage has been pretty good this year. We've had some clunkers, but I can't remember where they were. Actually, I do remember a gig in Portland, Maine, where I thought everyone should have gotten a refund.

Aside from the band obviously being on a roll, you personally seem so much more relaxed than you did in 1984. Some of that must be because you gave all your energy to the Dead this year and weren't coming home one day and going out with Bobby and the Midnites the next.
Right. I was killing myself. There was no sense in my putting out 150 percent all the time every day. I was exhausted all the time last year. I'll do another solo thing sometime, but what shape it'll take I don't know. It'll happen, though.

You've been very involved with SEVA over the last few years, performing at benefits and all. How did your involvement with that organization come about?

I was more or less brought into it by Wavy Gravy, who introduced me to a couple of [SEVA] people in Michigan when we were playing up there one time in 1979 or 1980. Then right after that, SEVA was having a conference—it used to be annual, now it's biannual—out here in Mill Valley [in Marin County]. Gravy had told me I should drop by and check it out, so I did, and I was most impressed by what I heard and saw, and so I attended the bulk of the conference, and I've been involved ever since on one level or another.

You guys have been hit up to do benefits by nearly everybody at one time or another, from the Hell's Angels to various American Indian groups. What about SEVA, in particular, appealed to you?

The collection of people involved with SEVA is a lot different than any other foundation I've run across. It's a public health organization, so to speak, or it has been, but they have a lot of emphasis on the philosophy of what they're doing and a lot of emphasis on having as paneclectic a view of things as could be digested by one outfit and still be of a workable and practical nature. It's not just doctors or philosophers. They've got all kinds of different people involved, and in that forum, when issues come up they're discussed from so many different directions. And that impressed me.

Didn't the Dead once do a benefit for the Black Panthers? That strikes me as being more political than the group usually gets.

That was another fiasco, I'm afraid. I wasn't real happy about doing that one, personally, but a couple of guys in the band got convinced by [Black Panther leader] Huey Newton, and I then went along with it. About halfway through it, though, I started getting the feeling that we were being ripped off, and I'm pretty sure that was, in fact, the case. We probably paid a lot of legal fees for people who were in jail for things they did. That's not where I like to put my efforts. We've all learned a lot since then.

How does the Rex Foundation [the Dead's philanthropic wing] determine who gets money from the annual Dead benefit shows?

It's done by committee. Each of the people in the organization gets to submit his or her ideas. It's the Grateful Dead crew and staff and a few others.

To what degree do you think a band has a responsibility to do benefits? Obviously, it's always been a significant part of the Dead's worldview.
We've always operated under the assumption that if you get some, you give some back, because that's what keeps things turning. It's not pure altruism. There's a real sense of fulfillment if you're able to affect positive change.

In the early 1970s, in particular, there were a lot of well-publicized benefits that didn't end up raising much money for the causes they were supposed to support. The Dead have been more careful in choosing benefits, it appears.
That's not entirely always been true. We've been through a number of real fiascos. Most recently we went through that Vietnam Vets benefit [with Jefferson Starship at Moscone Center in San Francisco in 1982] where almost all the money raised went to legal and administrative costs for the organization. I think we were hustled. But practice makes perfect, and you more or less learn how to separate the catfish from the trout, as they say, and we're still learning. We're getting better at it—getting better at getting the money to the right places, where it won't be squandered or pocketed.

Can you speculate on whether the Dead would have gotten involved in something like Live Aid?
My gut reaction would be, number one, we can't play a twenty-minute set [Laughs], and number two, they had all the help they needed. There's a lot of food rotting on the docks in East Africa, and I was afraid that was going to be the case. I think people could have done a little more homework on how the money could be spent or on data gathering. Obviously they did a fine job at raising the money and getting food over there, but distribution has been a real problem, and it seems as though a little more thought could have been put into looking real hard at the political situation there to make it all more effective.

I almost dare not bring it up, but do you think the fabled "next Dead album" will get made anytime soon?
We were talking about it at the meeting today, as a matter of fact. There

are a couple of plans that have arisen. It's not dead, I'll say that, and I intend to be working on it real soon. . . .

I guess I don't understand what the problem is. Is it just inertia? We hear other things about the band not wanting to deliver an album to Arista because of dissatisfaction with the label.
I think it's general studiophobia. The inability to come of accord in the studio is a real problem. It's so easy to do it onstage because it's demanded of us, but when we're in the studio, we're all so pathologically antiauthoritarian, to a man, that when someone makes a suggestion you generally get an instant six-way factionalization. Any agreement in the studio is more or less grudgingly conceded. Onstage that doesn't happen.

Was the band's experience with Gary Lyons [on Go to Heaven] that unpleasant? I think of that as a very well-recorded album that played to all of your strengths.
My major reservation with that record had nothing to do with him. I just felt that we didn't have good, mature material when we recorded it. Some of it we'd never even played live. But at this point that's *not* the case, so it's not an impediment.

Is there a danger that you've now played this material too much—that it's no longer fresh?
I don't think so. All the songs we'd record are still fun to play onstage, so there's no reason it couldn't be fun in the studio, too.

Has the idea of using another outside producer been rejected?
I don't think that idea would get a very favorable response. I ramroded through the last producer, and it worked for me—kind of—but again, I wish the material could have been in a better state of readiness. Our material isn't like a lot of popular groups' material. We develop our songs in different ways from most groups, and the kinds of music we play, the stuff we sing about and the whole aesthetic is a little different. It takes us a while to find the heart of a song, even after it's been written, whereas with most pop songs, it's a finished product by the time it leaves the pen, and it then becomes a matter of just getting a good rendition. With us, songs tend to evolve more, and it's a good idea for us to let our material evolve so we fully understand the heart of the song before we record it. We certainly have had that opportunity with the forthcoming record.

You've had songs evolve in the studio, too. Both "Esau" and "Throwing Stones" underwent some revisions after you worked on them at Fantasy Studios last winter.

Right. Anytime we take the time to really get next to a song, it undergoes that process. If we concentrate on it and do it several times in a row, something is going to emerge. That's also one problem we have in the studio, though—new ideas crop up all the time, and it makes it difficult to get the song recorded.

At this point, though, it would behoove us to get into the studio and start the task. I think we should get in there and just record them with as little belaboring as we can get away with. But the songs aren't going anywhere. We'll get to them. And sooner than later, I hope. [*In the Dark,* the album the band eventually recorded, came out a year and a half later.]

Who Was Cowboy Neal?

The Life and Myth of Neal Cassady

By Steve Silberman

Some families go to the country on Sunday afternoons, or to the zoo. When I was a kid, my parents took my sister and me to "the Village"— Greenwich Village.

We drove from Queens in a white Dodge Dart along the Long Island Expressway, past the Bagel Oasis, the three radio towers with red blinking lights, the World's Fair in Flushing Meadow Park, and the rolling graveyards behind which glittered the skyscrapers of Manhattan, into the Queens-Midtown Tunnel and down streets where men with the faces of demons spat on your windshield and wiped it off for a quarter.

The grown-ups walking purposefully past the huge monuments with briefcases, smoking cigarettes, full of worldly knowledge and sophisticated desires, seemed also doomed somehow, acting out stilted roles and robot fates, like the TV newscaster reciting the nightly body count from

Doris Delay (left), Black Maria, and Neal on October 6, 1966, the day LSD became illegal. *(Photo courtesy of* San Francisco Chronicle*)*

Vietnam who was part of a strange conspiracy that didn't allow him to scream or sob.

I vowed I would never grow up to be *like that.* I would tell the truth, not forget, and stay true to my feelings.

The Village in those years was changing over from Beat to Hippie, from jazz and hootenannies to music that screeched and thundered out of electric instruments, as if whole new technologies were needed to express this new—more than a feeling—*new way of seeing;* and the party was open to everyone, that is, you could invite yourself, if you were young enough, un-hung-up enough: if you *knew.*

I put up posters in my room with the new colors on them, and my room became a shrine, or an outpost, with Three Roses incense burning and the red Chinese candles that flickered like strobe lights and could maybe make you high just looking. I wanted to *know.*

I read Tom Wolfe's *The Electric Kool-Aid Acid Test,* and instead of Superman or the Lone Ranger, I had Ken Kesey and the Merry Pranksters—superheroes of the *it,* the way of seeing. Instead of inhuman powers they had something better, something you could actually, if you *knew,* get a hold of—LSD!—and the mysteries of the stars and time would open up to you in your own backyard, your own skull. And the most super hero of them all was Cassady, the driver of the Bus on its mission to proclaim the sanctity of the human soul and set up a Day-Glo freak flag over the Kingdom of the Robots.

I found Allen Ginsberg's poem "Howl," seeing there a reflection of my own yearning for the *it,* and Ginsberg's spirit in the poem seemed to speak directly and particularly to me. I figured out that the "secret hero" of "Howl," N.C., was the younger Neal. The Village blossomed and changed, but my naive vision of an earthly paradise—of a life lived fearlessly and spontaneously and lovingly *from the inside out,* in a community of lovers—remained.

At Dead shows, I discovered a community that shared that vision and practiced that human magic—community being the most powerful magic of all. And I found Neal had been there too, and had left his footprint by the silver stream flowing through the music.

It occurred to me that many Deadheads who could sing the words to "Cassidy" and "The Other One" by heart might not even know both songs were, in part, inspired by the same man—or if they had heard of him, might not know much more about Neal than that he drove the Bus, a long time ago.

It is difficult to live up to a legend, and Neal inspired several, in books by Wolfe, Ginsberg, Jack Kerouac, and Kesey himself, as well as many songs. Luckily Neal's spirit can't be trapped or contained by any idea of what or who he was, and this is just one version, my version, of the untellable story of a man's life. He's still *out there,* wheeling and flying through the storm.

Neal Cassady was the son of an alcoholic, an ill-fortuned August West also named Neal, whose own mother died giving him birth. Neal Sr. ran away from home at sixteen to escape his brothers' whippings, becoming the apprentice and surrogate son of an old German barber who struck up a conversation with him on a park bench.

Neal's mother, Maude, was a farm girl and maid who had first married a man who was elected mayor of Sioux City, Iowa, but died suddenly, leaving Maude with seven children. Neal Sr. saw Maude one night after the First World War at a dance at the Des Moines Country Club, and proposed to her on a Sunday drive in his new Star automobile. She accepted.

Soon after the marriage, Neal Sr. bought a two-ton Ford truck, and in a burst of what Neal called "unaccountable constructiveness, neither anticipated nor repeated," built a house with a sloping roof on the truckbed. In this road home the newlyweds and Maude's children by her first marriage set off for Hollywood in the middle of winter.

Maude went into labor outside Salt Lake City, and at 2:05 A.M. in the morning of February 8, 1926, at a hospital near the Tabernacle, Neal Jr. was born. After resting up a few weeks, the Cassadys continued west, discovering a barbershop on the corner of Hollywood and Vine that was for sale, which Neal Sr. bought with the last of the family savings.

The shop didn't do well, as Neal Sr. had a theory that the place could only be open when he was there; since he was often too drunk to work, he'd fire his helpers and hire more when he sobered up. Finally, he sold the shop and took the family to Denver, where he leased a two-chair barbering stall in a shoe-repair store, and moved his family into the rear.

The family ate dinner in shifts, and doubled up in the beds. Soon the older boys struck out on their own. Oldest brother Bill married a young widow who had inherited a swank dine-and-dance joint outside Denver, and Ralph and Jack made deliveries for various bootleggers, including the infamous Blackie Barlow.

Then the stock market crashed, and, as Neal recalled, "everyone in Denver seemed to go broke at once." Neal Sr. rented a tiny shop near a pie factory, and cut employees' hair behind drawn shades on Sundays

in exchange for pies, until his drinking caused him to lose the shop, his
last. Maude left him, and Neal Sr. and little Neal began their journey
through the mission soup lines, blue-light hotels, and railyard hobo
jungles of Denver's desolation row.

Neal Sr. was known among Denver's bums as the Barber, while little
Neal was called, of course, the Barber's Son. Father and son slept side
by side in a bed without sheets in an enormous transient hotel called the
Metropolitan, which offered sleeping space in high-ceilinged cubicles for
a quarter a night.

While the Barber drank wine or "canned heat" or barbershop bay rum,
little Neal listened to the bums' rap, already weighing the import and
sincerity of their words, and sensitive to the ways speech, even empty
speech, can bind people together:

> *Their conversation had many general statements about Truth and Life, which
> contained the collective intelligence of all America's bums . . . said in such a way
> as to be instantly recognizable by the listener, who had heard it all before, and
> whose prime concern was to nod at everything said, then continue his conver-
> sation with a remark of his own, equally transparent and loaded with gener-
> alities. The simplicity of this pattern was marvelous, and there was no limit
> to what they could agree on in this fashion, to say nothing of the abstract ends
> that could be reached.*

(from *The First Third*,
Cassady's autobiography)

Occasionally one of the men would ask the Barber if he should offer
his son a little nip, to which the Barber replied, "You'll have to ask
him." Neal—six years old then—always declined, but felt he had become
like a son to many of these broken-down men who had no other means
of expressing their affection.

In the dim cashier's cage of the Citizen's Mission, Neal took the book
where the lodgers signed their names and birthplaces into his lap and
contemplated its hundreds of pages, sounding the names to himself and
guessing which were aliases, pondering the web of destinies. Wondering
about the names, and where all the places these men had come from
were, Neal, through the strange dreaming power of words, had an insight
of the vastness of human possibility.

Soon after moving into the Metropolitan, the Barber signed Neal up for first grade, and got a Saturday job at the barbershop next to the Zaza Theater. Each Saturday morning Neal sat beside his father as he worked, reading *Liberty* magazine and waiting for the theater to open for the matinee.

The Zaza catered to a down-and-out clientele, but for a nickel, young Neal could sit behind the balcony railing, breathing through his mouth to minimize the stench, and lose himself in the shoot-'em-ups, thriller-dillers, and romances of the day, which he turned into stories to tell his father and the other barbers in the afternoon. . . .

It was also at the Zaza that Neal was introduced to literature, by watching *The Count of Monte Cristo* "pulsating with every scene in an intoxication of joy," actually eager to get to school on Monday so he could search the library shelves for the Dumas novel.

The book put a fire under Neal's eager imagination, and from then on he often got lost walking home from school, his mind spinning out threads of wild plot and cliff-hanging adventure. These kid-contemplations were elaborated on long walks along the Platte River, skipping stones over the black water and counting the splashes, pulling beer bottles from old tires, padding through the white-dusted interior of the defunct Pride of the Rockies flour mill, under railroad bridges and past whirring dynamos that transfixed young Neal for hours. Neal, who ran four miles to school every morning, vowed never to walk unless he had to.

Neal was initiated into sex by the time he was nine, playing discovery games with his girl cousins in Aunt Eva's barn, and another time, beside an uninhabited house, Neal was kissed by an older boy.

The Barber taught Neal to hitchhike and hop freights, eating Mulligan stews suspended on bent coathangers over sputtering flames by the railroad track and cultivating what Neal called a "trust-in-Providence" hitchhiking philosophy: Any ride is better than none.

In 1933, Neal moved with his mother into a huge Victorian residence hall called the Snowden, a broken-down bootleggers' palace on Denver's East Side populated by jazz musicians, whores, homosexuals, ex-cons, and other interesting characters, with continuous poker games—"strip and otherwise"—going on in the basement apartments.

Neal's older brother Jimmy's idea of an afternoon well spent was throwing cats up by their tails, and shooting them down with a .22. Jimmy also terrorized scared-of-the-dark Neal by locking him into the wall crevice their Murphy bed folded creakily into—sometimes keeping him there for hours. In that fearful prison, Neal experienced a sensation of the Wheel of Time in his head speeding up to about triple its ordinary speed, which was frightening but somehow pleasant. Neal got a similar feeling twenty years later when he smoked grass and took amphetamine, and found that he could, by holding himself absolutely still, turn it off and on again, as he described it in *The First Third,* "an increase of time's torrent that received in kaleidoscopic change searing images, clear as the hurry of thought could make them."

Neal estimated he stole 500 cars in four years while he was a teenager, scoping out parked cars for keys or hot-wiring them, and roaring up to secret love-nests in the mountains with girls. Neal's adventures in "autoeroticism," as he called them, resulted in his being sent to reform school.

There Neal had a dream of being in his forties, beer-belly protruding from his dirty T-shirt, missing teeth, trying to barter his filthy mattress for wine. His father appeared, wearing Neal's baseball cap and demanding in on the take. Neal woke sick and horrified, determined to change his life, drawing up a self-improvement schedule that included hours daily at the Public Library reading Marcel Proust, *Lives of the Saints,* and Schopenhauer.

After his morning paper route, lovemaking with an *amour,* and the library, Neal went to his car-washing and -parking gig at the Rocky Mountain Garage, then took a five-mile bike ride, paid another visit to the library, finally ending up at Peterson's Pool Hall.

In the atmosphere of smoke and great excitement of the Denver pool halls, where even Jelly Roll Morton had crooked an elbow to make his living, Neal was just another poor kid hanging around as the balls clicked and spun and ashes fell from glowing cigar-tips in snowy drifts.

But soon Neal picked out someone who had what he needed—that is, who could teach him how to play pool—and was perhaps open to what he had to give, which was earnest friendship. That was Jim Holmes, slump-backed snooker and rotation king, sad-eyed cardshark, and ace handicapper at the track, who never left Denver.

"Neal used to come in and watch me play," Jim recalled to Kerouac biographer Barry Gifford, "and I thought he didn't have any money, which I found out later was usually the case, so I bought him something to eat. The man was very, very energetic and he would actually flatter you in such a way that he would almost immediately be liked. I don't think it was a put-on. It was a technique, however. But it wasn't a con. He really respected the individual."

Neal moved in with Jim, and Jim bought Neal his first suit and taught him how to pick horses, though Neal's approach to gambling unnerved Jim:

"Neal didn't care whether he won the pool game or he lost it. It was the fact that he went through this process and played pool.

"He had a theory that the third favorite would come in at the track every day. So he would play the third favorite, and it would come in, and then he would continue to play until it came in the next time . . . and he would lose all the money he made—plus. But to him it was living an event. The fact he'd been losing for three days didn't make any difference. He was interested in the thing happening. He was a natural Buddhist."

Justin Brierly was an influential Denver lawyer, a high school counselor, a Columbia University alumnus, and a patron of the Center City Opera, but his calling and delight was that of recognizing attractive, intelligent young men and easing their passage into adulthood by sending them to Columbia.

One day Brierly was visiting one of his family's houses, and came upon Neal, naked, and with a hard-on by virtue of the fact he had been interrupted in his daily lovemaking with the maid. "How did you get in here?" Neal demanded. "I'm sorry," Brierly replied politely, holding up the key, "this is my house."

In 1944 Brierly was in New York visiting Hal Chase, one of his old students, and he met one of Chase's roommates, recently expelled from Columbia after being called as a witness in a front-page murder. This young man with a frank, open gaze had a theory and practice of writing that resulted in his typing the same scene over and over at a hundred words a minute, searching for the final right word that would resolve the tensions in the language like a tonic note in music. His name was Jack Kerouac.

The other roommates were Vicki Russell, a six-foot redheaded prostitute and ex–gun moll; author-to-be William Burroughs, then apprenticing himself to pickpockets who specialized in lifting the last few bills off drunks passed out in the subway and who hated Roosevelt so much he wanted to hire a plane in New Jersey, fill it with horseshit, and pitchfork it over the White House; Joan Vollmer, the woman who would marry Burroughs and be shot by him in a drunken game of William Tell in Mexico; and, occasionally, a young man from New Jersey with thick glasses and protruding ears named Allen Ginsberg.

"They looked like criminals," said Jack to a *Playboy* interviewer, "but they kept talking about the same things I liked, long outlines of personal experience and visions, nightlong confessions full of hope that had become illicit and repressed by war, stirring, rumblings of a new soul.''

Vicki had taught them all how to unscrew the Benzedrine-soaked wadding from asthma inhalers, which they chewed up with gum or drank with coffee. The apartment was like a laboratory for a life-style that wouldn't become popular in the mainstream for twenty years; instead of rock 'n' roll, they had a new sound roaring out of uptown clubs like the Royal Roost, played by young cats like Dizzy Gillespie, Charlie Parker, and Thelonious Monk, called bebop.

They were very serious about writing. They read James Joyce's *Finnegans Wake* aloud to each other to dig the sounds; they turned each other on to books, insights, the fruits of their own creativity; but even the production of interesting or successful new literature was not the desired end of their mission.

Walking through Times Square, which they experienced as a giant room glowing with red neons open to the heavens, the cornices and gargoyles the handiwork of craftsmen who had passed out of the world leaving behind these visible signs of their once-presence, even the whores and kid-hustlers and junkies stirring sugar in their coffee cups were fellow travelers on this strange road of impermanence; the whole panorama, with its minuscule dramas of life and death, acted out hanging in space . . .

They were after a *vision,* waiting and working for a miracle.

And Jack's intensity and spiritual earnestness and even his looks reminded Brierly of someone else—of Neal, writing letters full of philosophy from the reformatory. Brierly read the letters, and Hal mentioned to Jack that Neal might be a good character for Jack to write about.

Hal went back to Denver on a summer vacation and told Neal about the poets he was hanging out with in New York, and also said to Neal that the poet is superior to the philosopher, a statement that, as Ginsberg put it, "immediately clicked in Neal's mind. It suddenly delivered him from bondage to rationalistic thinking, and to the realization of creative humor, romance."

Neal, then nineteen, knew his own future was with this community of writers who turned their meditations into art and lived their philosophy, but he had concerns that kept him in Denver a little while longer—namely his new bride, a blue-eyed fifteen-year-old named Luanne Harrison.

Neal had decided to marry Luanne before he ever got to talk to her, seeing her in a Walgreens near the pool hall. The moment of truth came at a bowling alley, when Neal slipped Luanne a note that read "I'll call you in the morning."

After the wedding, Neal's ex-girlfriend refused to surrender Neal's clothes and books, so while she was out Neal sneaked up on the roof and threw his things down to Luanne, waiting in the alley. They hitch-hiked to Nebraska, where Neal got a job as a dishwasher and Luanne got a gig as a live-in maid for a blind lawyer—fourteen hours a day, six days a week, for twelve dollars a month. Luanne smuggled food down-stairs to Neal, and at night Neal read Shakespeare and Proust, going over passages with Luanne for hours.

One day during a squalling blizzard Neal came home to find Luanne scrubbing the front porch on her hands and knees, turning blue. "That's it," he told Luanne, "we're going." Luanne stole $300 from the strong-box, and Neal hot-wired Luanne's uncle's car.

The windshield kept icing over, so Neal had to drive leaning out the open window with a handkerchief over his eyes, finally switching to the passenger side to shield himself from the wind, with one hand on the wheel, and Luanne watching out the window for the cops.

The car conked out in North Platte, so they got on a bus for New York. They arrived at the Greyhound Terminal and walked to Times Square, where the Camel billboard man puffed Hula Hoop–size steam smoke rings over the Pokerino, teenage newlyweds on the lam.

The next day they met Hal at Columbia, who took them to the West End Bar to meet Ginsberg. Hal had cautioned Neal about Allen's "homo-sexuality and its disastrous effects." And Neal had formulated an over-wrought image of Allen (as he recalled in *The First Third*) as "a young college Jew, whose amazing mind had the germ of decay in it and whose sterility had produced a blasé, yet fascinating mask." But when Allen stuck his head into the booth, he was just—Allen.

Their true meeting of spirits happened a month later at Vicki Russell's. Allen was smoking a hookah on a stool; Neal got high for the first time; then, as Jack tells it in *On the Road,* "A tremendous thing happened . . . two piercing eyes glanced into two piercing eyes—the holy con-man with the shining mind and the sorrowful poetic con-man with the dark mind" *recognized* each other in the middle of Time. They began talking, each amazed and relieved to find a mind as keen and a heart as sacred-knowing as his own, and even Jack felt a little left out: "Their energies met head-on, I was a lout compared, I couldn't keep up with them."

A couple of weeks later, Neal and Allen found themselves at an all-night party in Harlem. With not enough beds, Allen volunteered for the cot, dressed chastely in his boxer shorts. When Neal lay down beside him, Allen eased over to the far edge of the bed trembling, until Neal "stretched out his arm, and put it around my breast saying 'Draw near me' and gathered me in upon him . . . my soul melted, secrecy departed, I became thenceforth open to his nature as a flower in the shining sun"— as Allen remembered in the dark bunk of a ship crossing the Arctic Circle a decade later.

Jack and Neal's friendship proceeded more hesitantly after a Neal-style first meeting: Neal answered the door naked as Luanne dived off the couch, and asked Jack to wait a moment while he finished.

Jack's first impression of Neal "was of a young Gene Autry—trim, thin-hipped, blue-eyed, with a real Oklahoma accent—a sideburned hero of the snowy West." Neal asked Jack to teach him how to write. Jack's first bit of experienced advice was "you've got to stick to it with the energy of a benny addict." Jack was working on his first novel, *The Town and the City,* piling up pages of memories of his childhood in the Massachusetts textile mill town of Lowell.

Neal hovered lovingly around Jack as he typed, the line-end bell ringing so often Jack's roommates thought an alarm clock was going off. Neal punctuated Jack's riffing with his "yesses" and "that's rights," head bobbing on his neck like a novice prizefighter's. After four years of New York nihilism and intellection, *Neal*—wiping Jack's face with his handkerchief—*Neal*—who looked so much like Jack himself, an athlete like Jack—celebrated lover of women and sharer of Allen's passionate dark soul—*finally* the long-lost brother who said, "Go ahead, everything you do is great"—"a Western kinsman of the sun"—"a wild yea-saying overburst of American joy."

And out of Jack's love for Neal, and Neal's for Jack, Jack crafted a character who was not Neal but was the Neal in Jack's heart, Jack's dream of an American hero, and the name of the character was Dean Moriarty, and the book was *On the Road.*

Yes, and it wasn't only because I was a writer and needed new experiences that I wanted to know Dean more . . . the sight of his suffering bony face with the long sideburns and his straining muscular sweating neck made me remember my boyhood in those dye-dumps and swim holes and riversides of Paterson and the Passaic. His dirty workclothes clung to him so gracefully, as though you couldn't buy a better fit from a custom tailor but only earn it from the Natural Tailor of Natural Joy . . .

On the Road spread its message of Natural Joy—that "life is holy and every moment is precious"—through a late-Fifties America that encouraged in its citizens insidious paranoia, distrust of one's neighbors (who might be Communist spies or perverts or beatnik drug addicts), and fear of one's own heart's desire.

> *His specialty was stealing cars, gunning for girls coming out of high school in the afternoon, driving them out to the mountains, making them, and coming back to sleep in any available hotel bathtub in town . . . Dean had the tremendous energy of a new kind of American saint.*

Dean Moriarty was the Adam in Jack's Paradise on Earth: Paradise found on the back roads of the very America that Allen said, in his poem "Howl," "coughs all night and won't let us sleep"—America under the spell of the soul-destroying unconsciousness of governments and men Allen named Moloch: "Moloch whose mind is pure machinery! Moloch whose blood is running money! Moloch whose fingers are ten armies! Moloch whose breast is a cannibal dynamo! Moloch whose ear is a smoking tomb!"

And the "secret hero" of "Howl," the secret nemesis of Moloch, was "N.C., cocksman and Adonis of Denver."

On the Road and "Howl" brought to those who read them what Neal gave to their authors—a life-affirmation, a profound *yes* that calls forth vision. Bob Dylan, Jim Morrison, Janis Joplin, and a young trumpet player in the College of San Mateo jazz band named Phil Lesh (who set "Howl" to his own music) were all inspired by one or both books, setting out on their own roads of creative effort and quest for illumination, "angelheaded hipsters burning for the ancient heavenly connection to the starry dynamo in the machinery of night."

Dean Moriarty is the Neal most of the world knows, one of "the mad ones . . . mad to talk, mad to be saved . . . the ones who never yawn or

Neal (left) on the road with Jack Kerouac.

say a commonplace thing, but burn, burn, burn like fabulous yellow
Roman candles exploding like spiders across the stars . . . ''

The Neal that only Neal and his friends knew suffered the life of a
man.

In March of 1948, Neal drove to Denver to annul his marriage to
Luanne. Neal had fallen in love with Carolyn Robinson, a blond graduate
student, and Carolyn was pregnant. A month earlier, on his twenty-
second birthday, Neal had sat for fourteen hours with a revolver in the
back seat of his car, finally deciding not to shoot himself. Neal made the
trip through the mountains to Denver in a sub-zero blizzard without

chains or antifreeze, which he must have known was suicidal. The car gave out, but seven hours later the road was plowed behind him and a bus picked him up.

Neal married Carolyn on April Fools' Day. "Her chief quality," Neal wrote to Allen, "lies in the same sort of awareness or intuitive sense of understanding which is ours. . . . She is just a bit too straight for my temperament; however, that is the challenge in our affair . . . the only reason, really, she affects me so is the sense of peace which she produces in me when we are together."

Neal and Carolyn moved to the Bay Area and had three children, Cathy, Jami, and John Allen—named for Jack and Allen. Neal did his best to be a good provider.

He got a job as a "brakie"—a brakeman—on the Southern Pacific Railroad, a job he was very proud of. "He was a family man," explains John Allen, now working for a computer company in Los Gatos, south of San Francisco. "He was everywhere at once, but at least he knew that his wife and three kids had a roof over their heads. He just drove us to school and stuff like that and went shopping like any other normal dad would."

He also grew six-foot pot plants in a lot beside the family house. "The heightened sensibility that one experiences after a good bomber," Neal advised in another letter to Allen, "is so delightful that it is absolutely imperative for one to really take it slow."

The letters Neal wrote to Jack and Allen while high on grass and Benzedrine—free as they were from inhibitions of syntax and "grammatical fears," allowing the confident, funny pool-hall rhythms of Neal's actual rap to tickle the reader's ear—were the major inspiration and model for Jack's newfound supercharged voice in *On the Road.* Jack had been writing long exfoliating evocations of Neal's pool-hall years in Denver on pot—waiting until his mother went to bed, "blasting" as he called it, and then staying up all night writing; but he still hadn't found the way *in.* Meanwhile, Neal was sending twenty- and thirty-page letters that blew Jack and Allen away with their hopped-up energy and humor and inclusiveness and sincerity and natural grace, especially a 23,000-word blockbuster Jack called "the Great Sex Letter," written in three days and nights on Benzedrine. Finally, in 1951, according to Jack's friend and fellow novelist John Clellon Holmes, Jack "literally said, 'Fuck it! I'm just going to sit down and tell the truth.' And that's what he did."

Jack was unable to find a publisher for *On the Road* until 1957. By the end of the decade, the media had begun its inevitable uncomprehending attack on the "know-nothing bohemian" Beats, typified by a *Life* magazine hit piece, complete with "bongo drums . . . dreary 'pads' . . . mom-haters . . . drugs and debauchery . . . homosexuality . . . fleabag hotels . . . cheap Mexican tarts . . . the dregs of a half-dozen races."

Neal was disturbed by both the shallow sanctification of Dean Moriarty's impulsiveness by weekend beatniks, and the caricaturing of Neal and his friends in magazines and on television as dangerous delinquents; after all, Neal had been one of Southern Pacific's best brakies for ten years and was, in fact, a loving, responsible suburban father to his children.

Another side of Neal's personality was enjoying his new status as a cultural hero in the coffeehouses and saloons of San Francisco's North Beach, where he earned a new nickname: Johnny Potseed.

In early 1958, two narcs posing as friends of friends gave Neal $40 to buy them some pot. Neal smelled a rat and blew the money at the track. Soon after that Neal made the mistake of offering some narcs two joints in exchange for a ride to work. He was arrested, set free, then rearrested the next day, and sent before a judge who, as he put it, didn't like Neal's attitude, and sentenced him to San Quentin for two years to life.

In prison, Neal turned his attention to religion, especially the Bible and the reincarnation theories of the trance-healer Edgar Cayce. In a letter to Carolyn that made it past the prison censor, Neal describes his strategies to maintain his spirit: "To overcome eardrum-bursting racket made by the cotton textile mill's 4-million-dollars' worth of 1745 rpm 68 × 72″ hi-speed looms, whose constantly collecting flug is my weary job to sweep all day from beside & beneath, I . . . incessantly shout into the accompanying roar every prayer known . . . saying them hurriedly it takes just one hour to complete their entirety . . . Don't demurmer, it at least eliminates clockwatching."

"To imagine what being so encaged is like," wrote Neal, "you might put car mattress in the bathtub, thereby making it softer, and if not as long at least much cleaner than is my bug-ridden bunk; then bring in your 200 lb. friend, Edna, or the more negatively aggressive, Pam. Lock the door, &, after dragging 11 rowdy kids into our bedroom to parallel the 1,100 noisy ones housed in this particular cell block . . . remain almost motionless so as not to inadvertently irritate armed-robber Edna, ponder past mistakes, present agonies & future defeats in the light of whatever insights your thus disturbed condition allows."

The morning after his "787th straight nite behind bars," Neal was paroled. The Southern Pacific refused to rehire a convicted felon, so Neal got a job busting tires for the Los Gatos Tire Company. "I remember riding my bike down there to watch him," recalls John Allen. "He'd race out to cars and change their wheels and then run back to the recapping machine and sling these hot truck tires back and forth and race back out. Nobody could believe he had that much energy and speed for this low-paying gig."

> *I could hear Dean, blissful and blabbering and frantically rocking. Only a guy who's spent five years in jail can go to such maniacal helpless extremes . . . This is the result of years of looking at sexy pictures behind bars . . . evaluating the hardness of the steel halls and the softness of the woman who is not there. Prison is where you promise yourself the right to live.*

> *Escaping through a lily field,*
> *I came across an empty space—*
> *It trembled and exploded,*
> *Left a bus stop in its place.*
> *The bus came by and I got on,*
> *That's when it all began.*
> *There was Cowboy Neal at the wheel*
> *Of a bus to Never Ever Land.*

Ken Kesey, like Jack and Neal, was a high school athlete from a working-class home. He had been voted Most Likely to Succeed by his senior class, and was the first member of his family to go to college— the University of Oregon, where he wrestled his way to the top of his weight class, acted some, and even went to Hollywood after college to try to be in the movies.

But inside all of that was another kind of spirit, one strengthened and tried by his father's physical contests, hunting and running and wrestling and whitewater—initiations really, with younger brother Chuck, for the greater and ultimate test we all come to in our own way. And the kid-spirit knew that the stories Ken loved in comic books, about Superman and Captain Marvel and mortals turned into super-mortals in secret caverns, Oriental rituals, magic stones conveying super strength or fatal weakness, were somehow true, that is *truer* than the accidentals of school and the drive-in and even one's own parents, because they were the story of the spirit-body on its road through changing matter: the *Test*.

And the spirit guided young Kesey to one possible means of its expression—as it guides us through various means—looking for a Way, a path, to realize its own nature and the nature of its home, the Universe; and Kesey began to write, *following,* as Joseph Campbell would have said, *his bliss.* And he was granted—O accidental means, O great and hidden end!—a scholarship to the Stanford University creative writing graduate program.

There Kesey was adopted by a circle of traditional bohemians living in Perry Lane, a bungalow arrangement housing graduate students, with dinners and discussions and contemplations over alcohol. They recognized in Kesey a certain . . . earnest spirit . . . but Kesey was not drawn so much to the award-winning novelists, but to a psychology grad student named Vik Lovell. Lovell told Kesey about these experiments at the Veterans' Hospital nearby in Menlo Park, where they were testing some new drugs and looking for volunteers; seventy-five bucks a day to sit in a white-walled room where a nurse technician would bring you a capsule that would contain maybe nothing, maybe . . . (What the volunteers didn't know was that the shadow-authority behind these and other similar experiments all across the country and in Canada was the CIA, which was *very* interested in these "mind-manifesting" compounds as possible truth serums, or insanity serums, or amnesia serums.) Sometimes the little capsule would give you what would later be called a really bum trip. Other times—even in the antiseptic room with the nurse coming in every twenty minutes to scope out your pupils, hiding her secret sadness behind a repertoire of mannerisms that were suddenly very transparent—the experience would be very beautiful, spiritual, though that word hardly expresses the sea of . . . not *only* thoughts or *only* feelings or *only* sensation . . . *being:*

And in that capsule would be LSD.

LSD quickly became the magic amulet around Perry Lane, and the prototype of electric Kool-Aid was not anything as campy and kidlike as Kool-Aid, but fiery venison chili, like shamans eating the flesh of the totem for a vision—and you could still mail-order peyote from Laredo, as the Beats had done.

Kesey was working up a novel about North Beach called *Zoo,* and Lovell suggested he take the night attendant's job on the psych ward, where he would be left alone and could write; but Kesey took the magic amulet onto the ward, and found that simply by looking into the faces of the residents he could see—behind the drooling or tics or mannerisms of dis-ease: *Spirit*. And through this literal seeing Kesey dreamed himself into the character of a schizophrenic Indian the fictional ward lackeys called, mockingly, Chief Broom: the narrator and muse of *One Flew Over the Cuckoo's Nest.*

Kesey called the Moloch shadow-authority in his armed madhouse the Combine, and the Combine's agent—a repressed, emasculating, lobotomizing pillar of soul-destroying efficiency—was called Nurse Ratched, or just Big Nurse. Though Big Nurse's ultimate nemesis is Chief Broom's faith in his own "undependable" subjectivity, her obvious enemy on the ward is a drinkin', fornicatin', and insubordinizin' rabble-rouser named Randle McMurphy, who disrupts the robot routine of the ward, allowing the residents to see, for a while, themselves as men again. McMurphy was a street brawler, gambler, disreputable menace, and lover of teenage girls. If this character profile is beginning to sound familiar, well, Neal read the book too, and knew McMurphy was, if not actually based on, a chip-off-the-old-block of—His Bad Self.

So, the story goes, one day Ken and his wife, Faye, came back from a trip to Oregon, and there in Perry Lane—head bobbing on his taut-sinewed neck, handsomest man you ever saw and talking a blue-white streak—was Neal, who had felt summoned by the book.

By this time Perry Lane had become a node of the New Thing—nothing so self-conscious as that, surely, but the venison chili parties were *happening* and attracting hipsters from the surrounding landscape, as these scenes do when they get going, drawing energy in, and soon everybody finds themselves with more energy than they ever knew they had on their own: tribal magic. And one of the habitués of the Perry Lane scene was *the* hot young banjo-and-guitar player around the Palo Alto coffeehouses at the time, named Jerry Garcia.

"We were playing around in this house," Garcia recalled, "we had a couple of Day-Glo super balls and we bounced them around and we were just reading comic books, doodling, strumming guitars. . . . All of a sudden you realize that you are free to *play.*"

And after Perry Lane was plowed under by a developer's bulldozer, the scene moved into the hills to La Honda, to Kesey's cabin, with redwood trees and a footbridge over a stream, like summer camp for big kids—big kids who had gotten a hold of the *magic amulet,* members of the tribe that would call itself the Merry Pranksters.

One day the idea was there:

"Why don't we have a big party? You guys bring your instruments and play, and us Pranksters will set up all our tape recorders and stuff, and we'll all get stoned. And that was the first Acid Test."

—Bob Weir

"Test," because acid brought you to that . . . *edge* . . . psychic white-water; to pass it was to stay in the moment, the beautiful or fierce or ecstatic or terrifying or peaceful moment that is the only golden road.

The idea of the Bus grew out of a modest intention to drive to the 1964 World's Fair in New York City. Early on, the Pranksters became fascinated with electronics as a way of both amping up the trip and documenting the scene. Also, Kesey's second novel, *Sometimes a Great Notion,* was to be published in New York in early July, so the idea was to bring along a few cameras and tape recorders, shoot some footage, and bring the Perry Lane/La Honda "free-to-play" spirit to the Fair. Then somebody saw a classified ad for a 1939 International Harvester school bus, with bunks and a sink and storage and other amenities for a comfortable life on the road—which Kesey bought for $1,500.

The Bus! That Grandfather of All Tourbuses, with a destination sign that read FURTHER, a sign on the back that said WEIRD LOAD, and on the side, the Pranksters' contribution to presidential politics: A VOTE FOR BARRY IS A VOTE FOR FUN. And Neal at the wheel.

Neal. Long-lashed eyes in the rectangular rear-view mirror, cannonball muscles popping under a too-small black-and-white striped shirt, with a penny whistle in his left hand and a big bomber in his right and both hands on the wheel, or one, or none, tootling and toking and navigating faultlessly and all the while keeping up an unbroken rap drawing into it the names of the Indy 500 winners, *Love Potion Number 9,* Edgar Cayce, memories of Denver, philosophical bits, thermodynamics—the minutiae of a lifetime of fact-seeking by Neal's triple-speed brain—intermingled with pure sounds, like tires screeching or pistons blowing up, as well as what Neal was seeing or hearing at that moment, road signs or the car in the other lane, and all rhyming and sparking in a way that, if you weren't really listening, could sound like nonsense. But if you *were,* you'd realize Neal was *jamming* like the jazz musicians he and Jack dug in New York—taking themes and elaborating and suspending and altering them in a flow the course of which was not determined by what you *thought* you'd do before you started, but by what you were hearing and feeling *now*, at the moment of composition.

> *Neal helped us be the kind of band we are, a concert not a studio band. . . . It wasn't as if he said, "Jerry, my boy, the whole ball of wax happens here and now." It was watching him move, having my mind blown by how deep he was, how much he could take into account in any given moment and be really in time with it.*
>
> —Jerry Garcia

"*In time*"—Neal's old buddy Jack had seen that too, and wrote that Dean "knew time." The Dead took that spark into their music, that time-knowing, that knowledge that in each moment a beauty is possible as intensely itself and newly created as the surface of the sun: radiance that still shines in the music, so that young Deadheads hearing it for the first time open their hands to the stage as around a warming fire.

And Neal knew his own body, which embodied his knowing by being taut and supple and beautiful. Watching Neal in the loving eye of the Prankster cameras is like watching Harold Lloyd, or W.C. Fields' fluid dance with a pool cue or a sheet of flypaper; rolling a straw boater off his head and down his arm to charm a girl, every moment—even when he drops the hat—lit from the inside with attention and wit.

Neal was a legendary lover, often choosing women who were thought unattractive by others, or even retarded or psychotic, to delight them with his lovemaking prowess and natural gifts. The first time he met Anne Murphy, his combative sidekick of the Prankster years, she was sick with hepatitis. "Hoping, I guess, to perk me up, he unveiled his mighty endowment while my eyes popped. We made a date for the following weekend."

Neal carried a hammer, a 4-pound jack, tossing and catching and flipping it, a mass to dance with his energy, keeping his muscles toned and his time sharp. "At his purest," Garcia said, "Cassady was a tool of the cosmos."

And Neal pushed that to the limit, hurtling around blind curves daring *it* to throw a vehicle in his path; or the time Neal guided the Bus down a hairpin-winding mountain highway in Virginia, everybody *wooooo-sssssssshhhhhhh*ing on the magic amulet—the edge!—without touching the brakes; or the snowy night in the Tehachapi Pass—with young Stewart Brand of eventual *Whole Earth Catalog* fame rolling his bombers—when Neal experimented with seeing how close he could come to the roadside telephone poles without actually clobbering into one, skidding from one side of the road to the other, all the while rapping about how God is in control. . . . Brand abandoned ship at the Big Sur turnoff feeling he'd been taught a lesson, and decided to get married and father children.

> *There was no space on him for other stuff—he did his trip, and he left no room between the sinews for other juices. Everybody who ever dealt with him felt this—this guy has a vision of the truth. "Oh my God! Is that what the truth is?"*
>
> —Ken Kesey

Kesey used to say there were no accidents around Neal—even when he dropped his hammer he was *showing* you something. Talking with Prankster Ken Babbs in 1981, Garcia recollected one Neal-lesson that changed the course of his life, the morning after the Watts Acid Test:

"He'd been on the road all night, driving back from San Francisco. That was the night everybody was terribly overdosed. Neal must have caught up fast. By dawn he didn't have his shirt on. No shoes. Just those shapeless gray pants. And for some reason he wasn't speaking. Sometimes he'd get to that place where he was beyond speaking.

"He was motioning George [Prankster George Walker] into a parking place, giving him signals, a little to the left, a little to the right, all with gestures. Neal directed him into a stop sign and the bus knocked it over and shaved it clean off.

"Neal immediately picked it up and tried to stick it back in the hole. Down the street come two little old ladies on their way to church. Neal's meanwhile walking away from the sign real fast, and it hung for a minute and started to topple and just before it hit the ground he caught it and put it back up. Then the ladies see him: Is it a disreputable drunk or what? He decides to clean up his act and hide the stop sign behind him until the ladies pass by. It was like an elegant physical Buster Keaton ballet.

"I hit him for a ride back to our house and it was just me and him in an old Ford sedan we used for a go-fer car, and most of the time when you got behind the wheel with Neal it was an adventure, at least, but this time we left the place at a speed of maybe eight, twelve miles an hour all the way without either of us saying a word. He'd look over at me every once in a while and we were strangely close. There was nobody out, the streets were bare and when you don't have to talk to the person next to you, that's real clean. Takes a certain thing not to try to keep anything up, not having to entertain one another.

"I remember flashing on Neal as he was driving, that he is one of these guys that has a solitary kind of existence, like the guy who built the Watts Towers, one person fulfilling a work. I made a decision: to be involved in something that didn't end up being a work that you died and left behind, and that they couldn't tear down.

"Neal represented a model to me of how far you could take it in the individual way. In the sense that you weren't going to have a work, you were going to *be* the work. Work in real time, which is a lot like musician's work.

"I had originally been an art student and was wavering between one man one work or being involved in something that was dynamic and ongoing and didn't necessarily stay any one way. Something in which you weren't the only contributing factor. I decided to go with what was dynamic and with what more than one mind was involved with.

"The decision I came to was to be involved in a group thing, namely the Grateful Dead."

Wavy Gravy met Kerouac behind a strawberry tart at an after-hours cafeteria on the Bowery called Sagamore's, a hangout for drag queens, poets, beatniks, musicians—"the whole mélange of wooga-wooga," as Wavy recalls over coffee in my kitchen in the Haight-Ashbury in 1989. Wavy had read *On the Road* while at Boston University, and started a jazz-and-poetry series after reading a *Time* spread on poet Kenneth Rexroth, who intoned his "Married Blues" over Duke Ellington's "Things Ain't What They Used to Be" at a club in San Francisco called the Blackhawk.

Wavy—who was still Hugh Romney in those days—became the poetry director of the Gaslight Café in the Village, integrating folk music into the poetry readings there. "In between the poems I started talking about the bizarre things that happened in my life," Wavy explains, "and some guy saw me and said skip the poems, and put me in a suit and started mailing me around the country, and the next thing you know I was opening for John Coltrane and Thelonious Monk."

Wavy was turned on to psychedelics by his conga drummer, whose hobby was synthesizing mescaline—he had all these tubes snaking around his apartment with black goo coming out of them. Wavy ate the crystallized Flesh of the Gods at Coney Island, and spent $50 on roller-coaster tickets: "It actually got scary when it *stopped*."

He got a gig with the Committee, a renowned San Francisco improvisational comedy troupe, while taking care of the "street biz" for Owsley with John Brent, who ran for mayor of San Francisco on the platform ANYTHING YOU WANT. Wavy and John's franchise was called Goon King Brothers Dimensional Creemo, and Wavy's *nom de commerce* was Al Dente—"a name I got off a Buitoni wrapper."

Wavy got on the Prankster bus after a marathon viewing of the ongoing Prankster movie—called "Intrepid Traveler and His Merry Pranksters Leave in Search of a Cool Place" or just "The Movie"—at Ken "Intrepid Traveler" Babbs' place in Capistrano, in Southern California. Soon Wavy and Neal were doing double raps at the Acid Tests.

"He'd say a few words and I'd say a few words, but there was no time to think. The only way it would work is, you couldn't be there"— that is, you couldn't let the past-and-future-you get in the way of Now. "What used to piss me off about Neal, and I finally called him on it, was he wouldn't take time out to laugh. He was too busy being three minutes ahead of time."

> *A person has all sorts of lags built into him, Kesey is saying. One, the most basic, is the sensory lag, the lag between the time your senses receive something and you are able to react . . . Cassady is right up against that 1/30th of a second barrier. He is going as fast as a human can go, but even he can't overcome it. . . . You can't through sheer speed overcome the lag.*
> —Electric Kool-Aid Acid Test

"Neal was the first person to teach me to trust my instincts," Wavy says. "To *not worry* about it—be open to the situation, not be in the past or future. Neal said fretting was the only sin. I've tried to take that one to heart."

Wavy graduated from being assistant tongue-dancer to riding shotgun for Neal on the big bus, "once I got used to the fact that he was doin' ten things at once and nothin' twice and wasn't going to crash. . . . He'd be peeling an orange and rolling a joint and having about four conversations, and there'd be all this *traffic* . . . the last thing you want to say is 'Neal, pay attention to the road,' 'cause that would *really* distract him— next thing you know you'd be heading into a telephone pole."

Annette Flowers met Neal in September of 1965. She was seventeen, and
had read *On the Road,* and walked into a friend's house in Los Altos, near
Foothill College where she was a student. There was Neal, playing chess
and blasting the new Beatles record, *Revolver,* turning it over and over.

That first day together they took some psilocybin mushrooms ground
up in gelatin capsules. Annette felt very comfortable with Neal right
away, intuiting the depth and rapidity of his mind and feeling gratified
to have met someone who could keep up with her.

Annette is a Libra, and her friend Cathy Mae was a Gemini, and Neal
was an Aquarius. The three air-signs came together to form a loving,
easygoing family that was, for Neal, an alternative to the ongoing psychedelic guerrilla warfare of the Pranksters and the tension of being with
Carolyn, who had asked Neal for a divorce. They called themselves "the
Trine"—the aspect of good fortune.

Annette's nickname in the Trine was either Anita or Mustang Sally,
owing to the fact she had a '65 Mustang, in which they dropped in, often
in the middle of the night, on Neal's friends—like Lawrence Ferlinghetti,
the poet-publisher who won the landmark obscenity trial for the right
to publish "Howl"; or Gavin Arthur, the eccentric astrologer whose
calculations were used to determine an auspicious date for the Human
Be-In and had been Neal's religion instructor in San Quentin; or Robert
Hunter, whom Annette met through David Nelson.

Neal also took Annette to her first Acid Test, at the Big Beat in Palo
Alto. The entertainment that particular evening was a band Annette had
heard about from David Nelson, but had never seen: the Warlocks.

"I spent most of the time under a table," Annette recalls in her office
at the Dead's headquarters, where she is now in charge of the band's
music publishing company, Ice Nine. Over her desk, in a charcoal sketch,
Pigpen looks back at us over his shoulder. "The Warlocks frightened
me. I sensed a tremendous amount of power up there, and I wasn't sure
if it was good or evil. I wasn't immediately comfortable with it.

"Like Deadheads'll tell you today, I was in one of those situations
where I was in the second row dancing, and all of a sudden I thought
Jerry looked over and was angry or something—like I'd pissed somebody
off—and I crawled all the way to the back and found a table and got
under it and waited till Neal came and got me and we went home."

Neal and Annette went to Quicksilver and Airplane shows at the
Fillmore together, and after one of these, Neal carried his little Anita—
still a virgin—down the stairs to introduce her to her first love, waiting
in the rear of Neal's big black Cadillac.

Like many others, Annette admired Neal's ability to carry on simultaneous conversations, or more precisely, to notice the simultaneity in conversations that were already going on, and highlight that synchronicity in his own rap, weaving the threads together. "He wasn't the motivator or the seed," Annette explains, "he was just picking it up to make people aware, to open up their ears and feel that three different groups of people, with different words, were essentially talking about the same thing. To see where it came together, what the common bond was."

Annette remembers one afternoon at a friend's house in Los Altos, when Neal decided suddenly to redecorate, "starting with the kitchen. He went through all the cupboards, juggling the dishes and silverware—pretty soon the whole house was a tornado. I swear he was twirling a couch on his finger.

"The folks who lived there, and the friends who were visiting, all eventually stepped out to the backyard—a whole group of us looking toward the house with just this *flash* going in any given window, around and around and around—'Oh God, he's gonna destroy the house!'

"And after a while he came out—'Where is everybody?'—'cause he was in there talking to himself, and finally noticed no people were in there any longer. So we all went back in and everything was in perfect order.

"That was like temporarily taking a place and putting it in another dimension. There's a point where you think the authorities or the brain police are gonna come down and—this house must be Day-Glo!—and the whole town of Los Altos must be on the phone saying 'What the heck, our electricity's shorting out, or juicing up'—are we gonna get away with this?

"But I guess people driving by were just—it's a regular house in the afternoon, friends hanging out together."

> *Flight of the sea birds*
> *Scattered like lost words*
> *Wheel to the storm and fly*

Speed—dull bitter powder that makes the mortal movie seem so . . . slow . . . but *booted up*—the Time-Wheel in the head faster and faster and the body able to keep up, hot stylus pushing forward into the molten wax of the moment and able to turn it into *speech, action, now, no time* for fretting or past-or-future but only I talking or running or fucking almost too fast for matter to keep up, keep *it* going, and where is *it* coming from? Not this slow body . . . but crackling *light of—damn—*

Peter Coyote was still Peter Cohon in the Diggers, the group he helped found with Emmett Grogan and Peter Berg, that set up milk cans of hot soup under the eucalyptus trees in Golden Gate Park's Panhandle for the armies of the Summer of Love, and set up a Free Store ("IT'S FREE BECAUSE IT'S YOURS"), and carried around a huge empty wooden frame called the Free Frame of Reference that could be placed around anything, re-investing it with its own natural meaning, which was FREE—FREE was not a *shtick,* it was a metaphysic: Being is Free.

Peter, now a film actor, remembers one night at a big poetry reading with Ginsberg and Ferlinghetti and the Diggers in the audience—"and we were very conscious that the mantle had passed to us. It was our time now, we were what was happening. It was palpable to everyone in the room—we just had a vision that was appropriate to that moment."

Peter met Neal hanging out at Paula McCoy's, across from the Dead's house at 710 Ashbury. Paula was the ex-wife of a real estate developer, an elegant blonde with an acid tongue who hosted Digger salons, walking around naked under a floor-length mink coat. One night Peter and Emmett were up in the front window when Neal walked out of the Dead house, and they threw some apples at him and called him over. Neal had some speed, they had some "works," and they all got high.

The *vision*—could be seen through different windows, you could say, different sub-scenes in the bigger picture of the Haight—"an urban cosmopolitan universe that went every place from beggars to millionaires, with corresponding differentiations of taste and style and politics and ideology," remembers Coyote. "The same people who are into channeling now were smoking $3,000-a-pound marijuana then and having these sublime upper-middle-class psychedelic aesthetic experiences."

And there was this *other* window, the speed window, that seemed to have *no frame at all*—"Speed gave you the energy to keep up, and the imaginative excesses to fuel a reality without limits," says Coyote, "to fuel the invention necessary to keep up with a reality without limits."

And Cassady, whose Prankster name was Speed Limit, who drove cars until they literally exploded, was the perfect driver for a bus whose destination sign read only FURTHER. But after the *flash*—the body's heavy meat is Home, after all. Peter gave up amphetamines and took up zazen, the physical practice of sitting body, breath, and mind in one place: here.

"I had failed to realize," Peter reflects, "that the body was the first legitimate limit."

The last time Kerouac saw Neal was at a Prankster party on Park Avenue. Kesey wanted to meet Jack, and Jack had praised *Cuckoo's Nest* to his friends. It was the long-awaited meeting of the two minds to whom the appropriate-vision-of-the-moment had occurred, each in his own time. There was the usual Prankster electronic din going on, speakers and wires everywhere and microphones feeding it all back on itself until it became . . . a *crackling* . . . all flood-lit for the Movie; Jack was tired, and wanted to sit down—but where he wanted to sit, there was an American flag.

> *But Dean's intelligence was formal and shiny and complete, without the tedious intellectualness. And his "criminality" was not something that skulked and sneered; it was a wild yea-saying overburst of American joy . . .*

Jack *believed* in America—not the America that dropped its bomb on Hiroshima, not the America of our own age that skulks and sneers and calls itself "kinder," but the America—*America!*—that Neal and Jack and Allen discovered *in their own living room:* An America that is discovered anew each moment with a truthful word spoken, a word of actual trembling tender feeling committed to Art, with the simplest act of looking into your friend's eyes, when secrecy departs, and you are thenceforth open to his nature as a flower in the shining sun.

So Jack—as he had taught his friends for years, not as a gesture but a physical enactment of respect for the America that is always waiting to be discovered and will find its flag in the Flag, its history waiting for it to realize its own promise entrusted long ago—picked up the flag from the couch, folded it, and sat down, and asked the Pranksters if they were Communists.

And when Kesey, wishing to heal a distance of differing mannerism, told Jack his role in history was secure—because Kesey knew Dean's jalopy and the Bus and any number of unforeseeable future travelers (you and me, reader) were all looking for that one . . . *place* . . . *here*—Jack said quietly, "I know."

Just before Neal left for his last trip to Mexico, Wavy and a friend took him to kidnap Tiny Tim from a place in the Village called the Scene, where Tiny was doing his ukulele-and-flowers act. Wavy's last, best memory of Neal is of Neal driving up West Side Drive toward the Cloisters: "And every now and then Tiny'd go, 'Oh, Mr. Cassady, not so *fast!*' and Neal, 'Well, Tiny, not to worry,' and Tiny, 'AUUUUUGGHHH!' But then the two of them broke into these Bing Crosby duets as the sun was coming up. It was just the most beautiful, beautiful thing that I ever experienced with Neal—just him and Tiny and the sunrise."

On February 2, 1968, Neal took a train down to Celaya, Mexico, and took a cab to San Miguel de Allende, where a young friend named J.B. was waiting for him. At noon Neal left J.B.'s house, saying he had to pick up a bag he'd left at the depot containing a Bible and some letters from Jack and Allen. He told J.B. he would walk to the station and then continue on to Celaya, more than fifteen miles away.

At the train station Neal ran into a Mexican family celebrating a wedding with traditional abandon, and drank *pulque* and tequila with them, along with the potent barbiturate Seconal.

About a quarter of a mile toward Celaya from the station, Neal died by the railroad tracks, wearing nothing but a T-shirt in the cold rain.

The police took Neal's body to the house of Pierre Delattre, the "street priest" of North Beach who had come to Mexico to avoid paying taxes that would fund the Vietnam War. The police told Delattre they had a body in their truck, the body of a man who had the priest's address in his wallet, and they told him the man's name.

Annette had moved to New Jersey that winter, away from the San Francisco scene, and lost touch with Hunter and Nelson and the other friends of her time with Neal. Cathy Mae moved East with Annette and her own new husband, and both the Libra and Gemini aspects of the Trine were pregnant—new lives beginning in every sense of the words.

Very soon after Annette arrived at her parents' home, there was a knock at the door—a hippie with a message for someone named Anita, that Neal was dead. No one knew how he had found her, "It was just one of those things—'I have a message.' That kind of thing happened all the time," recalls Annette, "and still does."

Annette says Neal is still with her. "He has appeared to me more than once in the form of a bird—if I'm thinking about something and I would like some confirmation, and I wonder how Neal would feel about this, a bird will fly by. In Kansas, a sea-bird will fly over . . . and there's my answer.

"Of course, you can just decide that, that that's what's happening, and that isn't what's happening. But I feel his spirit is very much a part of my life.

"I trash my friends sometimes. Everybody's going to sleep and I'm still talking—I find myself in a room with people crashed all around me, and I'm still up two hours later, nobody's listening—and I feel, 'Well, *Neal* understands, he's listening to me.'

"He lived his life, and he didn't waste time—even sleeping—putting it off. He jammed as much action and energy as he could into everything. My son says, 'But look—he burned out early,' and he did. He flashed through. Johnny says, 'It would be nice for the younger generation of Deadheads if he were alive today'... Yeah, it *would* be nice for the younger generation of Deadheads if Pigpen, Bobby Peterson, all those guys... He lived hard.

"I think it's really important to try to communicate with people, and that's where Neal was at—not building up a big bank account, but communication, getting to know each other. I live fairly hard myself, and I push it right out to the edge, and it feels like the most important thing I could do.

"I feel he shared and imparted to me the okay-ness to just *be* here, and try not to be too concerned about fitting in with what's supposedly okay. Being a rebel, a cage-rattler.

"Somebody who doesn't like it can tell me to leave, or we can get right into talking about stuff that matters."

Wavy says, "Thelonious Monk once told me, 'Everyone is a genius just being themself,' and most people don't get that. They want to be someone else, or they want to be Neal. I have spent my life walking down the road seeing the smoldering wrecks of burned-out beings who wanted to be Neal. They should concentrate on being themselves. Kids come up to me and say, 'You're my idol.' I say, 'Put your ear to your heart, that's your idol.'"

Robert Hunter

■ ■ ■ ■ ■ ■

The Song Goes On

An Interview: February 23, 1988

At this point, Grateful Dead lyricist Robert Hunter probably needs no introduction to most of you. Chances are his work is an indelible part of your consciousness. He literally (pun only semi-intended) writes words to live by: How many among our Deadhead ranks can say we have not been profoundly affected by the lyrics of this gentle sage? Who has not been uplifted by his stirring optimism, touched by his plaintive despair, felt true danger in his stern admonitions, empathized with his characters' soul-searching, confusion, or wanderlust? If the Grateful Dead's music is the soundtrack of our lives, then Hunter's words are the touchstones. They are points of reference along the way that seem to explain to us what is happening, where we've been, and even help us chart a course for where we might go next.

My personal experience with Hunter's lyrics has been that he has created a vast sea of swirling images, ideas, and connections of which I

Robert Hunter, 1988. *(Photo by Blair Jackson)*

have a vague surface understanding. Then, as if I've gotten a hearty whack of the zen master's stick (because I've asked yet *another* stupid question), I get flashes of true understanding when I least expect it, and the lyric fragment that once seemed dense and inaccessible suddenly becomes crystal clear. These bits and pieces then start falling together—sort of like a slow-motion film of an explosion, except in reverse, where the shards and fragments move from chaos to cohesion. There are Hunter lyrics I've heard, memorized, and sung along to literally thousands of times that are still completely baffling to me, but in general, living with the songs has been a process of seeing meaning constantly, if slowly, unfolding before me. Surely this is art's greatest function.

It is easy to take Hunter's work for granted, because at this point it feels so familiar, so comfortable, so emotionally *right,* that it's taken on some of the mystical glow of Ancient Wisdom—as if it's always been there to discover and we've just stumbled upon it. But take a moment and think about the incredible range of this man's work: the nearly Taoist simplicity of "Ripple" and "Attics of My Life"; the fractured psychedelia of "China Cat Sunflower" and "The Eleven"; the playful metaphors of "Deal" and "Run for the Roses"; the colorful portraits of working stiffs in "Cumberland Blues" and "Easy Wind"; the dreamy disconnectedness of "Row Jimmy"; mythological journeys through the psyche by way of "Terrapin Station" and "Franklin's Tower"; straightforward declarations of love like "To Lay Me Down" and "If I Had the World to Give"; the cartoonish whimsy of "Tennessee Jed" and "When Push Comes to Shove"; the world-weary existentialism of "Stella Blue" and "Black Muddy River"; and the steadfast stoicism of "Playin' in the Band" and "The Wheel." There are hundreds of songs in the Hunter cannon, most of them wildly different from each other, but all of them shoot points of light into humanity's mirror to give us fleeting glances of our inner selves.

Hunter has opted for a life away from the glare of the public spotlight, though he has made a substantial number of albums under his own name and has toured from time to time, with and without bands. He usually is reluctant to give interviews, though he is candid and compelling when he does. And, frankly, he knows that interviews are a way to promote his work, such as his new solo album, *Liberty* (on Relix Records).

It is a continuing source of frustration to Hunter that his solo records don't sell very well. At the same time, he acknowledges that they have been uneven for the most part; he says even *he* can't listen to some of them. Hunter's voice, a slightly unsure baritone rooted in folk-troubadour stylings, is an acquired taste, I suppose. And at their worst, his melodies have a repetitive, sing-song feel that's more cloying than endearing. But the fact is, Hunter's albums have been getting better and better, as his self-confidence has increased and he's learned to make better use of the recording studio and the musicians he's working with.

Liberty is unquestionably the best-sounding record Hunter has made in years, and it is also probably the most instantly appealing and accessible. While some might be put off by the record's pop veneer, I find the songs and the instrumental performances wonderfully infectious. The key players this time out are keyboardist Rick Meyers, who has adroitly steered Hunter away from his folkish proclivities with some nice, modern arrangements, and Jerry Garcia, who plays splendidly on every cut—sparkly, buoyant melodies here, pedal steel there, a bit of slide; the whole nine yards. Hunter has tried very hard through the years to distance himself somewhat from Garcia on his solo records (a position I admire), but the simple truth is that Garcia is the *perfect* player for these songs. It's no accident these two have been partners in one form or another for a quarter century. . . .

Though Hunter and I have spoken on the phone several times over the past few years, this was our first formal interview. We met at his house in Marin County on a beautiful sunny afternoon in late February. His living room was cluttered with books and musical instruments—about what you'd expect to find in the home of this supremely literate songwriter. Both articulate and engaging, he fielded questions on a wide variety of topics, like someone who actually enjoys doing interviews (though you and I know better). We began by chatting about *Liberty* and then ventured off into uncharted realms. . . .

Do you enjoy working in the studio?
I do now, because it's a place where I'm creatively, rather than passively, involved. With the Grateful Dead I used to hate the studio because it was a passive involvement. Once in a while I'd have something to say about phrasing, or I'd be Johnny-on-the-spot with a lyric where one wasn't working or singing right. But basically it was passive and terribly boring and tedious.

Then I made my first couple of records and was a little more involved, but I was still basically passive because I didn't understand any of the technology. So I'd let Mickey Hart or Barry Melton or a half-dozen other people who Garcia said had no business with their hands on a board [mixing console] do everything. Considering it was my presentation to the world, had I been a little more circumspect, I wouldn't have turned *Rum Runners* [his first album] out the way it was. In fact, I'm going to ask Tom Flye to remix *Rum Runners*. When I told Garcia that he said, "Good luck—you used every misrecording technique known to man on that. There's tape dropouts and all this other stuff. I know where it all is because I went through the hell of mixing it! This is going to be a long project!" [Laughs]

I feel like that record is very well regarded among Deadheads, crude though it may be.
I just want to give it a chance with automated mixing, which would allow me to do things like bring the bagpipes in and out differently and drop that sour note on it, too. I can do that now.

Aren't you afraid you're going to want to tinker with everything?
I *do!* I want to tinker with a couple of the early records.

Why not just rerecord the songs, then?
That would be too hard. How am I going to get Garcia to come in and
play the break that I love so much on "Tiger Rose," even though I *hate*
my vocal on it? There are vocals I detest on *Rum Runners* and *Tiger Rose*
and I just can't live with them, but I won't change those, either. I just
want to shine it all up a little. *Tiger Rose* still sounds good. Garcia and
Bob Matthews did a good job on that, but my vocals are terrible. I can't
listen to that record because of it.

*Do you feel better about your vocals these days? I think you sound much
more self-assured.*
I don't attempt so much. I think I know my limitations. I have the
wisdom at this age to know that I'm not a singer in the true sense of the
word. What I am and can be, I think, is a good phraser, and I think I
can deliver all the meaning that's intended in one of my lyrics, though
I can't make it sound as pretty as Garcia can.

Well, people have been saying that about Dylan for twenty-five years.
Yes sir, that's the alpha and the omega of that one.

*In fact, Jimi Hendrix once said that hearing Dylan's "weak" vocals on
that great material is what gave him the courage to write and sing at all.*
When I first heard [Jimi's] "The Wind Cries Mary," I recognized the
Dylan phrasing and this incredible voice at the same time that was as far
from Dylan as you could possibly get and still be using that phrasing.
And it hit me over the head that this was a song that Dylan would've
been proud to write. Then, with the way Hendrix could play guitar . . .
well, it looked like there might be *a conspiracy* out there, and I wanted
to be part of it. [Laughs]

*You have so many songs to choose from when you do a solo concert. How
do you decide what to sing and what to leave out?*
Mainly I'm trying to sing things that I think the audience will like. When
you're one man with a guitar up there, there may be certain things you're
trying to prove, but one of them *isn't* how boring you can be. And I
have gone on tours where I've just tried to satisfy myself and just sing
what I wanted to sing, and I've bored the audience in the process.

I've come to realize that when they come to see Robert Hunter, they are paying money not to see me get up onstage and be a prima donna. They're coming to hear a healthy number of my interpretations of Grateful Dead songs. It took me a long time to swallow that, but I think I accepted it with good grace, and now I give them at least half Dead songs. So I'll sing a bunch of my favorite Dead songs; they tend to remain the same favorites. Then I'll add in the solo material—things that were fun or worked particularly well from the last tour, and usually a couple of surprises. I try to mix it up. . . .

Were the songs on Liberty all written around the same time, or are they more motley than that? Certainly they sound unified.
Some of them are from the collection of seventeen lyrics that I got together for the Dead right before they made *In the Dark*. Of the songs on this record, I'd given the Dead "Liberty," "Bone Alley," and "Black Shamrock." From the collection of lyrics I gave them they took "Black Muddy River" and "When Push Comes to Shove," and Dylan took "Sylvio" and "Ugliest Girl in the World." So it was a fairly successful batch.

Have you ever been able to predict what Garcia will choose and what he'll pass over?
No, not really. He's avoided a great deal of stuff which both he and I think is good. What he does is put it all in a briefcase and then he carries it around with him, in case I ever get run over by a dump truck or something. [Laughs] Maybe it's his insurance policy. But he's got some real good stuff tucked away from years ago.

When he got busted a couple of years back, that briefcase got impounded for evidence, and I realized that all this work was in it! So I got his lawyer onto it—"For chrissakes, this isn't *evidence*, it's years of work!"—and he managed to get it back for us. I was worried for a minute. [Laughs]

Do you ever feel as though you're revealing too much in your songs? Or have you felt later that you obfuscated too much?
I think what looks like obfuscation in my work is a predilection to tinker with a good-sounding phrase, something that *fires*. I will sacrifice some meaning for the sound of something because that's a lot of what it's about for me—interesting turns of phrases and colorful ways of expressing things. So instead of saying "I went to the store," I might put a little spin on it—you know, "I rolled to the store and exploded from the cash register like a bomb" or something. [Laughs] I want color. I want variety.

Robert Hunter. *(Photo by Jessica Leopard)*

I think that my stuff probably does sound very opaque to people who are looking for a literal, left-brainedness in lyrics. But shift over to the right brain and you might find a lot of stuff in there.

Of course, you also have a partner in crime in Garcia. He's said that he'll deliberately cut out verses of songs if they seem to be explaining things too much.
Well . . . not very damned often. "One swallow doth not a summer make." [Laughs]

Can you think of instances when it has happened?
Well, he didn't choose to do the concluding songs to "Terrapin Station." There's a verse to "Friend of the Devil" that I do and he doesn't do, which I feel kind of ties the bow on that song in a certain direction. He's loath to change something once he feels like it's done, while I'll tinker endlessly with things, for whatever good it does me.

I've written up the lyrics for most of our songs, compiling them, and I still can't overcome the need to change lines that I've never liked. So I changed them, and I have an asterisk on the line and then an appendix which has the line as it was recorded. For example, in "Mountains of the Moon" there's the line: "Twenty degrees of solitude, twenty degrees in all, all the dancing kings and wives assembled in the hall"—

I love that line!
Yeah, well—"Twenty degrees in all"? Hmmm. I don't think so. It doesn't *mean* much. So I've changed it to "Twenty degrees of solitude, a fiddler grim and tall, plays to dancing kings and wives assembled in the hall." I think that's much better. When I wrote it originally [for *Aoxomoxoa*, 1969] we were in a pressured recording situation, I knew it was weak, but I just didn't have the time to fix things I wasn't entirely happy with.

There are other lines I'd go back and change, though I can't remember them right now. There's a line or two in "Playin' in the Band" I'd change, make it hit home better, express what I wanted better.

A phenomenon I've noticed, as someone who's been listening to a lot of these songs, really on almost a daily basis, for nearly twenty years, is that they are open-ended enough that they change with me—the things I saw in a song ten years ago are different from what I see now; we seem to adapt to each other.
Me too! Absolutely. These songs talk to me. I'll put them on and they'll

be addressing me at forty-six years old in a way I never could have predicted when I wrote them.

Does that surprise you?

I've learned not to be surprised by it anymore. As a matter of fact, in ways that are absolutely prophetic, there's one song, which I will not name, that has detailed certain experiences I've had in the last couple of months in an uncanny manner—and even told me what to do about them! This is a song I wrote quite a few years ago, yet it almost seems to me now that I was prophesying to myself. Prophesying to others I can understand, but prophesying to myself? Gimme a break! [Laughs] I was in the same aghast state as a Deadhead who suddenly realizes that his instructions are contained in this song, and it even names him!

I think "Black Peter" is an example of a song that has taken on a new life in light of Garcia's illness. The song's the same, but we—the Deadheads and the band—have changed in relation to it. That was a pretty spooky coincidence.

I feel that what we notice in this world is what is coincidental. When a thing happens twice, or when something is stated and then the event occurs, these are things we notice. What we don't notice are things that happen once. Coincidence seems to be the whole nature of what we find significant, and think about.

And I do believe that this sort of thing is just coincidence. I can't afford to believe that it's anything else or I would be afraid of everything that came out of my pen. I'd become a reader, not a writer. [Laughs]

I wonder if you could confirm or deny a bizarre story that's gone around about the writing of "Black Peter." The version I've heard a couple of different places is that one time at a Dead show you were so incapacitated on LSD that you more or less experienced in your brain what happens in the song.

[Long pause.] Let me see. I can't remember if "Black Peter" was written before or after the particular incident you described.

So there's some basis for the story.

Yes, this is a remarkable incident. Once I got dosed backstage with what someone figured was like a quarter-million micrograms—that was the end of my LSD career, by the way—and I went through every assassination I knew of. I was shot with Kennedy, I was assassinated with

Lincoln. The number of times I was killed that night! And each one was completely *real* to me.

I'm not certain whether "Black Peter" wasn't written before this incident. I remember "Stella Blue" was very present during these incidents. All the imagery in "Stella Blue" was very present in my mind at that time. "St. Stephen" was also very present.

I didn't realize "Stella Blue" and "St. Stephen" were contemporary.
This is around *Workingman's Dead* time that I'm talking about. I don't think "Stella Blue" had been performed yet, but it was written.

My time is still scrambled from that era. It took me a full two years after that to get back to where I felt creative or could feel any joy in life, or much of anything else.

Yet that was such a fruitful period for you and your partnership with Garcia.
That's true, but my experience of it was . . . This episode was very, *very* intense. I had a vision of a gold bar in the sky, this shining gold bar. But it wasn't shining on me—it was drawing my energy into it and there was nothing I could do to stop it. It's like it took two years of my energy. The amount of voltage going through my system . . . It really did flatten me for a couple of years and made me seriously consider what the wisdom of this drug-taking had been.

It was an accident, of course, that I got that high. I had taken a quarter tab, or half tab, of sunshine acid that night and washed it down with this bottle of apple juice that had been left on a table backstage. They found out later by asking around that four or five different acid assassins had hit that bottle with acid and mescaline! They found that out when they tried to piece together what had happened to Hunter! [Laughs]

That was the night Snooky Flowers got dosed, too, and Janis Joplin came in while I was starting to rush on it and starts screaming at Owsley—whose fault this was *not,* by the way—"You son of a bitch! You dosed my drummer and he's had to go to the hospital!" And all of a sudden I just saw blood pouring out of her mouth and going all over the room and oh, *the horror* of it all! I got up and went running through the crowd, down the stairs and out into the alleyway. And then the cops wouldn't let me back in because they thought I was just some stoned hippie. So I was just out on the street and I spent the whole gig out there.

They finally picked me up out of a pile of broken glass after the gig was over. The guys were coming out to leave and there I was. They got me over to somebody's house and then Garcia came over and spent the night playing guitar to me. And that helped a lot, because I was just dying over and over and over again. *Whoo-ee* what a night! *Shake it!*

Do you find the types of images and archetypes that drove you initially when you started writing are powerful enough that they still are fueling you? Or have there been shifts in your archetypes?
I don't think so. I don't think that happens to people. At a certain point, what is significant to you is formed in you and I think the only way you're going to change that is to get a new mind and a new body. [Laughs]

Although life and experience can alter it, no?
It can change the perspective on your values and your image system. You can get cynical about it. Or you can get senile about it—get a second childhood about it—and see it in golden lights. If you keep yourself healthy and get a certain amount of exercise, you'll perhaps run your symbols through a more logical and positive approach. But when you're talking about your symbol system, you're talking about who you are that makes you different from somebody else. You're talking about heredity, environment, and that *something else*. I think we're talking about what a being really is here; we're getting phenomenological.

What kinds of input from your environment do you find is stimulating you these days?
Well, Garcia has been coming over a lot and we've been writing some tunes toward a new album. Working with Jerry is very exciting. We each know how the other works and we just flash back and forth, working out changes and possibilities for phrasing. I'll throw him a phrase and he'll say, "Wrong accent," so I throw him another one. "Yeah, that accent's right." And we do that until we have sort of a dummy lyric that will work. Then, once we have an agreed-upon model, I can get cracking on it and hone it.

I can write fast once I have my model. I can put my ideas into pretty much any form. It's an ability—something I can do easily—so by the time he's out of here, we might have run through four or five drafts of a song, or maybe even two songs. Then I have a pretty good idea of how it should go and I work by myself on it, getting it to be coherent.

Using his chord changes?
Yes, on what we've been working on now. I don't need his changes past

the point where I have the dummy, and I have the scan and know where the accents go. Then I try to make a song out of it. It's not the way we generally have been working, but it's the way we want to work right now—close collaboration.

One of Garcia's greatest musical strengths is coming up with dynamic bridges—the music that accompanies things like "Goin' where the wind don't blow so strange..." or "I've stayed in every blue-light cheap hotel..." or "See here how everything leads up to this day...." My question is, when you're working on the lyrics, do you generally know that this is going to be the pivotal part of the song?
Oh sure, when I write a set of lyrics I'll label it "verse one, chorus, verse two, chorus, *bridge,* refrain, verse." This is one of the things we've worked on a lot together. I know that's one of the things he likes to do—construct real fine bridges. It's a nice pivot in the song, something to work toward.

How has working with Garcia affected your own music and your sense of melody?
There's simply no way to tell. It's like asking, how does listening to the radio affect your sense of popular music? I don't know, because it's the sense I have. He said one of the songs on *Liberty* reminded him of "Run for the Roses," and I said, "Frankly it would be strange if *every* song doesn't remind you of something of yours. You're my major musical influence."

I'm not trying to consciously copy anything of his, but then we've been playing together since we were eighteen, nineteen, and he's always been one step ahead of me in musical hipness, and that's a flat fact. I'm as much a fan of his compositions as any Deadhead. I love his songs and I feel honored to be able to supply the lyrics.

You two started out as folkies, and that music is still obviously important in your lives. What is it about folk music that it seems to have this sort of eternal verity?
It wouldn't be folk music if it didn't. It wouldn't have continued on in people's minds. That's the reason that it is folk music. There's a certain timelessness to the themes. Jerry favors a certain type of folk song. He loves the mournful death-connected ballad, the Child ballad stuff. This is a venerable source which has always spoken to him, and to me as well, which is one reason we got together writing songs—because of that haunting feel that certain traditional songs have. I just eat them up, and

so does he. It's a point of absolute mutual agreement. "Terrapin" gets that in spades, and even names a few of the songs. "Terrapin" was an attempt to entirely surrender and go in that direction. That's our little temple of that. It's full of ghosts.

Is it at all odd that you were both so into that at an early age? Most twenty year olds are busy feeling immortal.
[Laughs] Well, they can read that into this, too, if they wish. It's arche-typal. It hearkens to something in us that is built into us partly genetically and partly by the culture we assimilate, the values built into popular songs. I try to go for something real basic when I write a song. It's got to have these resonances to me or it's not right. Unless, maybe, I'm trying to write a rock 'n' roll song, and then I'm looking for rock 'n' rollish resonances. But I'm generally deep-sea diving in imagery and getting things that sometimes—as in folk music—you don't know quite what it means, but it's resonant. Like that line in that folk song: "ten thousand was drowned-ed that never was born." It makes the hair stand up on your arms. That's how I know I've hit in my own writing. You just know it. "Good line, Hunter."

Hunter onstage with the Dinosaurs, 1984. Peter Albin is on bass, John Cipollina, guitar.
(Photo by Ron Delany)

Do you feel that any of your songs have been widely misinterpreted?
Well, I think that people have often believed that the character in "Jack
Straw" who says "We can share the women, we can share the wine" is expressing my personal sentiments, which is certainly not the case. I heard a
lot from feminist groups about that one when it first came out. If you
really look at what happens in that song, you'll see it's a situation that ends
in tragedy. It's a dialogue between two people, and here's the outcome of
the various attitudes which Shannon is mouthing off in the song.

   The other one that comes to mind is "Driving that train, high on
cocaine, Casey Jones you better watch your speed." I said the bad word—
cocaine—and put it in a somewhat romanticized context and people look
at that as being an advertisement for cocaine, rather than what a close
inspection of the words will tell you.

   Then there's the line in "Candyman" that always gets the big cheers:
"If I had a shotgun, I'd blow you straight to hell." The first time I ran
into that phenomenon was when I went to the movie *Rollerball* and saw
the people were cheering the violence that was happening. I couldn't
believe it. I hope that people realize that the character in "Candyman"
is a character, and not me.

Oh, I think they do. I think people are cheering the attitudinal bravado
of the character more than the specifics of Mr. Benson's possible demise.
Maybe. I've gotten used to it. I expect it, but I'm never quite sure what
it means.

Through the years you've had so much Western imagery in your songs. Is
the West a subject you've always been interested in and read a lot about?
I don't think I know that much more than the average person. I did go
through a period in the sixth or seventh grade where I got caught up with
Wyatt Earp and read everything I could get my hands on about him. But
not too much beyond that. I am definitely a Westerner. I've grown up in
Oregon, Seattle, and California, all up and down the West Coast. My
grandfather was a cowboy. He could lasso me running across the yard.

"West L.A. Fadeaway" has a different lyrical flavor than a lot of your
songs. What can you tell me about how that song was written?
I think the initial hit on that was the old song—not the one I wrote—
that goes "stop on the red and go on the green but get my candyman
home salty dog, candyman salty dog, candyman." I liked that; it was

catchy. Little bits of old folk songs have a way of getting into my songs. But then I put that one on an L.A. freeway.

The character in there—his eyes are tombstones. Those are L.A. attitudes in there. Whew! And Jerry soft-pedaled those lyrics a little. There were verses he didn't do. I was out to create a real *bad* character, which is kind of what I consider an L.A. way of looking at things. I'm not a great fan of L.A. [Laughs] We recorded "Terrapin" in West L.A. out in some warehouse district where you had to walk through some real Shakedown Street stuff.

Are there certain characters in your solo work or your Grateful Dead work that you particularly like or feel close to?
Gee, I don't know. [Long pause] I guess I don't really look at them that way. I don't have a thoughtful, reasonable answer to that. Maybe if you gave me an example.

Well, for instance, even though the circumstances of the characters' lives in tunes like "Wharf Rat" and "China Doll" are tragic, I sense a lot of empathy toward the plight of the characters, a real loving attitude toward them.
I could tell you what "China Doll" means but I really wouldn't want to get into it. "A pistol shot at five o'clock the bells of heaven ring." Do you understand what that song's about?

I've always assumed it was about a literal or metaphorical suicide.
Good, 'cause one of my original titles for it was "The Suicide Song." It's almost like a ghost voice: "Tell me what you done it for/No I won't tell you a thing." It's a little dialogue like that. I don't know about *love* being in there. I think it's a terrifying song. And then it's also got some affirmation of how it can be mended somehow. There's a bit of metaphysical content in there which I kind of leave open, not that I subscribe or don't subscribe to it. At the time it resonated right. That song is eerie and very, very beautiful the way Jerry handles it.

I guess I've always sensed that there's another character there, literally or figuratively, who is empathizing with the main character and understanding why it's happening and saying, in effect, "It's all right."
Well, yeah, sort of like a guardian angel. Who knows who or what that is? This is a dangerous area for me to be talking about—the metaphysics of my lyrics. You don't want me to start passing judgments on this.

I'm sorry if this makes you uncomfortable.
It's fine up to this point, but I'd just as soon move away from the subject of lyric interpretation. All of a sudden my alarm started to go off because it's almost as if I'm starting to set something very delicate into concrete. And then, once I've set it in concrete I realize, "No, that's *not* what it means at all. That's not it anymore." Because if it is that concrete, if I can really explain it, I might as well write books of philosophy. The poet is touching and questioning. It's open to interpretation. I know to some degree what I intended there [in "China Doll"], or I know what some of the resonances in there seem to be *to me,* even if I can't put too good a logical head on it. It seemed right. I trusted it. I had to.

Grace Slick once told me that her one regret as a songwriter was that she'd never written a great love song—
[Laughing] What about "seven inches of pleasure"? [A line from a risqué song called "Across the Board" that Grace wrote.] That was a helluva tune!

Is there a type of song you've tackled but have never been satisfied with?
Protest music. Whenever I write a protest song I stand way, way back from it and it hits the garbage. I don't like the strident, protesting tone itself.

Yet you keep trying it?
Oh hell yes. In any given year I'll write a dozen or more. I just do people the favor of not laying them on 'em. [Laughs] I'm not a fan of the genre. I keep doing them, though, because I feel "protesty" about things. I'll read something in the paper, I'll feel righteous about it, and then I'll sit down and try to do what Phil Ochs would have done—I write a protest song about it. I don't record it, though. I throw it away. It's not my particular province. Perhaps it's the province of U2 or those who feel righteous enough about doing it and feel without sin enough themselves to be casting stones. Fine.

There's something I, specifically, can do, and it would be very wrong for me to say, okay, I will now take the world's causes upon myself and abandon the thing that I think is more important for me to do, which is . . . I have some little cracked pane into a little part of the subconscious. I've always felt that I'm conscious of the subconscious, and unconscious of the conscious. There are things that I can bring out of the subconscious that not many people can. I have feelings for the psychic waves, the psychological problems that people are going through, and it's those kinds of problems I want to address—more generalized things.

Do you have any thoughts on how the current younger generation of Deadheads is similar to or different from the first group that came up in the late Sixties and early Seventies?
I don't think you can generalize. They're all so different from each other. Once in a while I'll see kids who look like they just stepped out of 1969—their heads seem to be in the right place, and they're interchangeable with that era. Or perhaps those are some of the Heads who have been tripping back and forth between 1969 and 1988, for all I know. Maybe some of them have found a tunnel through. You never know. Maybe it isn't a new generation at all. First Deadheads were trying to get tickets to every city they could, now they're trying to get in every time. And they still can't get in—they're still standing outside saying "I need a miracle." [Laughs]

It's gotten pretty respectable to be a young Deadhead at this point.
That's true, there are enough young people into it that there's no shame in liking the Dead.

Hey, the Dead even made United Press' list of "in" things for 1988.
Oh no! Oh *no!* The lists, the awards . . . that's scary stuff. We've set ourselves up to weather all kinds of seas. The sea of fame and large, general middle-of-the-road acceptance may be one of the roughest ones of all, and we could founder here. We could have foundered anywhere on the way to here. I have to believe we won't. I don't know where this one goes, though, except *down*. It's impossible to think it's going to get bigger, because it seems like it would be impossible to be bigger. Where do you go from the stadium? To the point where you can no longer play gigs because it will be such a circus if we do? I hope not.

Who are some modern songwriters you admire?
There's this fellow Morrissey, who writes for the Smiths. I also like the guy in Love and Rockets. Then there's the writer in the Call [Michael Been]. He is just superb! I've played his records over and over. He's so literate! I also like Nina Hagen, because she's so weird. Some of what she writes I don't like, but some of it I like a lot. She's uneven insofar as pleasing me goes. I'm not sure who her target audience is at all. But some of her stuff is so remarkably weird it's almost shocking. She strews

around belief systems like they were handfuls of Cheerios. I would recommend her to the severely weird.

Have you ever written anything to be deliberately contrary or controversial in the way that in the Seventies punks wrote things deliberately to shock?

Well, I've thrown in a few forbidden words in my time. We got in "some other fucker's crime" in "Wharf Rat." The Jefferson Airplane said they used that word [in "We Can Be Together" from *Volunteers*], but did they really? I challenge you to listen to that closely. You can't hear it. I think we were the first ones to say "fuck" on a rock record and get by with it.

You know, it was fairly risqué to use the word *cocaine* in a song when we did, unless you were a folk song on public radio. And though it seems mild today, "goddamn" was a heavy word to use when "Uncle John's Band" came out. I don't like too many strictures on language. At the same time, I don't like using these kinds of words in a sloppy fashion. Sloppy language is usually indicative of sloppy thinking. You want language to be liberated, and I love what Lenny Bruce did, of course, but that doesn't mean you have to go act and talk like that. But you should *be able* to. It's a basic liberty.

In a recent interview, Robbie Robertson said something to the effect that he felt that most of the great song ideas in pop had already been mined. How do you feel about that?

Oh my! I think there's an infinity of great ideas; they just have to be uncovered. And Robbie Robertson most certainly uncovered some germinally great ideas. The direction he went with the Band earlier was one of the things that made me think of conceiving *Workingman's Dead*. I was very much impressed with the area Robertson was working in. I took it and moved it to the West, which is the area I'm familiar with, and thought, "Okay, how about modern ethnic?" Regional, but not the South, because *everyone* was going back to the South for inspiration at that time. I've done my share of back-to-the-South songs, too, of course.

I think knowingly or not people attach a certain autobiographical quality of your songs to Garcia, as if you're writing about his life and feelings. Do you detect that, too?

Oh yes. I think that's one reason I don't sell many records and why I've entirely escaped recognition. A lot of people do feel that Garcia has written these songs. I even had someone come up to me at a show years ago and tell me that he liked to believe that Garcia had written these songs and didn't really appreciate me singing them!

There are people out there who like to feel that [every Hunter-Garcia song] Garcia does is a unified being. Then they ascribe that unified being to Jerry Garcia himself and it makes him kind of uncomfortable because it isn't; that thing that's being sung is a mutual creation. I'm pretty much resigned to not receiving the credit for what I do, except among Deadheads who know. But even they don't think of it in those terms particularly, because it's a magic show and Garcia's the magician. You don't want to know who built the effects for [illusionist] David Copperfield. All you want to see is David Copperfield do his magic.

I've got a big ego, I'll admit that, and this has been a subject of unhappiness for me over the years. I like to get my little piece of recognition, and it doesn't seem to be offered me.

I'm really surprised you feel that way. Most people I know admire your writing tremendously. But you know, in a way you set yourself up for a life out of the spotlight by being somewhat reclusive.
I don't meet the public that well. I'm not inviting the audience back to my dressing room after the show, for sure. [Laughs] If I did, I'd just be answering a lot of questions I've answered before. Like, "How's Jereee?!" I live in a very Jerry-perceived universe, more than is pleasant for me really. We are, in fact, very different sorts of people.

Don't you think that your distance from the band is part of what's allowed you to write on some of the themes you have? So many rock and roll people fall into a rut in their writing when all they have in life is touring and recording, and all they turn out is bad on-the-road songs.
What was the major song I wrote while I was on the road with the band? "Truckin'." After that I knew it was time to get off the road or I would have been doing the same thing.

I guess what I'm saying is that one reason so much of your art is vital and people can relate to it is that unlike most rock and rollers, you've been able to live a life. A real life.
Yes sir. That's true. That's the trade-off. That's what I *have* got. So every time I go mealymouthing around about what I *haven't* got, I do look at the fact that I have had the blessing of living a life. And I have to ask myself, "Which is more valuable?" Well, *life*, of course! I *guess*. [Laughs]

Messages to
the Band

██████ ██████ ██████ ██████ ██████ ██████

What follows are comments from *Golden Road* readers directed to the band as part of a poll we conducted in late 1986.

It it's fun, keep doing it!... Grateful Dead is the understanding of "Lots of us and not much me."... I want to see Phil sing "New York New York" the next time the Dead are at Madison Square Garden.... Don't stop playing, at least until our unborn children have a chance to see fifty shows!... Try *closing* a show with "China Cat-Rider" sometime.... I really hope I don't piss you off when I yell so loud everyone in the country can hear me. But goddammit I just ain't ready to stop partyin' with y'all!... The diabolical experiment in which the band is effectively isolating the Pacific Northwest from personal appearances is beginning

to show the predicted results: scores of otherwise contented loyal fol-
lowers are beginning to join the ranks of the "un-Dead." There is only
one way to stop this—a string of concerts in Oregon (Hult Center, of
course)! We must stop the madness! We must make everyone cry "Iko!!"
. . . Stay tight but loosen up and explore more of the band (Phil, Mickey,
Billy, Brent) in the construction of new songs. . . . Remember the lyrics!
Pull more skeletons out of the closet! Don't play where cops are assholes!
Go out into the DEEP UNREAL! Fer chrissakes, JAM LONGER! But most of
all, remember we all love you, no matter what we might say about you
after a shitty second set. . . . Can my dog sing backups on your next
record? . . . Please don't cater to the crowd. It's become too rah-rah.
People applaud every lick and don't get into the shows. Just displease
'em for a couple of years, thin the ranks, and we'll all have more fun.
. . . "Grateful Dead" spells "love" in every language. . . . Heeeeeere
commmmmmes suunnnshine! . . . I'm getting married around the time
you'll be in Worcester. Please come to the wedding and play a few tunes.
. . . Please come back to Europe. Waiting for six years has been so hard.
Don't forget us. . . . As a student of geophysical sciences at a major ac-
ademic institution, I feel the need to constantly be classifying and cate-
gorizing to increase my internal/external harmony. As such, I have placed
what the Grateful Dead does under "metamorphic rock." Is that all right
with you? . . . Thanks for moving the tapers off the floor. . . . Oh hap-
piness! The Dead family and Heads have created a sacred space where
our spirits dance together, while our feet dance to blisters! . . . Thanks
for the inspiration and for giving me a fairly legal hobby. . . . Thank you
for all you've done to inspire my own musical style. Play for as long as
you want or need to. . . . You guys throw the best parties! . . . Eat shit
and die! (Oops, sorry. My brother's suggestion). . . . Let's start planning
for New Year's 1999. . . . Do you sometimes wish you were in the audience with us? I hope you get off at shows like I (we) do. . . . Thanks.
You keep us going. And there's no rush, so don't tire yourselves out
with endless tours. I'd rather see fewer shows for a longer time. . . . Next
stop, Moscow! The barriers have to come down for world peace to be
more than just visualized. . . . I really dig y'all and all that, but will you
PLEASE QUIT FUCKING AROUND?!? There's "barely time to wait," so would
you please play a "Dark Star," "St. Stephen," or "Cosmic Charlie"?
With so little effort you could make so many people so much happier.
. . . I can't imagine what my life would be like if I'd missed The Bus.
. . . Please play New Hampshire again—I've never slept in my own bed
after a show. . . . Let Mickey sing! . . . Greatness stands alone. Leave Dy-

lan at home. . . . Keep on being a band that most folks in the world can't figure out. Stay a mystery. Do an entire concert of songs no one has ever heard before. . . . If variety is the spice of life, you must cook Mexican. Keep up the salsa. . . . Through all my life's ups and downs with religion, drugs, jobs, women, and friends, the only thing that has never let me down, always been around and always come to town, is the Grateful Dead. . . . Love you a lot but would love to see y'all get back to more spacey, jazzy, extended improv in the second set. . . . Life hasn't been quite the same for me since Bobby cut his ponytail. Let's try it again! . . . Why not do a set "backwards" some time: "Sugar Mag"–"Wharf Rat"–"Not Fade Away"–Rhythm Devils–"Eyes of the World"–"Estimated Prophet"–etc. Shuffle things up a bit! . . . If you're ever in Cape Cod, Mass., drop by for lunch or something. . . . Four letters, Phil: S-O-L-O! . . . Now that more of us are doing fewer drugs, we need to either make the shows weirder and stranger (more exotic and different), or we need smaller shows with more participatory activities. Further Dead faster. . . . Billy, you've beaten your way into my heart and now I can't get you out. But that's not a complaint. . . . We do care about records, particularly carefully made ones. Audiophile-quality Grateful Dead records would be fabulous. . . . If you play Curtis Mayfield's "Freddie's Dead" at Alpine Valley, I'll inhale a large vegetarian pizza. . . . We're a softball team called the Ozone Pirates who use your skull motif in our logo. We live in Turlock, California, your favorite city. How about coming out for a game. . . . More Kesey! More Thunder Machine! . . . How about a frequent-flier program? . . . Thank you for making my day job bearable. . . . It can rain, snow, sleet, or flood, but you can bet that the Dead can bring in the sunshine. . . . It's been a pleasure growing up and growing old with you. . . . Let Phil SPACE! . . . Please, never wear spandex suits on stage. . . . Please try to start sending Deadhead newsletters again, like the old days. Even one a year would be great. . . . It's so obvious—HAWAII!!! . . . Please do the watusi. . . . As you have cultivated an extremely open-minded audience, challenge that audience (and yourselves) by subverting predetermined structure at all points. In the words of the sage, "Fuck the format—GO OUTSIDE!!" . . . Please take care of yourselves. NO hard stuff, but occasional sacramental drugs, with appropriate mind-set, would probably be GOOD. . . . Pigpen came to me in a vision the other night and told me to get 1,000 hours of Dead on tape by the fall tour or I'm dead puppy meat. Please send me tapes so I can avoid this horrid fate. Maxell UD-II's only, soundboards from your vault preferred. . . . Keep progressing but don't be afraid to go back and dust off some of the old gems many of us never had the chance to see you play. . . . 1. Thanks for all that's been. 2. I can't wait for what's next. . . . Billy, thanks for that smile back at Duke in 1982; Bobby, may your hair grow longer and your shorts shorter. . . . Vladimir Horowitz still tours in his seventies. Let those bones creak and keep jamming! . . . Here's a suggestion for a new format: ANY SONG, ANYTIME! The predictability of where in a show a particular song will surface lessens a factor that could increase the "high" between band and audience—namely surprise. Imagine a show where any tune could crop up anytime. We're up for it. Are you? . . . Keep on playing—your music is one of the few truly precious things the human race has produced in this century. . . . Jerry, please wear a tie-dye sometime. . . . Thank you for providing a vehicle for so much joy, love, laughter, insights, friendship, and warmth. For the musical ecstasy as well as the depths that were less than pleasant. So simple, yet so complex. . . . I'd like to suggest an alternative to the current taping scene: Broadcast every show on a limited-range FM signal within the concert hall and announce the broadcast frequency to those inside. This will eliminate the need for microphones and maybe even the segregated tapers' section. . . . Go for it. Space is the place. The rest is just passing the time hoping to get there. . . . AND LEAVE IT ON!! . . . There are few places I'd rather be than deep in the heart of the second set, sweaty, exhausted, oblivious, yet acutely aware, laughing, crying, ecstatic— thanks. . . . Thanx for trusting us with the taping. . . . The words to your songs float like clouds, in various configurations, suggesting infinite possible meanings. Below, the music flows like waves and the wind. . . . In a world full of confusion, aggression, violence, and self-centeredness, you serve as a clear message and influence that we matter, we will survive, that giving love will open the way to peace, and that each of us has our own unique gifts and corresponding contributions to the world. Oh, just for the record, I proposed to my wife on the third night of the three rainy Red Rocks shows in 1982. . . . When asked "What is the worst disadvantage to living in Alaska?" my answer isn't that it's frequently 40 below in winter or that there are hordes of mosquitoes in the summer. It's that I can't see the Dead without plane reservations. Please, please, please play Alaska again! . . . Phil, grow back your beard! And the rest of you guys—get your hands up and turn around real slow-like, 'cause we gotcha covered! . . . You have committed your lives to finding out what you want, working at it, excelling at it, and inspiring and overjoying people by doing it. My life will be spent that way, too. No matter what I do, I wish to do it as well and with as much spirit as the Grateful

Dead. You modern-day minstrels are a modern parable. . . . Grateful Dead tickets are better than money. . . . I would like to see a CD tribute to Pigpen with some of his best unreleased performances. . . . Please play "The Golden Road–The Eleven," and get me a real good job with long vacations so I can tour after I graduate and not starve. Then you might try walking on water. . . . Maybe a little international touring would be a good idea. It could do us and the world some good to provide a glimpse of that "other" America that we know exists, but that others may not have a clue about. It's a spirit that's not bound by imaginary, obsolete borders, so why not? . . . Throw an over-thirty concert so we can enjoy a night with all our old friends. . . . I'm sorry I asked you to play "St. Stephen" when I bumped into you at the hotel in Saratoga in 1985. . . . Don't pay attention to any of this "Poll" shit, because it's just bullshit. Just keep on playing what you want to play. . . . Mekka Lekka Hi, Mekka Hinee Ho! . . . Thank you for being such gracious channels and providing the atmosphere for many a shamanic journey. . . . JUST KEEP FUCKIN' WITH MY HEAD!!! . . . How about more verbalization on the whole trip, like the Joseph Campbell symposium? . . . What can I say to a band that is a way of life, a way of being, a philosophy of life, an ideal, an ideology, a "religion," a fundamental archetype, a consciousness-raising experience, a cosmic correction, a vacation, a new awareness, a thought, a feeling, a will, a way, a "band beyond description"? Thanks for being who you are! . . . I can't begin to count the good times the Grateful Dead have given me (and I probably only remember half of them!). I love to dance to the colors you play! . . . What will it take to get you guys to send someone into the vault, pull out maybe the one hundred best shows you can find, and release them on CD? You'll make oodles of money and we'll all be in heaven. In fact, may I volunteer my services to help pick 'em? . . . Stadiums are for other bands, not the Dead. You don't need the bucks that bad. . . . Thank you, Mickey Hart and Billy Kreutzmann for opening my ears to worlds of music I never imagined existed. Keep the weirdness coming! . . . The time has come for a Grateful Dead cruise— maybe a week island-hopping in the Carribbean. Trip around a different island every couple of days, shows on the boat every night or two. We could redefine "The Love Boat." . . . If parents paid an extra dollar or two toward special tickets, maybe we could sponsor a day- (or night-) care area at every show so those of us with kids could go to every show in a series without having to always find a sitter. My husband and I would go to more concerts if we could. . . . LET PARISH SING! (And then I can sneak behind Jerry's amp!). . . . I'd love to see T.C. up there onstage sometime sharing the keys. And while we're at it, how about inviting Donna back for a few tunes sometime. . . . I resisted the Grateful Dead for years because my sister played nothing else. A year ago I finally went to a show (reluctantly) and immediately "got it"! Now I wish I'd listened to my sister all those years. I would've seen some great shows. Better late than never, though, huh? . . . Jerry: "Mason's Children" sounds fine to everyone I talk to. It could be just the tune to wipe out "Throwing Stones–Not Fade Away" and "Around and Around" in our lifetime! . . . Please don't lose that old spontaneity in the quest for consistency. . . . To me, the best music of the Grateful Dead ranks as one of the greatest achievements of human life on this planet. It has taken DNA millions of years to evolve to the point where it could unleash the awesome magnificence of Grateful Dead space music onto the quivering masses of protoplasm that we call audiences. . . . Thank you, thank you, thank you, thank you, thank, THANK YOU, thank you, thank you, thanks, thank you, *gracias,* thank you, thank you, thank you, sure appreciate it, thank you, thank you, yowee, thank you, thank you, keep it up, thank you, THANK YOU! I love you. Peace.

Weird Notions

■ ■ ■ ■ ■ ■

Catching Up with Bob Weir

An Interview: June 26, 1989

When I arrive at the Dead's San Rafael recording studio in the late afternoon on June 26, the place looks uncharacteristically deserted. Usually it's a hotbed of activity, or at the very least, some serious hanging out. But this day the front lounge area is dark—almost spooky—and an eerie red glow emanates from a connecting hallway. At first, all is quiet, but soon I hear the warm, reassuring sound of Grateful Dead music coming from the main studio room. The red light announces that a session is in progress, and the tune that is bouncing through the sound-proofed door is "Foolish Heart," sounding as bright and chipper as I could hope for. Inside, Garcia and engineer/coproducer John Cutler are doing some mixing on what will likely be the Dead's first single in two years, and to these ears it sounds pretty damn good.

But I'm not at Club Front to report on the album sessions, which, as

Frost Amphitheater, 1989. *(Photo by Clayton Call)*

usual, are closed. My reason for being there is to have a chat with Bob Weir, whom I last interviewed for *The Golden Road* in the winter of 1986. He emerges from a back room puffing on a ciggy and looking typically relaxed. Always cordial and thoughtful, he graciously submits to a few rounds of questions about what he's been up to lately in the Grateful Dead.

Can you tell me a little about how "Victim or the Crime" came about? I know you played it solo for a while before bringing it to the Dead.
I had originally written it for the Grateful Dead in 1983 or 1984. I wrote a snatch of a chorus and then I showed that to my friend Gerrit Graham and we talked about it a little bit, and then he fleshed it out lyrically, and I fleshed out the music as well. When I originally brought it around to the band, the way I wrote it and the way it came together, it's a very complicated piece and it didn't get a whole lot of attention because there was a lot of other material we were working on at the time. So I did it a little bit with the Midnites, then did it solo, and then brought it around again a few months ago to a warmer response. So at that point we started putting it together as a Grateful Dead song.

Was there a specific inspiration for the tune? It's hard for me to gauge the attitude of the song.
It's introspective. It's just something that occurred to me. That chorus came to me—words and music—out of the blue, and then Gerrit and I had at it.

I think it's got an integrity of its own. I understand it's not a real popular tune. [He chuckles]

I think people are warming to it as it develops more. What do you think when you get that kind of negative feedback?
[Smiling] It doesn't matter that much to me because I have to do what I have to do, and I can't cater to a bunch of directives that are handed to me by a board of my peers. I'm a fairly specialized individual. If I try to satisfy a whole lot of tastes, my output is going to be pretty watered down.

Beyond that, when I get met with adversity, I tend to bite the bit and run with it. I sort of revel in it. Anyone who knows me fairly well knows that about me. It's not unlike a lot of my friends, and not unlike other members of this band.

I think the rap is, "If you want Weir to do something, tell him the opposite of what you actually want."
[Laughs] Right. We're all a little perverse.

Is there something about "Victim or the Crime" and the subject it deals with that would have made it harder to do with the Dead five years ago, given the band's problems in that area?
Well . . . I don't know. There's that reference in the first line to the junkie, but that wasn't meant to be specific in any way. It's a line that had to be there. Hey listen, I tried to replace that like a billion different ways, but nothing would do it. It's a powerful, intact image that gets the point across with a great deal of ease, though not with kid gloves certainly.

There's a lot of ground to be covered in the issue that we approached in this song.

Which is what, exactly?
Well, you know, it takes the whole song to describe it. The chorus pretty much states it: "What fixation feeds this fever/As the full moon pales and climbs/Am I living truth or rank deceiver/Am I the victim or the crime?" It's about self-doubt in the face of all that one amounts to. It points up moral terror and all that sort of stuff. I guess not everybody wants to hear about that, and I can surely understand that.

Anyway, given the ground we were trying to cover in the tune, there isn't a whole lot of room to lightly suggest the subthemes that are going through it except by saying things plainly. If I were to try to pull that "patience runs out on the junkie" line and replace it with something that gets to the same point with a little softer punch, it would take me the whole verse just to say that, and I just can't do that in that song.

I gather some people were touchy about it because we had some problems with junk. But I wasn't pointing a finger at that. I wasn't shying away from it, either. I was addressing a subject and that line came up. It was necessary to get to the place where we were going. I know some people stumble on that line and can't hear the rest of the song. In that case it's their challenge to either overcome it or discount it if they don't want to look into it.

It has a real interesting chord progression; those ascending steps and all.
I listen to a fair amount of twentieth-century music, and actually there's a thematic line that's sort of a suggestion of something I copped from Stravinsky's "The Rite of Spring." I'd actually been working on little

permutations of it for a long time, and it's popped up in a couple of places. I can't remember where.

"Saint of Circumstance"? When you played that at Shoreline the other night I really noticed its similarity to "Victim or the Crime."
Yeah, it's in there, too. All that sort of stuff that I play on my bass strings on both of those tunes particularly—root and five, root and flat five, root and six or root and nine—and if I hammer those intervals on a quarter-pulse or a sixteenth pulse, that's basically stuff I've lifted from "The Rite of Spring," which I consider to be early rock 'n' roll.

The ascending passage that happens after the second verse of "Victim or the Crime," and then again during the instrumental part at the end, is sort of a variation on a passage that Bartok did in "Music for Strings, Percussion, and Celeste"—all that dissonance. What I've done is sort of a condensation—in a different key and with different intervals—of something he did in the first movement of that piece. I took a couple of lines and had them ascend in sort of a spiral so that the whole feeling of the music there would point the listener up at the moon to set up that image in the chorus.

The thing hangs together. I'm happy with it. But we'll see how it comes out on the recording and how it seasons as a performance piece for us. It's complicated.

How about "Picasso Moon"? Barlow told me that you'd originally written that tune for another set of lyrics, but that Brent worked up those lyrics independently.
That's right, which meant it was time to start over. So I took the music and went on a vision quest—I went on a good, long bicycle ride is what it amounted to, and in the middle of it I came up with what I wanted the song to be about.

Is bike riding a good catalyst for inspiration for you?
Yeah. I get into an aerobic state and things strike me. I was looking for something that fit the various movements of the music and then Barlow and I hammered out a scenario. We're not quite done with it; it's maybe 90 percent finished.

To what degree do you think about the singability of your songs when you write them? On that one you seem to be struggling in a few spots.
It still has a ways to go. I still have some work to do in that area,

Bob Weir, 1990. *(Photo by Jay Blakesberg)*

definitely. Usually, if I can't handle the melody that was in my head when I was writing it, I'll change it or cover it somehow.

What is it that appeals to you about the imagery in the song—this flashy night world? Is it something you relate to particularly?
Not necessarily. It's just a common theme in music, and every now and again I like to hammer a common theme and see what I can do with it.

The main character in the song seems to be unsure if he wants to be where he is.
Right. And where he is is getting progressively weirder. From what I can see, too, he doesn't get any more sure of himself as it goes on. His frame of mind stays pretty much the same.

Does it feel at all autobiographical, either emotionally or actually?
No, not really. When you're singing a song like that you're wearing a mask. Most of our songs are that way. Like the guy in Garcia's song "Deal"—is that autobiographical? I doubt it.

Well, the metaphor in that is pretty general and universal.
Right. That's true. But my point is that when you're writing a song you're painting a picture, and it doesn't necessarily have to come from your own life for it to work.

Are there songs you've written that you would consider autobiographical on some level?
"The Other One" was autobiographical. "Truckin' " was autobiographical. All of the rest of them certainly have facets of my personality. None of them is an attempt to be a complete representation of what it's like to be me or anything.

It seems there's quite a bit of alienation in a lot of the songs you've written with Barlow in recent years. Alienation and a certain amount of darkness, really.
There's darkness and doubt in all of us, so that's natural that it's going to come out somewhere. I'm not sure "Sugar Magnolia" falls into that category.

That was written twenty years ago. Most of your songs, from "Estimated Prophet" on strike me as mainly dark portraits.
I can see that. "I Need a Miracle" isn't dark. I'm maybe a little close to it to really analyze that. I'd need to have more distance from it to actually comprehensively comment on that. It could be. Everyone has loneliness and darkness in their lives, but I don't think I have a disproportionate amount in mine.

Would you say you're basically a happy person?
Yeah, I'm doin' fine.

Can you talk about how your songs evolve with you onstage?
Well, after a few years of seasoning, a song will generally get better, and easier to deliver. Oftentimes when I'm writing a song there are lines in there I don't fully understand.

What's an example of that?
Most of "Cassidy." I really couldn't have told you what it meant way back when, and I really don't know that I could tell you now, though I know for myself it's come to mean certain things. It hangs together better for me now, whereas when we first wrote it, it had an integrity I could recognize right away, but I didn't understand parts of it. As we've done it over the years, each of the lines has come to mean more to me.
   There was a song that wasn't without its dark undertones.

How does the infusion of new material affect how the band plays?
It takes us in new directions, hopefully. Often when I'm writing a song,
I'll engineer it to be a stretch for me—something I either can't sing or
play to some degree—and then work on it. I usually won't bring it around
to the band until I can more or less handle it, but I like there to be room
for growth. I like to give myself a challenge, and when you challenge
yourself you make yourself more capable in the long run. You expand
yourself. I view every song that's presented to this band—by myself or
by anyone—kind of that way: that this is a song I can't play, but if I
work at it I can. To varying degrees, others in the band view it that
way, too, so we all have to stretch to learn the new material. It's good
for us. And in so doing, a lot of what new capabilities we have to achieve
to be able to play new material splashes over into the other tunes we
play.

*What processes do you go through when another band member brings in
a new song? For instance, in the background I can hear that nice rhythm
line you play on "Foolish Heart." Is that something you came up with,
or was it suggested somehow by Garcia's original presentation of the
song to the band?*
On that one, Garcia originally had a line that he was going to play
between the verses and then again between certain lines of the verses,
but he suggested that I play it so he could play a rhythm part on it. So
I played his line and then started coming up with variations on it, and
then tying it in to my own concept of the rest of the part. So my part
grew out of his suggestion. But it varies from tune to tune.

Do you feel like your role in the band changes much from year to year?
Not really year to year, but epoch to epoch, period to period. You know,
there's our beginning period, our early middle, our middle, our late-
middle . . . [Laughs]

*I always wondered what sort of historical perspective you might have on
the band's different phases. Is it determined by personnel changes in your
mind?*
Not completely, though that's certainly affected it. But then the Keith
period overlaps the Pigpen period, and running through that was our
country-rock period, so you can get pretty detailed about it. We've
covered a lot of ground. [Laughs]

What makes you stop playing a tune for a while? Does the music feel stale to you?
It can be any number of things. Sometimes I get tired of the words. That happened with "Black-Throated Wind," for instance. . . . It's a good tune but it needs a rewrite.

Because it doesn't resonate with you?
Right, it doesn't resonate with me. The character in that particular tale is not somebody I can get behind. It's always been a poor fit for me. There's stuff in there I just didn't want to be singing; that seem like words to fill out a melody rather than something I really cared about, and that finally got in the way. I've always felt like the words I was singing in some specific places—I won't list them—were like wearing lead shoes in a track race. I couldn't carry those words through the melodic and harmonic changes that the rest of the song had suggested to me. So it needs some adjusting.

I'd think it would be difficult to try to rewrite something so long after the initial creative burst.
I'm sure it can be done to some degree. [Weir introduced a new version in the spring of 1990, then returned to the original that fall.]

Does "Lost Sailor" also fall into that category?
Yeah, that's going to take some reworking as well before I bring it back around.

The music you've been playing in your solo shows with [bassist] Rob Wasserman is going in some interesting directions. Do you miss not having your own band and the input of more players outside of the Grateful Dead?
I don't miss it now, but I probably will eventually, in which case I'll do something about it. But for the time being, for getting outside the Grateful Dead in the limited time that I have these days, playing with Rob works real nicely for me, because it's interesting to me musically, and from a practical standpoint I don't have to do much coordination compared to having a band. I just call him up, ask him if he's free to play some dates, and then we take our instruments and go. It travels easily, and it gives us the flexibility to each do a lot of other stuff.

*Do you find that after twenty-four years, you can pretty much predict
what kind of musical input you'll get from the other members of the
Dead when you bring in a song?*
Not really, which is part of what keeps it interesting for me. You get a
lot of good surprises, and a few bad ones as well. But we iron things
out.

What would be the nature of a "bad surprise"?
A bad surprise is something that I feel is inappropriate for the song,
either to the feel of it, or the melody. And a good surprise, obviously,
is something that goes beyond what I expected to hear and delights me.
For a song to sound right, it's real important for the writer to be able
to communicate with the guys in the band what he had in mind, at least
to start with. From there it can go on its own course to an extent, and
probably should, as it develops in performance. That's the way we generally work, anyway.

*Can you usually tell what kind of night you're going to have onstage
early on in a show, or does it change a lot over the course of the evening?*
It varies. Sometimes it starts out well and stays that way and it seems
relatively easy. On the other hand, there have been a few nights where
it's started horribly for whatever reasons and it's ended up great for us.
Generally, if it starts poorly and you fix your attitude that it's going to
be that way it tends to be a self-fulfilling prophecy. In fact, if you fix
your attitude in any way, you're going to limit how expansive the show
can get.

*At the end of a show, are you generally in tune with what the rest of
the band thought about it?*
More than half the time. There are times I'll feel like I've had a good
night and then somebody'll say I'm crazy, that we had a horrible night.
[Laughs] But more often, on the really good nights we all agree.

*What sort of factors determine your choice of songs from night to night?
One night you might follow a hot "Scarlet-Fire" with "Looks Like
Rain," another time it might be "Estimated" or "Man Smart Woman
Smarter."*
Well, some of it is just what tunes are up in the rotation. And some of
it is just how it feels like it will fall together best. The first set we'll
usually set the first two or three songs and then go on from there. Usually

Dylan and Weir at Oakland Stadium, 1987. *(Photo by Ron Delany)*

we have a little huddle before the second set and try to plan out the first half of the second set, based on how it's gone so far—how the night feels—and what the singers feel like singing. Often enough, though, that gets tossed aside. Sometimes we don't even start with the song we just agreed on. [Laughs] Somebody gets a different idea once we're on the stage. And sometimes what seemed like a good idea is a good idea, and we'll do it like we planned it. . . .

How often are you actually surprised by what the other guys in the band play?
Pretty much nightly. It's a bad night when I'm not surprised by anything. I think we've been playing generally pretty well recently, and I find myself surprised at some of the places the music is going. We're just feeling our way to some new stuff.

You seem to have become very comfortable with your repertoire of Dylan songs. How has that affected you?
They're great stories. If a song is like a painting, then these are great paintings to present. It's a lot of fun to play songs that very nearly play themselves, like those do.

"Play themselves"?
Well, everything in them works so well together—the melody, the words, the chords. They're so well written, they're just a real pleasure to play.

I'd think the experience of singing them the past couple of years would affect how you view them compared with when they came out in the mid-Sixties.
Actually it's not that different. They always connected to some facet of me. They're the same songs for me. They haven't tended to grow for me the same way our own tunes do, so I'll bring up some new ones, and some of the old ones aren't done quite as much as they were, like "Desolation Row." I have a feeling the ones that I'm singing now will stick with us for a couple of years and then they'll drop back and we'll do them only rarely. Then I'll try to find some new ones, because I do like playing the Dylan tunes.

When you've been playing short tunes in the first set and then you get into something more expansive, say "Cassidy," do you have to make much of a mental adjustment to get into that space?
Somewhat. I generally try to place a song like "Cassidy" later in the set so we're pretty much warmed up and loosened up and have some sense as players what our parameters are for the evening, so we can just let fly. I think "Bird Song" is the same way for Garcia.

I'm always amazed, then, when you can open a show with a long, spacey version of "Feel Like a Stranger." It must require a different mind-set from opening with "Jack Straw."
Right, though "Jack Straw" has on a few occasions gone more outside than I expected within its structure. "Feel Like a Stranger" obviously requires more instrumental work and its structure is more open.

You, Phil, and Jerry seem to be enjoying your new guitar synthesizers during "space" these days.
It's a lot of fun. I'm playing a Casio guitar with an on-board synthesizer.

I'm constantly modifying it, but I'm getting close to what I want to play for a while.

Do you envision a time when the synth guitars will be integrated into the regular songs rather than just being during "space"?
Last year around this time I would have thought that there would be more synth guitar on the new record, but it hasn't worked out that way. I would assume that sooner or later it'll happen.

Have you sensed it affecting your writing at all?
A little. But I'm still just getting control of the synthesizer, and I don't want to do anything in my writing that I can't perform comfortably. Basically, I'm a guitarist first, and when I'm sitting around my living room, I don't play a synth guitar; I just pick up whatever guitar I have lying around. I rarely even plug it in. That's how I do most of my writing—just messing around at home. I have a studio and a [synth] setup there, and I imagine that a lot of the writing I do from now on will probably have some synthesizer guitar on it.

Would you say that your overall feeling about the band's current state of evolution is very positive?
Oh yeah. It's a lot of fun right now.

It's too bad there are so many problems with the fans right now.
My suspicion is that if we fastidiously see to the music, that everything else will fall in line. That may be a sort of Pollyanna viewpoint, but I can't help feeling that way—that if we put out the right vibes, things will arrange themselves.

I understand that on summer tour last year, you actually donned a disguise and went out into the campground to check out the scene.
A few times. It was interesting. I've tried to peek into it from time to time through the years to try to get a feel for what's going on out there.

How did it look to you?
It looked like fun. I was impressed by the size of it, which if not staggering, is at least considerable. There's a pretty wide diversity of people out there, albeit a lot of them wearing tie-dyes and looking fairly similar. But you've got street people and professionals and students and all these other types. I think it's great. If I were a kid on summer break, I can't think of anything I'd rather do.

Bill Kreutzmann

Long-Distance Drummer

An Interview: July 19–20, 1989

One of my favorite moments in the entire body of the Grateful Dead's music comes during the August 27, 1972 (Veneta, Oregon) version of "Bird Song." After the vocal part of the tune, the band embarks on a twisted, obviously acid-drenched jam that spirals up and up until it resolves at the main riff. There's a moment of pure silence, which almost feels like it might be the end of the song, but then Bill Kreutzmann unleashes this amazing rolling drum figure that instantly propels the jam in a completely new direction. In *The Grateful Dead* filmed two years later, Billy explains that when the band is really happening and he's at this best, playing the drums is like dancing. And that explains, in part, why the Grateful Dead's music swings so sublimely.

Earth. Air. Fire. Water. Both of the Dead's drummer/percussionists bring all four of those elements to the music in varying degrees at different

Billy in 1987. *(Photo by Herbie Greene)*

times. But when I think of Bill Kreutzmann I think mainly of air and water—of perfectly placed cymbal splashes and flowing tom fills; of subtle stick work that has a nearly transparent quality, it is so well integrated into the band's gestalt. Of course we've all seen him throw himself into his drums with ferocious, even frightening, intensity on many occasions. Billy can definitely rock with the best of them, but to me he is part of what makes the Grateful Dead first and foremost a jazz band. It is not at all surprising to learn that one of his major influences was the great Elvin Jones, who helped propel John Coltrane's music for many years.

Throughout the Dead's twenty-five-year history, Kreutzmann's drumming has provided both a rhythmic anchor around which the front-line guitarists weave their parts, and an expressive current that courses through songs and jams like some free-swimming electric eel. It is no accident that the Dead's freest music came during the periods when he was the lone drummer—first during the era surrounding the Acid Tests (when he was known as "Bill Summers" because that was the name of the fake I.D. that allowed him to play in bars), and again from 1971 to 1975. Listen closely to the drumming on 1973 to 1974 tapes and you'll be astonished how effortlessly (or so it seems) the band moved from fat grooves to deep space and back again with just a few flicks of his powerful wrists. And one need look no further than the *Mars Hotel* version of "Scarlet Begonias" to hear how brilliantly he fit into a more complex polyrhythmic attack. In short, much of the Dead's very essence derives from his drumming.

Of course from mid-1967 through 1970, and for the past fourteen years, Kreutzmann has been teamed with Mickey Hart in what has to be the most potent long-term drumming duo in modern music. Billy readily acknowledges his debt to his partner, occasional teacher and good friend; their onstage rapport is obvious. Since the introduction of the Beast in 1979, following Hart's work on the soundtrack for *Apocalypse Now,* the percussion jam in the second set of Dead shows has been the most consistently unpredictable and open-ended portion of each concert. Together they've explored percussion realms that have taught us all much about the power and language of the drum. I know much of my own appreciation of world music stems from hundreds of hours locked in Billy and Mickey's spell.

Because Kreutzmann doesn't really do interviews or have the self-promotional flair of some other band members, he has never received the press attention he clearly deserves. He is basically a very private person; indeed, he lives hours away from the other musicians, on a rustic ranch in Mendocino County with his wife, Shelley. So we're especially pleased that we can offer the first in-depth solo interview with him in many, many years.

Our interviews took place over the course of two afternoons in late July. The first day, we talked at the Dead's studio, where he was re-cording tracks for *Built to Last.* The following day, we jumped into Billy's jeep and drove up Marin County's Mount Tamalpais, stopping for a while on a beautiful rocky bluff overlooking Stinson Beach to watch a hang glider begin its long descent to the shores below. Though reportedly he can be volatile, my dealings with him through the years have been nothing but pleasant. And much of his intensity is positively directed: he's a man who cares deeply about his work, his family, and his friends, and I think much of his inner passion and warmth come through in the interview that follows.

What are your first musical memories growing up in Palo Alto?
My mother was a choreographer who taught dance at Stanford, and when I was real young she'd have me sit down in the living room with this Indian drum—a tom-tom—and she'd have me pound the quarter-

time for her, and she'd write out the choreography and try out steps.
I'd even go to her classes sometimes and I'd beat the drum there. Everybody thought it was real cute, of course. [Laughs]

Is that what got you interested in drums?
It probably contributed to it. At first, though, I wanted to play piano
or trumpet or some lead instrument, but I ended up getting into drums
instead. When I was about twelve, I met this cool drum teacher named
Lee Anderson who taught in Palo Alto, and he just had a neat vibe about
him. He was going to school at Stanford to become a physicist—which
he is now—and every Saturday he'd give me a lesson up on Perry Lane
right near Kesey and that whole clutch of people. Kesey was writing
right next door, but I didn't know it at the time. Anyway, Lee would
give me a lesson for half an hour or forty-five minutes, and then he'd
let me loose on the drum set for hours. And at that point, that was the
only time I was able to get onto a full set. All I had was a pair of sticks.

What sort of stuff were you listening to back then?
I remember liking Elvis Presley when I was small; for some reason he
cracked me up. I got into Fats Domino and liked New Orleans music a
lot, though I didn't even know it was New Orleans music; I just liked
it. Just like everybody else, I'd go down to the music stores in town
every day and hit every one of 'em and see what new records were out.
And in those days you could listen to the records in these booths. I spent
hours doing that.

Do you remember your first set of drums?
Sure. There was a drummer in town who was older than me and who
I sort of looked up to. When he decided to get a better drum set I bought
his old Ludwig set—which he'd refinished white for some reason—for
$250, which was a lot of money back then, especially for a kid.

*Were your parents supportive of all this? I can't imagine being a parent
and having a twelve year old around pounding the drums day and night.*
They were totally supportive of me . . . still are.
   One time I was away at prep school [Orme, in Prescott, Arizona] and
I was playing football there until my grades got too low. I got so bummed
out that I couldn't play football that my dad crated up my drums and
sent them to me by train so I'd have something to do outside of classes.

I set them up in a little barn there and I practiced like crazy, and that helped me make it through the year.

Did you play music with other kids?

There was one other kid I knew who was really into music, and he played saxophone. So he and I would jam hour after hour—it must've been really musical! [Laughs] But I learned a lot from that experience.

Then I went back to public school in Palo Alto the next year and people tried to get me to play in the school band, but I wouldn't have anything to do with it. I went and heard the band one day and said, "Are you kidding?!" It was just lame orchestra stuff, with nothing for the drummer to do.

Luckily, later on down the line, I got turned on that Jerry and Pigpen and sometimes Bobby were playing bluegrass at a place called The Tangent in Palo Alto, and I went down there very faithfully and listened to them all the time. I really got off on those guys; I really just liked them a lot. My heart just said, "This music is really cool."

Hadn't you played some rock 'n' roll before you hooked up with those guys to play music?

A little. I played in a band called The Legends, and we'd play at YMCA dances, and there'd be fights and the usual stuff. The kids liked us for some reason, though I can't imagine that we were really any good. We'd play Chuck Berry and whatever was popular. It wasn't too soulful, though, and I think I was probably the most serious about music then; we were just teenagers.

Once I was going to leave that band to get into this other band called The Sparks, who were all guys in their twenties. This was going to be my big move! But I had this showdown with the other band and the guys are asking me, "Are you gonna leave the band?" And I got this vibe that if I said yes, they were going to take me outside and knock my lights out, so I said, "Nah, I'm not leavin' the band!" [Laughs] It sounded like a setup. So I stayed with The Legends a while longer and it was cool. We got better, and eventually we got this black singer who came down from San Francisco, and he fronted the band real neatly. I liked him a lot; in fact I was the only guy in the band who'd let him stay at his house. People in the neighborhood, which was all white, apparently were pretty freaked out by this, but I didn't even think about it.

Had you listened to much jazz at this point?
Not really. Phil was my big influence in jazz. During that first rough
year after Phil and I joined the band and we were playing around at
Magoo's Pizza Parlor and joints like that, Phil lived near me in Palo Alto
and he turned me onto all sorts of stuff—not just jazz, but Charles Ives
and people like that. It really turned my head around. Then, when we
lived together in San Francisco, he turned me on to Coltrane and I just
bit on that. [Laughs] I thought, "Jeez, I gotta learn to play this stuff!"

Was that Elvin Jones' drumming mainly?
Yeah. I really listened to him a lot. He was a major influence on me, no
question about it.

*By the time the Warlocks got going you must've had a bit of experience
playing R&B.*
I didn't think of it that way. It was all just music. I didn't really get
locked into the idea of different styles until we got further along—in my
mid-twenties—and I started to really differentiate between different
styles. It got real neat when I met Mickey because we really concentrated
on rudiments and we got all that done and over with. It allowed us to
play real fluidly.

*In the very early days of the Grateful Dead, was there any other music
out there that you could use as a model for how to play these long, extended
pieces the band got into?*
Not really. And we played extended pieces from the very beginning.
We just never thought of stopping; it never crossed any of our minds to
play three-minute songs. [Laughs] We played this bar called the Inn
Room before Mickey joined the band that was a terribly weird gig on
some levels, but a great learning gig for us—six nights a week, five sets
a night. The weekends were all these heavy straight juicer types, and
they'd be looking up at us as we played all these long, long songs and
they didn't know what to make of us. They wanted us to quit, but the
men didn't want to admit they were tired of dancing and look shitty to
their girls . . . [Laughs] We played every new Rolling Stones song that'd
come out, and Pigpen would sing some blues. We just kept playin'.

*What did LSD do to your drumming? The Acid Tests came so early in
the band's development.*
It changed the tempo a lot. [Laughs] Actually, a lot of the time there

was no tempo. It also created more extendedness and amplified what was going on—it made things go on longer, or just seem like a blink, depending.

How musical was it?

It was totally musical or not musical at all. Who knows? When you're high on acid you can't really be expected to be too analytical about things; you're going more with a free-flow, and sometimes that would be synchronous with what the other guys were playing, and sometimes you'd just be in your own world playing. But we weren't examining what we were doing. I remember once when I was high on acid it took me what seemed like fourteen years to take my drums apart. It seemed like lifetimes had gone by—I'd gone gray, grown old, died, been reborn all in the time it took to put one cymbal in the case. [Laughs]

Where did you meet Mickey?

We met at the old Fillmore; I can't remember if I was playing a gig there or not. Michael Hinton, who's now a musician in New York, was with him; he was one of his students. Anyway, they met me, we went outside, and they pulled out some sticks and they did this shit and it was like, "Oh yeah, I gotta learn *this* stuff!" [Laughs] So I did. I worked out with Mickey for a long time. We worked on all sorts of different drumming things and we did a lot of neat things together. One time he even hypnotized me, which was great because you get real relaxed and into a total learning space. There was a lot of growing that got done by both of us.

His first gig with the Dead was one night at the Straight Theater when he sat in with us. And after that he just seemed to fit in.

Do you think it changed the music drastically?

Not drastically, at least at first. But what happened was during that period we really rehearsed a lot at the old Potrero Theater, and a lot of what we'd do was rehearse different times—we'd do sevens, or nines, and I think "The Eleven" came out of that stint. We'd play for hours until it was practically flawless. The drumming became really unitized, though. We'd lock into one time, and sometimes it would be hard for us to get out of it. We were locked into playing bar lengths instead of phrases; and a phrase is much better in my opinion.

It's funny, somebody once asked Coltrane what his favorite time was and he said 4/4. [Laughs]

Were you listening to people like Joe Morello [Dave Brubeck's drummer], picking up on the 9/8 in "Blue Rondo" or the 5/4 in "Take Five"?
Oh sure. I like the nine more than the five. Back then, "Take Five" seemed very hip, but I don't think it's stood up that well. It sounds a little corny to me, but "Blue Rondo" had that nice fresh bounce to it. I listened to Morello and all those guys—like Shelly Manne, who was really great with the brushes.

Anthem of the Sun *sounds so dense rhythmically, with all the layering and all. That must have been a weird record for you to make.*
It was kind of strange. There was a lot of layering and manipulation in the studio, obviously, but if the end result is cool then that's fine with me. To be real honest, I wasn't all that involved with *Anthem of the Sun.* I didn't feel like I participated that much in that music; it didn't "get me," if you know what I mean. It wasn't my cup of tea particularly. If I listened to the record right now I might eat my words, but my memory is I wasn't that thrilled with it. I thought then—and actually I still feel this way sometimes—that some of the double drum stuff makes the music seem less concise. Sometimes less is more.

Did you like it, then, when the band moved into a softer realm with **Workingman's Dead** *and* **American Beauty**? *I always thought the drumming on those was nicely understated and tasteful.*
I liked it, too. It was a neat period; a lot of fun. We were adding so many new songs and the whole feeling of the music was very different from what we'd been doing. For me, it was a lot more satisfying than playing the music of *Anthem.*

Did you and Mickey ever sit down and try to define what your respective roles were?
No, never. Then and now, we'd just go out there and see what works and what doesn't work. The stuff that works we try to keep. The nice thing about having the drum suite, or the crazy suite, or the free space, as I like to call it, in the second set is that's a nice place to experiment. I can do anything I want that I feel like playing. My rule to myself is to be as musical as I can; I try to play that way. I'm not up there just trying to play a million hot licks to show I'm the fastest.

How did you feel about that trend among drummers in the late Sixties to show off their alleged virtuosity with interminable solos?

I kind of felt it wasn't too musical usually, even though there were good drummers out there. It sort of seemed like showing off a lot of the time. If you can be musical and show off, fine. Otherwise, fuck it. I like playing in an ensemble; that's the most fun for me—complement the lead player, lay off a little when the vocals are going . . . there are a million things to do in ensemble playing.

I bet you don't remember that Elvin Jones and [Cream's] Ginger Baker had a drum-off sometime in the late Sixties.
Actually I do remember that, and I think everyone was really disappointed with it, me included. I hate that kind of competitive shit. You might think that being in a band with two drummers I'd feel competitive, but I don't feel that way. Or maybe I am and I don't know it. If anything, I think Mickey just sparks me to play better. If I get into a competitive thing it just shuts me down musically, so I stay away from it. At the same time, you're a human being and you have emotions and you have to play through those emotions; but if you dwell on them, you can get hung up on them.

I've had some real sad nights on the drums before, when people in my family have died or a friend or whoever, and we've had to play. Everyone in the band has gone through this, of course. And in those cases, the emotions that come out are sometimes just so overwhelming that you can't help playing in that mode. Sometimes you're so shocked under those circumstances—under that strain—that playing music is what eases the pain for you; you're so happy to be able to do it. A trauma has happened and you can't stop the feelings, but maybe you can channel the feelings musically. Some songs will make you cry your eyes out, because they're so close to what you're going through. I'm sure a lot of our fans relate to the music that way, too. Through the years I've tried to learn how to use that emotion to play more sensitively.

How did you feel when Mickey left the band at the end of 1970?
It was okay with me, frankly, because I felt at the end of that period we weren't really gelling that much. It's hard to really explain what was going on. Those were real complicated times for him and real private times, and I'd rather not talk about it.

Fair enough. Did you feel a greater sense of freedom as the lone drummer again?
I wouldn't put it that way. I had a sense that the music became a little

more clear. The rhythms and the grooves had a clarity you can hear on tapes from that period.

The music of that era was the jazziest the Dead have ever performed. There was a real swing to a lot of the jams, even when they'd be pretty out there.

It was definitely the most open music we've played. I loved it. It's never quite been that way again—which is fine; you want things to be different, to change.

How did you view your solo slot during that time?

Well, I didn't always have a solo. Some of them were good and some of them weren't. Frankly, I've never enjoyed doing drum solos alone that much. With Mickey, at least we can bounce ideas off each other and it seems a little more interesting. When I was with Goathead—that's what I like to call Go Ahead—the other guys in the band wanted me to do a drum solo, but I just didn't dig it; it didn't feel right. Like I said before, it sort of seems like showing off. Sometimes virtuosity is lost on me—on any instrument. So that guitarist can play two million notes in one-quarter second—big deal, did he play any music, anything that hit you in the heart, and grabbed you and moved you? That's what I want from music, whether I'm listening to it or playing it.

Did Keith's joining the band affect how you played? He was such a percussive pianist.

I loved his playing. I remember when we auditioned him, Jerry asked me to come down to our old studio and the two of us threw him every curve ball we could, but he was right on every improvised change. We just danced right along on top. That's when I knew he'd be great for the band. He was so inventive—he played some jazz stuff and free music that was just incredible. He had a heart of music.

How did Pigpen's death affect you?

Shitty. I hated it. It's funny you ask me that, because I just drove by his old place in Mill Valley and got a little choked up. I really liked that son-of-a-bitch—he had a lot of love in his heart. He was a guy who was jokingly mean . . .

I don't think anyone believed he was actually mean, though.

That's true, because you could tell he was this sweet guy. Though I have to admit, when I first met him in Palo Alto I believed it. [Laughs] He had sort of a motorcycle jacket that was a little scary; he had that look. He was unkempt, to say the least. But he was the leader of the band.

He went to Europe with us in 1972 and we could sort of feel him slipping away a little. He was emaciated. But it was a really sad day when he died.

Weir once said that when the band went back to two drummers in 1976, it became a little harder to turn the corner in jams, that a certain amount of flexibility disappeared.

I can see what he's saying. Things maybe didn't flow quite as easily for a while. You know, I don't know what it's like for him to listen to me and Mickey from his point of view. It was a little more cumbersome, which I think you'd expect, but it smoothed out over time.

In the late Seventies the band started working with outside producers. How was the Keith Olsen experience [he produced **Terrapin Station***] from your perspective?*

Everybody told us that he was a real motherfucker on drummers, and he made me do some stuff I didn't want to do, like playing with big sticks. I think he wanted me to be some Top 40 drummer. He was kind of a megalomaniac, which isn't the kind of person who should be working with the Grateful Dead.

*How about Lowell George [***Shakedown Street***]? At least he was a musician who understood the band's strengths—although I didn't think that album was very good.*

I really liked Lowell a lot. Whereas Keith [Olsen] always wanted to be the director/producer type and wear the higher hat—to work in the upper office, so to speak—Lowell was really like a member of the band more. If we were working on a song and he didn't feel it was going right, he'd just grab a guitar and come into the studio and show us how he felt it. That was one of the ways he'd communicate, and it worked great. I had a tremendous amount of respect for him.

Basically, though, I think the Grateful Dead produces itself best. It's not the fastest way for us to work, but that's not important.

Let's talk about the present and how you experience a show. What do you do before the show?

Well, actually, for me the show starts way before the day of the show.

Generally I'll try to visualize a tour before we do it. I can actually visualize myself onstage playing, and other things like checking into hotels, sitting backstage. I tend not to look at the itinerary to see what the specific gigs are, because it sometimes makes the tour look long to me. But it helps me relax and puts me in the right frame of mind for playing music. At this point I don't "plan" to do the visualization—it just starts happening, and I'm not even necessarily aware I'm doing it. I guess it's my way of psyching up.

Most of the visualization occurs right before the gig. I'm in the hotel a couple of hours before showtime and I'll just start thinking about how it feels to play; I get together with that feeling. I get really anxious before every show. After all these years I still get stage fright. It's really important that I be mentally ready when I go on, because otherwise I'll play lousy.

We get a half-hour call before we go on, and then about fifteen minutes after that I'll go up on the back of the stage and put on my armbands and stuff like that. If it's at all humid I have to wear wristbands, because my hands get so sweaty I start dropping my drumsticks. Then, before we actually go out onstage, I'll sort of look out in the crowd, maybe make eye contact with somebody. Somebody'll see me looking at them and they'll wave, and I'll wave back, and that relaxes me some more. Now you're not just in yourself; you're starting to relate to the crowd. And then when you do finally go on, the applause and the screaming and all really makes me feel good, and it gets me pumped up so I have even more energy than I thought I did before I went on.

It took me a long time to learn about that, though. Years back I used to fill a lot of the off-time before we went on doing stupid things, and I'd go on so screwed up I didn't feel good about playing; it was like an overload. It's easier for me as a player to come from a relaxed place and make myself play hot than if I'm antsy from whatever. But like I said, it took me a long time to figure that one out.

Garcia and Weir have told me that during the first couple of songs they're out there trying to feel out the vibes and the sound and reestablish connections within the band. Do you go through the same experience?
That's true for me, too. That's really where the true warming up takes place, because even with all the mental preparations and actual practicing you've done backstage, it still comes down to playing in this ensemble and adjusting to the musical dynamics—How does the room sound? How's the mix?

Talking about connections with the other guys in the band, I really make it a point all through the show to try to establish eye contact with the others. In fact on this last tour I even moved a cymbal so that I could see Jerry better. I like having that visual contact. I think we communicate really well onstage, and a lot of time it's not even verbal, of course. We'll be in a jam and I'll look over at Jerry and he'll look at me and it's like, "This is great! You havin' fun? I thought so!" [Laughs]

It sounds very intimate.
It is. It's great. After so long we can read each other pretty well.

Through the years, I've learned how to play with all the other musicians at the same time. The bass drum goes with the bass—with Phil—and I'll do the right-hand lead stuff with Jerry, complemented on cymbals or crashes with Bobby, and then I'll use the left-hand high-hat stuff for the rhythm pocket with Brent and the bass and the rhythm guitar. I'll do all of that at the same time. I found myself doing that once and I thought it was a cool thing to do instead of dedicating the drum set to one player and moving it around the band that way. It's not something I could ever teach another drummer, because it's really a matter of listening and being able to separate the functions.

Am I correct in believing that most of the song tempos are determined by the guitar players, by how they go into a given tune?
Yeah, but I'll void a tempo on them if I feel somebody's started it way too slow or way too fast. I'll just pull it back if it's too fast, or nudge it up if it's slow, and keep a big smile on my face the whole time because I don't want them to think it's not intentional. It's my way of saying, "Hey, c'mon, there's an hour and a half between each quarter beat. I could go out and have lunch between beats. What're we gonna do here?" [Laughs] But that's just me; maybe the guitarist really wants to play it that slow. But I have to trust myself, trust my body feeling. I like to play from inside.

Do you ever feel like you have to compensate if one member of the band is obviously "off" that night?
Oh, we all have our off nights, of course. That's the way it goes, you know. I don't think you really make an adjustment when somebody is off. Just play as well as you can. You'd be surprised, too—sometimes when someone's having an off night they'll pull some weird shit out of the bag and the sets go in interesting places. You never know. But you

don't want to sit there and be judgmental—"Oh this is too fast, or too slow." You want to just get on top of it so you can just roll with the wave instead of trying to pull the wave back or push it ahead.

Have you noticed any slowing down with age?
Not really. I'm forty-three and I'm feeling great right now. I don't think of age chronologically. It's how you feel inside. If anything, I think it's gotten better for me through the years. I'm more confident, and I'm having more fun than I have in years. Part of it, though, is how well I treat myself. If I'm feeling good like I'm feeling now, I might as well be a kid. I'm pretty young at heart, too.

It must be quite a challenge as a drummer to play Grateful Dead ballads.
It's definitely the hardest for me, though not so much anymore. They used to scare me a little, because it's harder to find a groove on them. Not "Stella Blue," which is pretty straight ahead, but on something like "Row Jimmy," for instance, I just wasn't sure the band had the groove on it; or maybe I just didn't have it in my heart. But I've learned how to deal with it, and now I'll just sit right in the middle of the quarter beats. I used to feel hesitant about certain songs because I didn't think we could just jump into the feeling. Ideally the groove should start at the beginning; you shouldn't have to sit there and twist it around to find it. It should come right on. You turn on the faucet, water comes out.

How about more conventional first-set tunes, like "Mexicali Blues" or "Mama Tried"?
Those are a lot less interesting to me.

Does you're playing on them then become somewhat mechanical?
No, it's not ever mechanical, because I can always find something to interest myself. Somebody might play something that'll make me laugh, and I'll do a little add-on to that. It's like a little tease going on—"You did that? Okay, check this out!" Or me and Garcia will play some licks together. That's what keeps it interesting to me. Even though we play a lot of songs more or less the same lengths, we really do change the interiors of them all the time—change the carpet, so to speak; paint the walls.

I don't know why we still do some of those songs. We've had so many years to put new songs in there. If we're going to do cover tunes, there

are a lot that would be better. In general, I like playing our stuff more
than cover tunes.

*I'd think that the order in which songs are played would affect your
experience of them night to night. Like if you followed "Big Railroad
Blues" with "Bird Song" . . .*
That's a great combination! "Big Railroad Blues" is real straight-ahead
and "Bird Song" is lilting. The contrast is great for me, because one is
this bam-bam-bam on the beat, and the other is this free, jazzy, open
song that has all these other possibilities. I love playing "Bird Song."
   A harder trip to play is when the two songs have similar grooves, like
a couple of 12/8 songs—like Bobby's done "Little Red Rooster" and
Jerry does "Sugaree." They're both 12/8 but they've got totally different
feelings.

*A tune like "Eyes of the World" seems to change tempo almost with the
seasons.*
That's another one I love playing. Yeah, we've never really locked down
into a groove. It's one of those kind of songs that's remained changeable,
which I like. It keeps it more interesting.

How does the song right before the drum solo affect how you go into it?
Well, if we've just done "Man Smart, Woman Smarter" my thinking is
generally that I'll hang with that rhythm when the guitarists and Brent
leave the stage. Mickey might get off the drum set and start playing
something else, or sometimes we'll both stay on the drum kits and talk
back and forth there for a bit. If it's coming out of something like "He's
Gone," I'll tend to play a much more open drum solo, because I don't
have to be on the pulse. So yeah, it totally affects it. But each one has
its own place. That's the nice thing about our band—if you didn't have
that simple variation, it would get boring really fast.

*Do the drum solos ever have a conceptual theme? Garcia and Weir have
both said they sometimes predetermine a broad subject area for the
"space" segment.*
We do the same thing. We didn't use Tiananmen Square or anything,
[Laughs] but we'll be back there saying "Earthquake!" or "World War
III!" and we'll do big bomb shots on the big toms—that's a little influence
from *Apocalypse Now*. It's kind of fun to have a theme going through
your mind.

The other thing we do is program rhythms, sometimes before the show, or during the break. We'll be back there doing these rhythms that are stored [by computer], and then we use them during the drum solo.

Is the flow of the solo based mainly on the mood of how it's going, or do you sometimes decide in advance that, say, you'll move to the roto-toms at some point, then play this or that instrument?
No, that's too premeditated for me. I wait for sounds to come along that I want to play with and use, or if Mickey's doing something that I'm not locking in with, I'll take the initiative and start something else. I'll always use whatever drums I think will work for the sound I'm looking for. And if none of those seem right, I'll play my electronic stuff.

Which is what, exactly?
I have real basic stuff compared to Mick. The main one I use is a [Roland] Octapad.

Billy and Mickey clowning backstage at the 1987 Bay Area Music Awards. *(Photo by Ron Delany)*

And that's loaded with samples?

Right. It's got eight switches under these black pads, four on top, four on the bottom, and you activate it by hitting it with a drumstick.

So who has control over things like decay and other signal-processing info?

I work it out with our sound tech, Bob Bralove. Bob has been such a wonderful addition to our band. He's a great human being. He really listens to you when you try to describe a sound or feeling you want to coax. He'll really help you get what you want. He's helped me tremendously.

So we work together getting sounds for the Octapad. I have a whole long list of sounds on a big sheet of paper near me, and then I have to initiate the number [of each sound] on a switching box that I can hit with a stick. And each number corresponds with a different sound. So number one might be "high jingly thing," and then there's a single boom on the number four pad, handclaps on three, a shaker on two. It's neat. And sometimes I'll use things during the regular part of the set, too— I'll throw a hand-clap into "Gimme Some Lovin' " just for fun.

If the band isn't playing well, does it color the drum solo much?

It can. If we haven't been playing well, for whatever reason, sometimes by the time we get to the drum solo it can seem like a chore—not in the sense that I don't want to do it, but because I'll occasionally feel like it's my job to try to make it all better; I can put this drum solo Band-Aid on there. Unfortunately, it doesn't work that way. [Laughs]

I wondered about that. There are nights I get the sense you and Mickey are trying to exorcise weird energy from the stage.

I'd like to be able to, and damned if I don't try to, and I know Mickey does. It doesn't usually work, but we give it the best we can.

What do you do during "space"?

Usually I'm right back there listening to it. Those guys are doing stuff with their new MIDI setups that's been blowing my mind! I've really been enjoying it because that's when I get to be the audience, too. So I'll sit back there and close my eyes and just drift.

It's a nice time for me because I get to rest and cool off, get some water, and hear them play.

I've been thinking lately that I want to take a shorter rest, though, and maybe get back out there and play some free music with Jerry, like we did in the early Seventies—not to repeat that space, but because I'm hearing such neat stuff in what he's doing and I'd like to add to it; I hear drum parts on it.

I know a lot of people who would be thrilled to see that happen—to get back into that jazzy place again.
Well, you're not locked to tracks or stops or left or right turns. It's free and open; you don't know what's going to happen. It's got a three-dimensionality that I love because it can go in any direction.

I know you said earlier you don't consciously think about how you play in relation to Mickey, in terms of whether you're doing more straight drumming and he's doing more accents, or whatever, but can you talk at all about your different roles?
It's hard. The best I can do is tell you how I see it.

Some people call you a drummer and him a percussionist.
Nah, that's wrong. We're both drummers and percussionists.
I sometimes see that there's double-drums stuff that we're doing where we don't need to be doing it; where the music might sound better if he were doing more percussion, like on tom fills and lead-ins to changes and choruses and bridges—setups they're called. A lot of times he'll be playing the backbeat on the snare drum and I'll be playing the backbeat on the snare drum. He'll be riding on his tom-tom, I'll be riding on a cymbal or a high-hat, playing the eighth-note or sixteenth-note pulse, or whatever it is; dotted shuffles or whatever's going on. Personally, I find that to be a little redundant. I'd rather he played a different role—maybe a lead rhythmic role, while I hold down the fort.

In other words it gets too locked in?
Yeah. Maybe that's what Bob meant about "turning the corner." Because the way we sometimes work it gets so steamrollerish the music doesn't bend.
But I'm not being critical of Mickey here. I'm sure there are things I do that drive him up the wall. What it comes down to is that everyone in the band hears music differently. That's why the band works as well as it does.
Like I said, to me the neatest thing is playing with everyone in the band—true ensemble playing.

When we're really playing well is when we take the most chances, and that's the most fun for me. I love to go out and take a gigantic risk someplace in a song. Sometimes they make it, and sometimes they don't. When they make it, it's amazing. Jerry once described it: "Kreutzmann, it's wonderful—you sound like you're falling down a flight of stairs but landing on your feet!" [Laughs] I just get this weird idea in my head and then see if I can do it.

You get the infamous arched eyebrow from Garcia...
Or if it's really off the wall, you get a real good chuckle. [Laughs]

Let's talk about recording. I know you've been laying down some drum parts for the new album the last few days. Is that a pretty intense experience for you?
It can be. It varies. It requires a lot of concentration, and in a way a different kind of concentration from playing on stage, partly because at this point I'm playing with tracks that are already down. I get into it ...

Sometimes I wake up at 4:30 in the morning and I can't drop back to sleep, so I'll get up and work on songs. Last night when I woke up I worked on "Victim or the Crime" because that's what I'll be doing all day today. I got up, put on the earphones so I didn't wake up the family, and listened to a tape from yesterday and really thought about the parts I was hearing—Phil has some really great things on there that got me thinking in a certain direction. So from there I visualized myself playing a part in relation to him. Now today when I go in, it'll take me a couple of times through at the drums to get it, but the idea I have will probably be right because I worked it out in my mind first. It's like doing a storyboard for a movie instead of just going out and being loose and shooting a movie.

"Foolish Heart" sounds like it would be really fun to play.
"Foolish Heart" is a wonderful song. When Jerry first laid that song on us, everyone liked it so much they played everything they knew all at the same time. [Laughs] It was a mish-mash, but we were excited. It was like, "Settle down, cowboys! Rein 'em in a little!" But after a few times we got the feel for it better. It's evolved nicely. It's come around to the point now where I can't wait to play it onstage. I get so excited sometimes when I like a song I'll push it a little.

I can almost be like two people sometimes. I can sit up there and be like a timekeeper and let that happen. Though actually, I'm not really keeping the time—I'm playing with it. The time is already there—you're just picking parts of it out to show people. And then I can also be real excited inside and that makes me play in another way.

Are there certain Grateful Dead songs you relate to lyrically more than others?

Different songs different nights, just like it is for Deadheads. I'm finding that in nearly all the songs we do—except for the cowboy tunes—there are good lines in there; a minimum of a couple of dynamite lines. The poetry is such a wonderful part of our songs. The words are really important to me and definitely affect the way I play the song. It becomes close to acting in a way, except with sound rather than words.

Is a tune like "Morning Dew" difficult to drum to?

Oh no! It's such a wonderful song. When the words are out there and they're so beautiful and they take you away, like those do, you can really lay into the music; you can really play your heart out. It's the songs you can't relate to, where you feel like you're bullshitting, that kill you. But a tune like "Morning Dew," that grabs you, is a cakewalk to play.

What are some of your other favorites to play onstage? How about "Fire on the Mountain"?

I love that song because it's got that big, big half-time groove and the line is real neat. I love "Wharf Rat"; that has some neat parts in it. I love Brent's songs. I love how he sings and plays piano, so any of those are good for me.

You guys seem to have a pretty close relationship. You've been in a few bands together . . .

We trust each other and we like each other. We've been through the best of times and the worst of times and come out of it with good times, so I'll take that to the bank. We're friends; what can I say?

Did you enjoy the experience of playing the clubs with Kokomo and Go Ahead?

Not really. I enjoyed playing the music, and I loved the musicians, like Alex Ligertwood and David Margen, who are real top-dog players, but I didn't like eatin' other people's smoke and smelling booze and seeing fights and all that stuff that happens in places like that. But also it was too much trying to work in two bands. It didn't give me enough time to do things by myself and with my family.

Do you listen to a lot of music at home?
Oh yeah, I have a huge collection of CDs, and of course I have a lot of records, too. Like this morning I happened to put on Stevie Ray Vaughn's new CD, made myself some strong French roast coffee and that woke me right up! [Laughs] I did my exercises and then came down to the studio. I listen to every kind of music. I still love jazz a lot.

I just love music. I love listening to it and I love playing it. I feel incredibly lucky that I've been able to spend my life in music. And it's still getting better for me; that's the best part.

The band has certainly been playing great recently.
We've been having such a good time lately; that's a big reason. And also we've been playing a lot, which is important. You gotta keep playin'. I don't like sitting around in hotels on an off-day watching TV. It's like, "What the fuck am I doing here?" [Laughs] I can get in a weird head space. But on show days I usually wake up and all day I look forward to playing. Playing is what makes it all worthwhile.

We Want Phil!

An Interview with Phil Lesh: April 18, 1990

It seemed somehow appropriate that on the morning of the day I was to interview Phil Lesh, I was jolted from a sound sleep at 6:54 A.M. by a rumbling 5.4 magnitude earthquake. Talk about a rattling bass sound— Phil's got a ways to go before he matches that one! To make matters weirder, it was also the eighty-fourth anniversary of San Francisco's 1906 quake; I instantly thought of Phil's famous "Earthquake Space" during a Hartford Civic show April 18, 1982, the seventy-sixth anniversary: "SAN FRANCISCO IN RUINS!!"—*Bwonnnnnnnngg!!*—*thuddddd-thud-thud!!*

Actually, through the years there *have* been times during "space" at a show when I've been sitting there with my eyes closed, and Phil's bass emitted such a ground-shaking low note that I honestly wondered if the ceiling above might start to crumble. Crushed at a Grateful Dead show— what a way to go! These fantasies are rare, however, and more often I

Phil at the Greek, 1985. *(Photo by Ron Delany)*

associate Phil's bass sound with less threatening natural forces: I keep thinking of that line in "Crazy Fingers"—"Peals of fragile thunder, keeping time."

The thunder analogy is obvious, but apt. (And in part of "Let It Grow," it's even literal.) His playing conjures other images, too: There've been "Other One" jams where the bass line reminds me of some jungle beast chasing its prey; others where it's our very cosmos spiraling out of control. Are Phil's sonic booms on "Morning Dew" the end of the world, or a prayer for redemption? Maybe they're just notes in a musical piece. Depends on the listener and the moment, I suppose, like everything else.

The point is, it isn't *just* bass; some solid rhythmic anchor married musically to the drums. In a band where no one player is setting *the* rhythm, and in fact *all* the musicians are setting the rhythm all the time, Phil's bass is able to dance through the music with peerless fluidity and grace. (Would anyone be offended if I fondly compared it to the hippo ballet dancers in *Fantasia*?) To say that his playing owes more to jazz bass than rock 'n' roll or R&B bass doesn't exactly capture it, either. Yes, it's rooted in continual improvisation, like Mingus or Scott La Faro or Charlie Haden, but there's the matter of *electricity*—Phil's style and touch are rooted to his mastery of the possibilities of his electronic instrument. Indeed, he's been a true innovator in this area, involved with aspects of the design of nearly every instrument he's used since the halcyon days of his gargantuan Alembic axes.

Unlike most bassists who came up during the mid-Sixties, Phil didn't learn his instrument by copping James Jamerson licks off Motown singles, or Paul McCartney riffs off Beatles records. Rather, he learned on the job, playing with the Grateful Dead in bars and ballrooms. At the same time he was building his chops, the band was getting high and experimenting with *demolishing* conventional musical structures. The group's eclectic approach forced him to continually explore new areas as he grew: It's an R&B band! No, it's a cowboy band! Wait, it's a space band! No wonder he doesn't sound like anyone else.

Though he's adept at every style the band plays, Phil shines brightest when the music is most open and challenging. Quickly tripping through the years in my mind, I hear Phil lending a fluttering accompaniment on a jam at the end of "New Potato Caboose"; rumbling like a Harley over the other instruments as Pigpen raves during a hot "Lovelight" rap; moving determinedly through musical asteroid fields and gaseous clouds en route to a distant "Dark Star"; prying open the jam in "Playin' in the Band"; darting around, under, *through* Garcia's leads on "The Other

One"; cascading in a baroque waterfall of notes at the tail end of "Crazy Fingers"; twisting in a unison downward spiral with Garcia and Weir in a late-Seventies "Dancin' in the Streets" jam. I love that counterpoint that sounds like a Latin motet progression he sometimes plays at the end of Garcia's solo on "Friend of the Devil"; that high, dramatic descending figure he plugs in before "Maybe I'll meet you on the run" in "Sugaree"; his snaky lead over the opening bars of "Help on the Way"; and the air he leaves between notes on the quietest parts of "Stella Blue".

For a while there in the early and mid-Eighties, I wondered if Phil was going to stick it out with the Dead. Onstage he often looked positively bored, and his playing frequently lacked both the crispness and assertiveness that characterizes his best work. I think it's no coincidence that this was also the period when Garcia was struggling hardest with his personal demons, becoming insular both musically and socially. So much of the Dead's power depends on the special musical camaraderie between Garcia and Lesh, yet there were shows—*tours, even*—when they didn't seem to connect onstage. As Garcia slowly emerged from his addiction during the second half of 1985 and early 1986, though, Phil perked up noticeably, too, and all of a sudden you could see them interacting again. It's been a steady climb back for both of them since Garcia's near-death in the summer of 1986.

These days it really does seem like we're hearing the Phil Lesh of old at most shows. (As the bumper sticker says, LESH IS MORE!) Sure, he still has his crabby nights, where he spends much of the show scowling at his amps and yelling at the crew. I can assure you that *all* the members have those kind of nights; Phil's moods are just more transparent. But lately, more often than not he's been downright frisky onstage. He looks more relaxed than he has in years, his voice is stronger, he's obviously in great physical shape, and I'd argue that he has reasserted his role as one of the band's musical leaders. He's even out onstage for "space" most of the time; always a good omen. Evidently a happy family life and his (and the band's) relatively clean living agree with him.

As proof of his renewed commitment to the band, Phil has even taken on the production chores (with engineer John Cutler) for the Dead's upcoming live album—the first time Phil has taken an active role in production since *Steal Your Face*. (Uh, we won't hold that against him this far down the road.) In fact, it was after a session of listening to tapes from the spring 1990 tour that I caught up with Phil at the Dead's Club

Front recording studio. Sitting around the giant Neve mixing console there, we chatted about what he's up to, in and out of the band.

How is it that you're the one producing the new live record with Cutler?
Well, it sort of fell to me by default. I wanted to do *something,* and I felt like we've been playing a lot better recently—especially on this last tour [spring 1990 East Coast]—and Jerry's got other things he wants to do, like make a live Garcia Band album and actually take some time off. He practically lived in the studio when we were making the last record *[Built to Last]*, plus he worked on our videos and all, so he deserves a break.

John [Cutler] actually is the one who called and asked if I wanted to take a whack at it, and I said, "Oh boy, yes!" I haven't done anything like this in a while and it's been very exciting so far, though we're still just listening to stuff.

Are you starting back at the beginning of when you started recording, which was June of last year?
No, we're starting with the latest stuff, which I remember most freshly, and I'm hoping we'll be able to get the whole record out of the last tour [spring 1990] we played. There was also some stuff from the Mardi Gras shows that was good, and I also understand there was some good stuff from New Year's. I'd like to keep it in as recent a time frame as we can. We actually have [multitracks] from 1987 on up, but I don't think we should go back that far. We'll have to see what we have.
[Editor's note: In the end, all but one song from *Without a Net* came from the spring 1990 tour.]

What are you hearing in these tapes that you don't hear onstage?
A lot of the details, and some of the real specific interactions—like from where I am I can't always tell how Mickey and Brent are interacting, for instance. Or Brent and Jerry.

I also hear the tone of the instruments differently, and some nuances—inner voices—I can't make out onstage just because it's so noisy up there. There's something like seventy to ninety db [decibels] just of crowd. That's the noise floor when we're playing, comparable to driving a car with the windows down at fifty-five miles per hour.

Does that affect the recording?
Not really. It doesn't leak into the microphones, but it does affect the

level onstage when you're playing. When you have a noise floor like
that, the quietest thing we do has to be louder than that or it will be
inaudible.

*I assume that the audience is on separate tracks, though, so you can make
them as loud or soft as you want.*
Yeah, and we hardly ever make them real loud on our records. I don't
know—maybe when they start chanting "We want Phil," I'll make it
real loud. [Laughs]

*Is listening to tapes something you've done fairly consistently through
the years?*
No, not for a long time, because frankly there have only been about four
or five gigs in the last couple of years that I've wanted to listen back to.
The rest of them I'd sooner forget. But things have changed. I think
we're playing better.

Why?
I don't know. Maybe it's because everybody's *there*. Everybody wants
to be there, and all of a sudden it's exciting to play music again. The
proof of it is that at the end of this last tour everybody agreed that for
about the first time since we've been touring in this format—three times
a year—everybody wanted to keep going after it was over. That was
amazing, we all agreed. [Laughs]

*Is it the infusion of new material and the reintroduction of interesting
older material that's reinvigorated it? Or is it not that simple?*
I think that's part of it, but I don't think it's that simple. Because if it
was the new material, it would be harder to write new songs than it is
already, I'm sure.
   No, I think it's mainly that everyone's attitude has changed toward
making the best of this thing we've all built up together.

You're stuck with it!
[Laughs] Well, it really is like we've been married for twenty-five years.
We've had our ups and downs, and for a while it's felt like we're on an
upswing. Not in terms of any kind of career success, but just in the way
it feels to play the music, and people's *desire* to play the music.

I gather you were partially responsible for Branford Marsalis jamming with the band at Nassau [March 29, 1990, one of the best shows the Dead have played in years.]
Indirectly, yeah. I've been a fan of his for some time. I heard him and his brother [trumpet ace Wynton Marsalis] when they were playing with Art Blakey, and I've sort of followed both of their careers, separately and together.

We were going to connect in Albany originally, but that didn't work out because he was leaving the stage there around the same time we were. So when we got to New York we told him to come on over. Then the next day we found out he wanted to bring his horn! I was totally surprised. "Branford wants to play with *us?* Great!" [Laughs]

How did you decide what to play with him?
Oh, he just sat in on our set.

Gee, it seemed a tad more adventurous than the "regular" GD set.
Well, we didn't want to bore him.

There's something amazing going on in the music you played with him, and I can't quite put my finger on it. I don't know whether it's that you folks in the band had to play differently to put more air in the arrangements to allow him room to blow, or what, but the music has a different twist, a different flow, that's really exciting.
Yeah, I think you're right, and I think the band played differently the four shows after that night than in the shows that preceded it; after that we played more adventurously all around. Jerry and Bob were using their MIDI a little more in regular songs, getting some outside tonalities, and I think in general, in terms of the playing, we weren't sticking to the program quite as much.

So that's one level in which that performance reinvigorated the band. "Oh yeah, we used to do this all the time!"

That's what a lot of the crowd is saying.
I know. We still have a lot of bad habits. Like sometimes when we're doing lots of tunes strung together the transitions are too short, so there's not enough trail-out or tail from the tune in front, and often there's not enough intro to the tune in back. But we're working on that, trying to make it more interesting.

Garcia told me he felt like a lot of the transitional pathways were worn out.

I think it's more that we *haven't* really explored a lot of the variables, getting step-wise from one tune to another, in the sense of key and modulation. You change one note in the scale, from, say G sharp to G natural in an A scale and you can go smoothly from "Eyes of the World" to "Uncle John's Band." But usually we don't take the time to do that sort of thing. Usually the tunes are just juxtaposed brutally—which is one way to do it. There are many other ways we haven't explored.

So what determines if that sort of thing will ever occur?

The fates. Destiny of the gods. [He chuckles] Certainly not anything we do!

The best thing to do would be if we're sitting together, say, during the drums, waiting to decide what to do next, we could really focus in on some transitions: actually say, okay, at the end of this tune we'll use such and such a scale, or set of chords, or drone. After we've said everything we want to say, let's change it in this way, to this scale, which will put us in the right key for the next song. But we hardly ever do that.

Is that because of laziness?

Yeah, or just thoughtlessness, or force of habit. Sometimes it might be just wanting to finish the tune, finish the set and get on with the encore. [Laughs]

I've heard you basically never play the bass offstage. Is that true?

Yes, and it's a drag, too. I'm going to do more of it in the future, because to be honest I'm not satisfied with how my chops have dragged down.

You feel that way? In relation to what?

To where I want them to be.

How do you judge that?

Well, when I can basically play anything I can think of, which I can't do right now. It's a matter of working at it more, which I have started to do.

Do you have a warm-up routine before a show starts?

Not much. I'll try to play the instrument a little before we actually go on, but I don't usually have too much time; I generally get there as late as I can, because I don't like to hang out at coliseums and wait to go on.

Your new bass sounds tremendous. What's the story on it?

I like it a lot. It was made by a guy in New York named Ken Smith, who makes instruments and has a whole line of products—strings, pick-ups, straps. When Jerry was so turned on to the Chick Corea Elektric Band and their guitar player, Frank Gambale, he had me check it out, and they had an outstanding bass player, as well, John Patitucci. I picked up one of his records and saw him holding this bass, so I looked into it more.

The neck looks so wide.

It is wider than what I'd been using, and actually it's forced me to reexamine my whole left hand technique, which was getting really sloppy. The position it requires is the *correct* position—in other words, it's the position that allows you to reach as many of the strings as possible as quickly as possible. Whereas my other instruments with narrower necks tended to give me more of a guitar positioning where the hand is dropped from the wrist, rather than the wrist dropping from the fingertips, as in bass or violin technique.

I'd been getting lazy, so the new instrument is a good excuse to put myself in shape, because I won't be able to play well unless I really work at it. It's been fun.

Have you ever played a fretless bass?

Yeah, a couple of times. I like 'em, but it would take a lot of practice to get used to, and also the MIDI setup I have wouldn't work without frets.

Do you listen to other bassists at all?

Yes and no. When I'm listening to music that has a bassist in it, of course I do. But I don't study other bassists, and I don't think I've really drawn much from them. In my own style of playing, such as it is, I've been influenced more by Bach than by any bassists. Actually, you can go back even further—Palestrina, sixteenth-century modal counterpoint.

What's your monitor mix like onstage? What do you hear best and worst?

Well, I have my huge stack behind me and I hear that pretty well. [Laughs] I wear earplugs it's so loud. I have control [in his individual mix] of everyone except Jerry and Mickey, but they're loud enough that I can hear them. Jerry, in particular, usually cuts through it all so I can hear him clearly. I have monitors for Billy, Bobby, Brent, and the vocals. Obviously I want to hear what everyone's doing. I'm continually having to change my mix because everyone's continually changing how loud they play and the sound of their instruments. So for me it's a continual dance.

When you're playing, is it just an instinctive thing of who you might be interacting with more, musically, at any given moment?
It depends on who I can decipher sometimes.

Billy told me, for instance, that he tries to play with you with his right foot, Jerry with his right hand, and so on, simultaneously. Is there an equivalent for you?
It's not that specific for me, no. Usually, I'm listening for someone doing something meaningful, or just something I can decipher in the wilder places. In a regular song I try to listen to the whole thing, because you know how it's going to go. In the wilder flights, when everyone's diving in different directions—like the Blue Angels—sometimes it's best not to go with anyone, and just play what you want. I find myself doing that a lot. But then I'll find that actually I *am* playing with someone, and that's kind of neat, because I haven't necessarily consciously tried to lock in with that person, yet there we are together. Usually, I'm playing with somebody, even if I don't know it. I've discovered that listening back to the tapes. And part of that could be that they're trying to play with *me*. It's hard to tell sometimes exactly what's happening.

Sometimes my mix will be set wrong and I'll suddenly discover that I can't hear Brent, and I'll hear him doing something meaningful way off there in the distance and I'll try to work with that. It's not predictable.

And if I'm completely lost, which does happen, I'll play something that relates to where we've been, or guess at where it seems like we may be going, or I'll just lock on to someone else's tail. I play counterpoint with Jerry a lot, but I also lock in a lot with Bob, and I have to combine that with what the drums are doing as well. We're all doing that to differing degrees.

Do you differentiate between Mickey's and Billy's roles?
It's hard to now, because I'm not between them like I used to be. I'm closer to Billy, but I still sort of hear it as one big drum set.

Four arms, four legs . . .
Right. The demon!

I would think it would be very difficult as a musician to predict how the spaces in the arrangements develop. For instance, sometimes Garcia will go into a double-time attack on a lead, and Bob will be playing something way in the upper register and Brent's playing block chords and then you have to figure out where to lay your part.
Sometimes it's hard and sometimes it isn't. There are no hard and fast rules about what I'll do in any situation. Usually what happens on stage is that if Jerry starts double-timing and Bobby goes to either extreme of his registers, it sounds like Bobby just disappears pretty much. That's just the way it is acoustically on the stage, because his speakers are below the drum riser, which is lower than my knees. So I don't really hear that directly, and my monitor doesn't always pick up the extremes in texture in his guitar sound. It's very strange when that phenomenon occurs, because I can see Bob's hands moving but I can't really hear what he's doing. I can maybe hear the attack, but not the pitch or the sustain. In those cases, or when the sound in general becomes indistinct for some reason, I'll usually just play whatever I feel until I can hear something to play *with,* as it were.

How conscious are you of the evolution of tunes from tour to tour? For instance, on a tune like, say, "Stuck Inside of Mobile," are you aware of how it's developing over time?
In my mind, a lot of those tunes have stayed static for a long time because . . . well, I don't know why, but they have. And now I feel like they're taking on new life. For a long time I think we had trouble with the grooves, getting the right tempo. Some of Bob's tunes are a little hard to decipher, in part because of the speaker placement below the drums. Sometimes the tune starts out and you can't really hear at first which side of the beat it's on—whether you're tapping your foot on the on-beat or the off-beat. Sometimes we'll come in and it's backward: 0-1, 0-1, 0-1. [Laughs] That happens on "Queen Jane" from time to time. It just gets hard to find a groove that everyone likes, because everyone has a different desire of what they want to do with it.

Now that we're getting a little more consistent, I imagine we'll probably dump a bunch of those tunes and hopefully bring in some new first-set cover material.

Is it fair to say that the way you're playing now is closer to the—dare I say?—"lead bass" style of your past?
God, I don't know. I never really thought about it as "lead bass," and I never thought about retreating from it, either.

I'm only speaking for myself here, but I felt that often in the early and mid-Eighties, when the music would start to expand—say, at the beginning of a "Playin' " jam or some of those other spacey passages—you'd lay back a little, while now you seem to be laying into those spaces and taking a more prominent melodic role with where the jams are going.
I suppose that's true, yeah. A lot of it, I think, was a question of attitude. I guess maybe I didn't like what people were playing that much and it didn't involve me as much as what I'm hearing now.
     Those were the Heineken years. Those are over now.

So you think everyone is listening to each other better now?
Absolutely. I know I am for sure, and I care a lot more about what I play in relation to what everyone else plays. I hope it shows, because I am listening a lot more productively than I was in the early Eighties.

Is it difficult to sustain interest through a whole set when some of the material is less than fresh?
Not really, because for me—and I suspect the others feel this way, too—there's always the challenge of performing the material better, in a new way, with a better feeling—to deliver the whole package, the whole body of the song, in one gesture, which is frequently not done by us. You know, a lot of times there'll be good parts and . . . not so good parts. [Laughs] There's always the possibility that you can throw it out there and make that magical curve in which all the parts are perfectly proportioned. That to me is one of the major excitements of working with this band. I still feel it's always, potentially, right around the corner, and that we can lock into that at any time. That level of performance is what musicians strive for; what they *live* for. We're closer to it now than we have been for quite a while.

I guess the natural question then is, why not play even more material that points you in that direction—that opens up to allow those magical possibilities?
Well, all we have to do is get together and play things that we can orbit around. That's a question of material. I mean we could conceivably do

Lost in the music, 1989. *(Photo by Bruce Polonsky)*

an hour and a half of "space" and it's possible that it would be as coherent as any set of songs. Going through these [spring tour] tapes, I just heard a ten-minute segment of "space" that was just really amazing! It started out with a drone and big harmonic structures over this drone, and then I guess it was Jerry who started to play this demented [MIDI] horn thing that sounded like Mahler's Third deconstructed—there's this trombone passage in Mahler's Third, and it was like he was parodying it. It was silly, very funny. I don't even know if he knows the piece, actually. Then at the end of it there was a great E cadence and some well-developed craziness. And then we dropped into "I Need a Miracle."

From the sublime to the ridiculous.
I don't know, I think there's a lot to be said for those kind of discontinuities. We have them in life, after all.

When you're going through a first set and a tune like "Bird Song" crops up, do you suddenly have to think in a different way as a player?
No, I think the same way all the time—how can I open this sucker up? [Laughs] I've always felt that every one of our tunes has got the potential to open up and flower like "Dark Star."

You really believe that?
Yeah. Every one of them. I guess there are some that might have some

kind of rotating chord sequence that's kind of restrictive. But most of them have some kind of connecting passage or bridge or instrumental thing that can open up.

And the reason it doesn't is . . .

I think we get used to playing something a certain length and it gets comfortable in that way. Perhaps other ideas would crop up if we played the instrumentals longer or tried to vary them a little more. God knows we play our songs long as it is. I think they *average* at seven or eight minutes.

Probably the best way to break out of that would be to actually sit down before we play a tune and agree that at a certain point we'd open it up, do what we wanted to do with it, and then close it up at the same point. It's happened that somebody *has* suggested something like that, and we've worked on it, though I can't think of an example right now. Bob or Jerry or Brent will say something very specific, like, "At the end of this tune, let's try these chords, or this scale"—like I was saying before—"and see where that takes us."

There's a beautiful jam you did after "Terrapin" a couple of times on the spring tour that brings that process to mind. It was a lovely little melody that sounded a little like "Dear Prudence."

Right. It is a little like "Dear Prudence." That's an example of where Garcia had an idea that moved into a scale that's different from the one we'd been in, but is somehow related to it. I think that one first surfaced three or four years ago—just once—at the end of "Terrapin Station," after all those big chords and all that madness. Then it was dormant for the longest time and I kept trying to figure out what to play to remind him of that. I suppose if we'd listened to the tapes together it would have been simple. [Laughs] But nothing was that simple then. Then it surfaced again this tour.

I've noticed your bass generally sounds more prominent at outdoor gigs— places like Frost and Laguna Seca. Why is that?

That's because standing waves in enclosed spaces tend to cancel out entire registers. Then there's the huge cave underneath the stage that resonates and artificially resonates the very lowest notes. The severity of the problem indoors depends on the hall, how loud the p.a. is, and so on.

Healy told me he thought you lost two years off your life from playing in Winterland!

[Laughs] You mean from having the bass sucked up night after night after night? I wouldn't doubt it.

Your work with the MIDI bass has been fairly limited so far. Is that because the triggering is slow because of the lower frequencies?
That's partly true, but I have an instrument now where the triggers are built into the frets.

What is that instrument?
It's a Modulus bass that's been specially modified. Unfortunately, that system is only good for a four-string mix, and I hate switching instruments, so hopefully they can build it into the Smith [his regular bass]. If they can't build a six-string system, I could have one where the center four strings are MIDI and the outer two won't be, and then I'll be able to switch back and forth—like Bobby and Jerry can.

During "space," what are you looking at when you're looking at your rack?
I'm not looking at it, I'm staring into space. I'm staring into the molecules of air between me and my nose hairs. [Laughs] I'm using pedals to control what I'm doing, and I have them back there so I won't trip over them during the rest of the set. If I had MIDI in the instrument I play all the time, the pedals would probably be out by my monitors and I'd be facing forward because I'd have the same instrument and I'd be using MIDI during songs and everything. That's what I'm after eventually.

   The triggering is a matter of touch. It's very tricky. There were a few places at these last gigs in Atlanta where I was actually playing the MIDI in a song for a few bars, and it worked out okay. I was able to add some nice harmonic color to my part, and a delayed attack at one point.

Does the bass have the same kind of MIDI potential as a conventional guitar? Could you do some low-end instrument like a bassoon or something?
I'm sure you could. In the show that Branford played with us, you'll hear some flute—that's me. It's not as fast as Jerry playing it, or a real flutist, but it's a good synthesizer flute sound. I've finally got the octave shift the way I want it so I can have real high sounds as well as real low sounds. But I have to reach over and push a switch, take my hand off the instrument, to do it.

Does it change how you play with the other musicians if Garcia is suddenly playing "saxophone" or "flute," or, my personal favorite—"pipe organ"?
[Laughs] Not really. It just cracks me up. I love it! Some of the things those guys come up with! I don't think even they know what it's going to sound like when it comes out sometimes.

I hear a lot of people wondering aloud why you don't play bona fide solos anymore.
Did I ever?

Yes.
Oh. I guess since every note we've ever played is public property, I should have known the answer to that one. [Laughs]

I guess I never felt terribly comfortable playing solos. In the context of our music, the idea of standing out there and doing a solo just seemed alien to the whole idea of what we were trying to do.

It is an ensemble, first and foremost.
Yeah. Essentially, that's what I feel it is. Or that's what it is when it's at its best, because the whole *is* greater than the sum of its parts.

Actually, it's curious you should ask that because I was thinking of playing something like that sometime. Or maybe a duet with somebody else. But I have to practice a little more, so I'll be satisfied with how I'm playing.

You're a tough taskmaster on yourself, aren't you?
I guess. No tougher than I want everyone else to be. Slap me around if I'm loosenin' up.

To what degree do you have a vote in the material that gets played from moment to moment?
As much a degree as I want to put in there, which usually isn't that much since I'm not singing most of it. So I pretty much let them decide what they want to sing. Which may be a mistake, since we do get into ruts. What we need is a song list hanging everywhere we look that lists all our songs. . . .

When you're playing one of Bob's or Jerry's tunes are you able to experience the lyrics they're singing fairly well?

Occasionally. Not as often as I'd like, though, because of the ear plugs and because vocals don't come through the monitors clearly at the volumes we use. So yes and no. Most of the words are in my subconscious by now anyway. We have been doing most of these songs for a few years.

Do different tunes resonate with you more than others at different times? One night it's "Black Peter"—
And the next it's "Morning Dew" or "High Time." Sure, it changes all the time, from night to night. They *all* resonate in part of me, because I'm part of them and they're part of me.

"Dark Star" is a tune that's evolved a lot in its different incarnations through the years. The late-Sixties versions sound markedly different from the early Seventies ones, and now the Nineties versions are different again. Does it feel like a different space to you?
No, it feels like "Dark Star," which has always had the potential to go absolutely anywhere. We designed it that way in the first place. And it turned out to be a very appropriate vehicle for trying a whole lot of different things through the years. That was the one we sort of tacitly agreed upon where anything was okay.

I guess it might not have the sort of mythic dimension it's attained if it hadn't been absent so long.
I guess maybe in some way we felt for a long time that if we couldn't do justice to it, we didn't want to do it at all. Or for whatever reasons, the impulse to do it just wasn't there. Maybe it didn't feel right. I don't know.

Beyond that, all I can really say about what it's like now is that it evolves because we evolve. It's grown or shrunk or disappeared because we have our ups and downs. Anyone's work will do that—it grows and shrinks with them. It rises and falls.

I don't really subscribe to the decades of nostalgia division, where everything gets divided up into Sixties, Seventies, Eighties, and Nineties. I don't think human events follow the divisions of the calendar.

I don't either, but I think a reasonable way to talk about Grateful Dead history is to divide it by the membership in the band.
You mean by the keyboard players? [Laughs]

Yeah, and the change in drummers. I mean, if you listen to a "Playin' " jam from 1974, Keith is doing things with that Fender Rhodes that sound sort of like **In a Silent Way**–*era Herbie Hancock, which is very different from what Brent is doing ten years later. Keith is playing in middle registers more, and Brent is doing more high-end stuff. It changes everything, including how you others play around it.*

Right. I think that's true, but I also don't think that's something the musicians try to analyze, especially in our band. In a way, that kind of thinking is in the past and we can't recapture that, and don't even want to try, because we're going to play it differently next time, and that's what we're after. So it's up to you folks to decide about those kinds of things.

I'm not making any judgment. I'm simply saying that a lot of the changes seem to have been dictated by changes in personnel.

That's logical. In the past, I guess the reasons people usually left the band or rejoined or whatever, usually had to do with the music, so in a way it's the music that dictates the personnel, as well as vice versa.

Can you see playing "The Eleven" again?

I don't think so. It was really too restrictive, and the vocal part—the song part—was dumb.

Garcia said it was a hard tune to "play through."

That's because of the three-chord structure. When we put that together with a drone it was much easier. How was it we used to do it—"Dark Star," "St. Stephen," "The Eleven," and "Lovelight"? It fit well in there, I guess. It was almost like an alternative to "Alligator"—"Alligator" was the one that was in four. "The Eleven" was another one that was in a compound meter [11/4].

Was that written with the drummers primarily?

Yeah. It was really designed to be a rhythm trip. It wasn't designed to be a song. That more or less came later as a way to give it more justification, or something, to work in a rock 'n' roll set. We could've used it just as transition, which is what it was, really.

Every tour we hear a lot about the possible revival of "Unbroken Chain."

I've had a lot of requests to bring that one back.

We're always hearing, "Oh, they sound-checked it here." "Oh, they're going to play it on Phil's fiftieth birthday!"
[Laughs] I really wish I could have done that. It would've been great.

Have you ever even sound-checked it?
No, that's bullshit. I'd have to completely relearn it. I'd have to learn the guitar part over again so I could teach it to Bob. I'd have to relearn the words. I'd have to figure a way to play bass and sing it at the same time. It's fairly complicated. I wrote it on guitar and could play and sing it all the way through as a performance. It was meant to be performed, but there were so many changes in it, it proved to be very difficult. We had a lot of trouble even recording it.

By the end of it I was in that brutal state of mind where I said, "Fuck this," and dropped it. It was too embarrassing to try to perform it live because it just fell apart. But we'll get it better this time.

So you think that'll happen?
Oh yeah. I'm pretty sure it will.

Does singing a song during a set give you some extra juice to go on?
Sometimes, sure. When we did "The Weight" for the first time [in Nassau] I was terrified I was going to forget the words, so I was really nervous—and in fact I did. That was a lot of fun.

Whose idea was that?
I don't remember. Somebody just came up with it. There are a lot of Band songs I'd like to do. I like so many of their songs: "Stage Fright"; "King Harvest" is another of my favorites. We'll probably bring those in one of these years.

Are you writing at all?
I'm trying, but I haven't had much time lately. I've got two kids, you know.

Would that be with Hunter most likely?
Hunter and Barlow hopefully.

I think most Deadheads probably don't know much about Bobby Peterson, with whom you wrote "Unbroken Chain" and "Pride of Cucamonga." What can you tell us about him?

He was a mad beatnik poet, I guess; a road character and a storyteller. A road *pirate* actually. He was my oldest friend. He's got a book of poetry out [*Alleys of the Heart,* Hulogos'i Books] that tells you more about him than I ever could.

What are you listening to these days?
Just about everything I can find—mainly jazz and classical, I guess. It's hard to keep up. I try to find good jazz on the radio, but that's difficult around here. I don't have that much time to listen to music except in the car. Like I said, my kids keep me pretty busy at home.

However, I would like to inform your readers and anybody else who wants to know that I have no intention of retiring to tend my garden and take care of my family. I may have been misquoted as saying that somewhere, but it ain't true. My family goes with me wherever I go so it's not a question of missing them when I'm on the road. Just slanderous rumors! [Laughs]

How about scaling back touring?
I've come to feel that the amount of touring we do now is just about right. Three weeks, three times a year is really a lot of work, when I consider how many people we play to in that period of time. It's okay. I can do it.

How was your experience working on **Built to Last**?
It was interesting. It was very easy to do the work because all the instruments were isolated, and you could mix them and set them up to your heart's content so you could have the perfect mix to play with. I'd come down here alone and work the machines myself and do it till I was happy with my part. That's one way to do it, but it certainly lacks the feeling of the other way. It's a real dilemma for us because when we play live with two drummers [in the studio] we can't get the isolation on the instruments to make a good record. When we play separately in the studio, we don't have the right *feeling,* but it sounds good on a record. We do one or the other; hopefully one of these days we can figure out how to do both.

I do think *Built to Last* was one of the best-*sounding* records we've ever made. You can hear everything real clearly. But it didn't hang together all that well.

Do you have any desire to play music outside the Dead?
No. I want to compose and hopefully write some songs for the Dead.

Phil Lesh, 1974. *(Photo by Bob Marks)*

As far as performing's concerned, I have my hands full with the Grateful Dead. I've never wanted to have a band of my own.

What's happening with your orchestral work, "Noosphere"?
I still have it in my drawer, and I still plan to complete it. The last time I talked to Kent Nagano [director of the Berkeley Symphony] he said, "Finish it and we'll play it!" I'm also working on another piece simultaneously.

What is it about so much modern music—by that I mean the type of stuff you play on your Rex Radio program—that makes it difficult for people to listen to?
It's just different from what we usually hear. People find it difficult to comprehend, difficult to follow the story, so to speak. It's difficult because it usually doesn't have even rhythms or a euphonious tonality that it always comes back to so you always know where you are. It's music that's relativistic in the sense that the parts relate to each other, but not to any common ground necessarily.

Do you find that you're able to bring some of those concepts into the Dead, whether in "space" or in your regular playing?
Somewhat. In any amalgam, any alloy, there are several components, and there are parts of those components that get melted away in the joining, as it were. I think the whole "space" section, which essentially evolved from our feedback experiments, is a response to electronic music and concrete music, found objects music, tape music; that sort of thing. Some of the discontinuity that we get going—the heterophony of everybody playing something different—probably comes from those worlds to a degree.

Are Garcia and Weir pretty hip to this sort of stuff?
Oh sure, because of their instinctive musicality and all the listening they've done. They're adventurous enough that if they don't hear a particular landmark in what they're doing they'll just keep going until they *create* one. [Laughs]

It's great that there's a vehicle for that kind of music to be made, night after night, in front of thousands of people. That's the stuff.
It *is* great. I don't know of any other band of any kind that has that built into it. Jazz players mostly improvise on changes. True collective im-

provisation is pretty rare. I guess some of Ornette Coleman's bands have come the closest.

Did you see Ornette's last tour?
No, I was either on the road or home with the kids. I did see [avant jazz pianist] Cecil Taylor with a quintet, and that was truly awe-inspiring. That was like a force of nature! What a phenomenon he is!

When you see an act like that, how does it make you feel about your own music?
Why it makes me proud to be an American! [Laughs]

In terms of the music, it makes me proud to be part of the Grateful Dead, because I think we're also doing something that is that interesting, though in a different direction. It's kind of hard to say exactly what our direction is, but that's also part of what makes it interesting.

Mickey Hart

Drums and Dreaming

An Interview: September 1, 1990

I first met Mickey Hart in the fall of 1978, about a month after the band returned from their historic trip to Egypt. Mickey had agreed to write an article about his Egypt experiences for *BAM, The California Music Magazine,* and as that rag's resident Deadhead, I eagerly took on the assignment of helping Mickey and his friend Cookie put Mickey's thoughts on paper. A couple of nights before our meeting, the Dead had completed a series of shows at Winterland in San Francisco that had been dubbed "From Egypt with Love," featuring projected slides of the Dead in Egypt, as well as some exquisite Egyptian music by Mickey's friend Hamza El Din. I can't say that those shows quite made up for not going to Egypt, but hearing Hamza and encountering the hypnotic rhythms of the *tar* that week opened me up to a new world of music. And when I finally met Mickey at his ranch a few nights later, he was sitting in his

Mickey plying the tar, 1989. *(Photo by Mariah Healy)*

recording studio (The Barn), which was illuminated by only a few large candles, playing a *tar* as a steady percussive rain beat down outside. It was quite a moment for me. Over the next few hours, Cookie and I sat rapt as Mickey spun his tales of Egypt; I was impressed by the lucidity of his perspective and the depth of his spirituality.

A year later we met for another interview at The Barn, and this time he was playing some strange-looking South American shakers that he'd gotten from his friend Airto. He blew my mind with a tape of an early version of "Lost Sailor," which the Dead were recording for the album that became *Go to Heaven.* Mickey's work tape of the song was punctuated by humpback whale noises he'd added. I was very disappointed they were nowhere to be heard when the album was released a couple of months later.

When Regan and I interviewed Mickey in the late fall of 1983 for the first issue of *The Golden Road,* his instruments of choice—the ones he seemed to be *living* with that day—were a Brazilian rainstick and The Beam—the former an instrument of incredible delicacy and clarity; the latter one capable of mimicking a napalm bombing. That's two sides of Mickey in a nutshell: ethereal beauty and unrelenting bombast. Of course there are a million shades in between, as well.

My point is that Mickey Hart has constantly surprised me through the years, both on and off stage, and that's why I find him so fascinating. In some ways he represents the purest embodiment of the Grateful Dead's original searching spirit—even though he is not a founding member of the group. A musician of seemingly boundless energy and imagination, he is always up for leading us to new places, and nine times out of ten he has the goods to make the trip worthwhile. Sitting, figuratively speaking, by his side at hundreds of Dead shows, I've been exposed to a universe of percussion that has enriched my life tremendously. I've gotten lost in the chantlike twang of the *berimbau*'s lone string; let my own heartbeat merge with the gentle flow of the *tar;* welcomed into my brain the high, clear voice of his Tibetan bowls; been shaken viscerally by the booming thunder of The Beast; danced merrily to the *balafon*'s rhythmic song. And when you follow him into his world, you can't help but meet some of his friends: Olatunji, Flora and Airto, Zakir Hussein, Batucaje, Hamza, and others whose names I don't know but who have moved me with their playing. These are heavy cats; all of them masters of *the zone.*

As compelling as his work with the Dead has been through the years, Mickey's outside projects have often been most broadening for me: the Diga Rhythm Band, The *Apocalypse Now* Sessions, Yamantaka, his various ethnic music productions, etc.; music where he wasn't even necessarily the clear leader, but was instead a facilitator and fellow traveler with a knack for coaxing and capturing the magic from different situations. This is going to sound like hyperbole, but it isn't: Mickey Hart has done more to popularize world percussion music than anyone else on the planet. And his efforts are still gaining momentum.

His latest endeavors outside the Dead are a book titled *Drumming at the Edge of Magic* (Harper & Row) and a "companion" CD/tape called *At the Edge* (on Rykodisc). The book, which he cowrote with Jay Stevens (author of the excellent book about LSD, *Storming Heaven*) is tremendously enlightening and entertaining. It's part autobiography, with lots of interesting anecdotes about his childhood and his early fascination with drums; part ethno-musicological treatise on the myths and history of percussion in different cultures; and part adventure story about his quest to learn about the power of the drum. It also contains dozens of superb photographs of Hart, the Dead, and drummers from around the world.

Anybody who knows Mickey well will tell you he can be brash and egotistical at times, but I was struck by his humility throughout the book: he casts himself as an eager pupil who has learned from many masters, including his father, Lenny Hart, Billy Kreutzmann, Airto, Zakir, mythologist Joseph Campbell, and other scholars of different stripes. He is more than generous in his praise of those who have helped him on his journey.

Some readers may be disappointed that Hart doesn't write more about his life in the Grateful Dead, and others may be frustrated by his and Stevens' breezy approach to mythology. But it's a *good read,* as they say, and Hart points out that there's more to come: a giant volume of photos and stories about percussion, called *Planet Drum.* (It was published in fall 1991.)

The first time I listened to *At the Edge* I was a little caught off guard by how *quiet* most of the music is; frankly, coming from Mickey I expected more flash. But successive listenings with headphones have revealed the album's beauty, mystery, and amazing sonic depth. Each of the nine compositions on the disc has its own distinct character, yet there is an unmistakable continuity to it all. Hart and his percussionist friends, including Olatunji, Zakir, and Airto, create a wide range of textures with relatively few instruments: tabla, wood blocks, cowbells, slit gong, hex bells, beaded gourds, rattles, and a few others. There is a dollop of subtle synthesizers and a pair of tracks with Garcia playing guitar, but in general the "melody" on most of these pieces is established by the interplay of different percussion feelings and the sometimes very musical overtones of the individual instruments. It starts in the rain forest and ends with a wonderful percussive vocal piece by Airto. What's in between is sometimes dreamy, sometimes insistent, deceptively simple, but always compelling. This stuff will definitely take you on a trip.

A week before the fall [1990] tour I met with Mickey to talk about his recent projects and his approach to music in and out of the Grateful Dead. We did the interview in the Dead's boardroom, which is in an old house near the band's Marin County headquarters. What a cool place: the big meeting table is surrounded by huge, high-backed Knights of the Round Table–type wooden chairs, with the skull-and-lightning-bolt logos carved into the arms, and a beautiful Asian-looking pattern sewn into the chairbacks. There were also colorful streamers draped across the ceiling, as if there'd been a party there recently. Now that's what you want to see in a boardroom! We plopped ourselves down in two of the big chairs and rapped for a while. Slowly now, shake that rainstick. Cue the tablas . . .

Can you talk a little about how your new CD is a "companion" to the book?

I composed it at different times during the period I was researching the book. I was heavily into reading the literature on the subject day and night, and it was even in my dreams. The instruments that naturally come to life in those dreams should come to life in your dream songs; become part of your code. So these are just little rumblings that I brought back from that side; little dream songs.

So the work you did on the album parallels the research you were doing to a degree?

Right. When I was reading about *djembes* and old trance-inducing instruments, the compositions I was working on started taking on some of the characteristics of what I was researching during the day. I was starting to mythologize them in my own mind, trying to see how they related to me in the past and the present.

I didn't set out to make a "popular" record. I wanted it to be a companion to the book; sort of a soundtrack, but not a literal one. I didn't specifically try to re-create things I was writing about in the book. It wasn't linear like that. It was more the spirit of what I was writing about; the spirit and the imagery. It was like me waking up in the forest as the first man, before there was sound, and the world slowly coming alive for me. In that dream I was lying on my back in the forest and I just looked around and I started hearing nature, and all of a sudden nature becomes like a symphony; it's the forest talking. And then my imagination started to develop some sort of contour, or soundscape, and *voilà!* All of a sudden it turns into almost what you'd call "music." But I didn't want it too "musical," you know what I mean? I wanted to keep it drums.

Clarence Clemons originally played on one track, and that was fine—he's a beautiful musician—but he turned it into a song, and that's not what I was looking for. Jerry got taken off a couple of tracks. Pete Sears was on there; I took that off. Same with David Freiberg. All these musicians got the ax, because when I got right down to it, I wanted drums, percussion. But it's processed percussion and it has melody. Most of what's on the record is processed from acoustic sounds. I took those sounds and shaped them—put them on the computer or whatever and manipulated them. We had 161 individual raindrop sounds that we collected. We had wind and distant thunder . . .

Did you do that recording yourself?

Most of it. George Lucas allowed me to use his special-effects library. I'd trade him four raindrops for distant thunder. I'd give him running water and he'd give me something else. We'd trade these sounds back and forth. It was like a soundscape for me. It was primal because I was studying prehistory, a time before man organized sound. The whistles and sounds of nature—that's where we got our language and our music. We started mingling with these sounds until it became music.

I really like how much ambiance there is on all the tracks. What sort of rooms did you record in?

Well, that's not the rooms you're hearing. I created that ambiance with an enormous amount of spatial processing. I spent a lot of time trying to come up with beautiful digital stereo-processed reverberation and other kinds of sophisticated delays, and what I tried to do was fit one kind of reverberant feel into another so they all sit phase-coherent in each other, so you're able to see deep. I didn't want to just load it up with a bunch of reverb.

It's a great headphone album.

Yeah, it is. I mixed it at the appropriate listening level. Working on the mix was like the ear falling in love with a new lover every time there was a playback, it was so rich and sumptuous. There's no guitars whining, no bass thumping. You can hear the overtones of all the instruments, so the few instruments I did use all sound really huge. I let the voice of each instrument prevail, rather than loading the tracks with a lot of instruments and using combination sounds.

In the past you've been so successful at using natural room sounds on your records. This must have felt a lot different to you, in a sense manufacturing the rooms with delays and reverb.

It's virtual reality, man! [Laughs] Through the years I've learned what different acoustic spaces do to different instruments, and I've learned how percussion is affected by electronic processing. I can sit there and say, "I'll add this kind of delay to this sound," and I'll know what it's going to sound like before I try it. On this album I didn't have to spend 10,000 hours searching for things because I knew what I wanted. I *already* put in the 10,000 hours over the past twenty years to get to the point I'm at now.

It's interesting that you talked about dreams earlier, because the album as a whole has a really dreamy quality.
That's what it's supposed to be. It's not a dance record. It's not a popular music record.

It's also not like **Rhythm Devils Play River Music.**
No, it's not that kind of image at all. That was inspired by *Apocalypse Now,* of course, and that was a brutal, dark foreboding image. It was the image of war, so it had all those nuances. My dreams aren't like that. I wanted people to drift; that's what this is all about to me—the flow of consciousness. That's what you get into when you get down to theta— that's where all this stuff starts rippling across your consciousness and you figure out the universe: right before you fall asleep. [Laughs]

Do you drum in your dreams?
Oh yes, of course! My dreams are filled with sounds and music. It's not limited to drums, though; it's sounds. Clusters, batteries of sounds . . . sounds that only come in my dream time. Having my own studio, I can spend unlimited amounts of time trying to realize some of these odd sounds I hear in my dreams. I can sit and just play in these strange arenas of sound. And it's not like it has to be any *thing*—it just has to be a good version of itself.

Were most of the pieces on the record constructed track by track, or were you in the studio with Zakir or Olatunji, or whomever, laying down your parts together?
Most of it is constructed. Zakir and I laid a couple of the basics together, but most of it is overdubbed. When Olatunji would come in we'd talk about it for hours and try different things. Sometimes he or Zakir would come in, I'd talk about what I was after, and *wham*—"That's it!" But it's hard to describe what you hear in a dream, and sometimes it's hard to remember your dreams clearly. So you have to search and try to hold on to that original vision as well as you can. That means you have to really concentrate on what you're doing and not get sidetracked down blind alleys. But at the same time you have to relax and let it flow. If you find that seed sound you're after, then you've been successful. If you don't, you've mutated your vision a bit, and that's okay, too. I settle for that all the time.

Do you write down your dreams?
I do something better. As soon as I wake up I run down to the studio,

where I have a tape machine. I always like to have a tape machine with me. If I'm in a car and I get an idea, I'll pull off to the side and talk the idea through, being as specific as I can: "Okay, it's a pan delay of seventy-eight milliseconds" and this and that. And I try to pull the sound through all the devices it's going through: "We'll take the woodblock, run it through an octave divider and run it back through this device, put it in a sequence of sixteen beats," and so on. It can be very specific or very vague. As long as it gets me back to that place where the original flash was. And if I forget it? So what. I'm on to the next thing. You're going to forget most of them, but the few you bring back from the other side make it worth the effort. This album has stuff from there and stuff from the waking state.

How often do you spontaneously come up with some new musical idea during the Rhythm Devils section of a Dead show and then later develop it more?

It happens occasionally. It tends to develop itself over the course of a few nights. We'll explore an idea. More often, though, I'm trying to be as spontaneous as I can from night to night, and not repeat myself. It's more dangerous that way, and maybe not as fulfilling sometimes—because you're not always going to come up with something great—but when you do hit it, you know you've got something truly original; something that's never been heard before.

It all depends on what you're after. People play music for different reasons. I go for the spirit side of things; not necessarily to be perfect. What I'm after is changing consciousness—transition; changing from one state of consciousness to another. That's what music is all about to me. Entertainment is just a by-product of that other search.

Speaking of consciousness, given your collaborator and the band's past history, I felt that the importance of LSD was downplayed in your book.

I don't know. This isn't a book about LSD. I did say that some of the Dead's music came out of experimentation with psychoactive drugs. Beyond that . . . read Jay's book [*Storming Heaven*]. It's brilliant on that subject.

But not in relation to you and music.

No. But that's not this book. That could be a whole book in itself. To really treat that subject right I would have had to spend a lot of time thinking about it and looking into it. It's not the kind of thing you can throw out in a quarter of a chapter. I'd really want to do it right. I really haven't studied it—I've only experienced it, you understand? To write about it intelligently I'd need more than just my experience, and it's such a big topic, I just didn't feel like I had the time or space to get into it properly. I didn't want it to distract from the drums, and it might have if I'd dwelled on it.

In the end, some of it was really a space consideration. I cut out a lot on the subject. I cut out a lot on all sorts of different subjects. I just couldn't tell the whole story in one book. I'm not even going to be able to tell it all in two books!

What can you tell me about the second book, Planet Drum?
The first book is sort of the preface to the second book. The second book is really the lumber I gathered. It's the anaconda; the time line. All the pearls, all the ornaments, all the jewels I picked up on the search for the Holy Grail. It's the information that backs up the conclusions of the first book. The first one is an adventure story. The second is a pictorial survey of the world's drum archives. It's going to be a beautiful book; it's a honey. It's got something like 450 images in it, all sorts of great full-color stuff; a real coffee-table book. It's the *stuff.*

Actually, though, these are two parts of the same book. We just couldn't put out an 800-page book. [Laughs] I probably have enough for eight books. Hey, I got *into* it. I just woke up one day with this dream to do something. It became a passion that I couldn't let go. I was just following the muse and it was driving me madly, night and day.

I knew it would be a book, but it started off just as pictures of my collection [of instruments]. I had this huge collection and I realized I didn't know shit about it. I knew these drums intimately—I played them!—but how well did I *know* them? [Laughs] I didn't know my heritage. Doctors know. They have books on the subject. But drummers don't. Yet drums have been with us from prehistory, part of rites from ancient times until now.

I was intrigued by your discussion in the book about how in Western cultures the drum ceased being used for religious purposes and was taken over instead by the military, to marshal troops and such.
Right. That's because Western religions didn't like the way drums were used in other cultures to induce trance and altered states. They wanted you to be praying to that guy on the cross, not going into a trance state.

They still don't.
No. Religion killed the drum in Western culture, until it made its way
back through rock 'n' roll—the devil's music. [Laughs] Why did people
try to suppress rock 'n' roll? Because the back beat, the groove, took
people to the other side, and that's not considered acceptable in Western
cultures. And where does that beat come from? From Africa originally.
It came across with the slave trade, found its way to New Orleans,
mutated into rhythm and blues, and all of a sudden you've got rock 'n'
roll—check it out: they're dancin', they're mamboin'; they're goin' crazy!
It's rhythm-dominated; it's got percussion galore. So it's made a tremendous revival, and melody and harmony are assuming their proper
place alongside it, as part of the trinity.

*The Dead have always been more interested in polyrhythms and odd
time signatures than most popular musicians. There isn't much of the
thump-thump-thump we hear on the radio year after year.*
Well, they're extremely personalized rhythms. Our shuffles are Grateful
Dead shuffles. It's very specific.

Garcia said part of it is just observing how bodies move.
That's right. The band as a whole moves as an organic unit, and the
people dancing to our music are finding their own ways to dance to it
and lock in to a rhythm that they feel comfortable with. We're not trying
to make the beat fall right on the two or right on the one or wherever,
and that gives everybody the freedom to find what they want in it. It
allows for personal nuance. It's not assault music where we're dictating
how to respond to it by laying down some fixed thing. It's participant
music. And when everyone's really into it, that's when you get this giant
animal breathing as one, and that's what's so thrilling about the Grateful
Dead. You can have all these guys playing polyphonic parts, but we're
playing as one; it's just different pieces of the pie. And the same is true
of the audience. Everyone's dancing differently but they're part of the
same thing. That's magic. It's fascinating.

Do you think it's accurate to say that everyone in the band is a rhythmist?
Yeah, we rely heavily on rhythms. After all, it came out of jug band
and that whole rhythmic tradition. It's very rhythmically articulate, and
everyone in this band is good at rhythm. Bob is very strong on the
rhythm side, and not strong on melody. Jerry is strong on both sides.

And Phil, of course, is a rhythm machine. He knows exactly where he wants it.

Is there any drawback to having two people sitting at the drum kits, instead of having one person playing drums and another assorted percussion?
There's a downside to just about everything, I suppose, and the main downside to the way we do it is when Billy and I aren't playing together; when we're out of sync. It can sound plodding at times. At the same time, it's the bed that the Grateful Dead rides on, and we do have a certain feel when we play together that each one of us doesn't have individually. We sort of search out each other's groove and then agree on a way of going. We're trying to play *together;* not just lay down individual parts. There's so much power you can get with two drummers locking in together. An incredible amount of power.

I talk a lot in the book about entrainment. Well, that's one of the major laws at work in the Grateful Dead. Billy and I are entraining when we're up there—beating efficiently together. There's a lot of power in that, and a surprising amount of subtlety, too—a lot the band can play off of; little nuances we can add because we're playing together and off of each other, and don't have to be totally concerned with just keeping time. We can drift off a little bit, maybe even go into trance states, and then pull each other back. If I go a little too far out, the band won't fall apart; same with Billy. It's not like losing consciousness, really; it's changing consciousness. We're actively courting that space. When we can relax and things flow seamlessly—with no effort, with no thinking, just feeling it—you're *there,* man. But you can't force it, either, and you have to be ready for change every second. It's the razor's edge. It's dangerous. But when the music is right and the feeling is right, it's heavenly. It's as good as making love.

I was wondering about all this, and I knew the Grateful Dead had the ability to do it. I wanted to find out more about the ecstatic states and trance, and what the difference was. So I started reading Rouget's *Music Trance* and Eliade's *Archaic Techniques of Ecstasy, Shamanism in Siberia* by Douschegy. I read all these accounts of how shamans use drums to move in and out of altered states at will, and I thought, "Jesus, *we* move out of these states as well. Let's talk about this stuff." When I met Joe Campbell, he was gathering myths and noticing that all these shamans had drums—they were riding their drums to another world, *doin' business* there, and then comin' back. Those guys are professionals. Well, so are the Grateful Dead. There's a need in our community for what we do, just like there's a need for shamans in other types of communities. We're not shamans in the classic sense, but we fulfill some of their function.

It seems that in the late Sixties there were so many more people involved in that pursuit musically. Or at least consciously trying to blow people's minds.

Well, I think a lot of what was happening back then was that people were discovering themselves and discovering their priorities, and finding they weren't always what they expected they might be. Music was like a skeleton key to the inside of you. Music has always been used to loosen you up, open you up.

People were experimenting back then; they were freer. The demands of daily life weren't as hard, and everyone was getting high and discovering things, separately and together. It was an incredible environment to make music in—very exciting and supportive.

Why did so many people fall away from this path?

I imagine because it was just "time out" for them. Then they went and got jobs to make money. They didn't follow their bliss. Most of them got jobs in areas they didn't have a passion for. Maybe they became doctors because they felt they had to make money. Maybe they became lawyers because they know the world is run by lawyers.

Obviously there's something in the chemistry between you guys in the band that allowed you to prevail, against all odds.

Sure. It's the music. The *music*. This is just a classic example of a musician chasing the feeling. Only we found each other and the group years ago and we've been chasing it *together*—this collective sound. We've been on the tail of this dragon for years, and every time we get it and grab a hold of it, it slips away. But it's so good we keep chasing it, because sooner or later we'll grab it again.

Right, for a minute or two.

That's okay! That's okay! Because most people never get a chance to touch it at all! It's the miraculous that we're after; nothing short of that. Why else would we be trying so fucking *hard,* going through all these scenes on this trip? [Laughs] This is business, but it's not for the bucks. It's the spirit business.

Are you surprised that it's become a big money business, too?
No. I thought that sooner or later if we kept going and got our business straightened out, we'd be able to make some money at this. But that's really only been pretty recently. We had to get the flakes out of the office. All that bad stuff is in the past now . . . thank God!

Were the band's business problems a distraction through the years?
Only when we came off the road. Not when we were out there, certainly, because we were flyin'. When the music's going, all is well. When the music stops and you come home, that's when art meets reality.

But we always had faith in the music and it worked out just in time. I mean, here we are, and it's just fine.

When you listen to a Dead tape from the late Sixties, does the music sound primitive to you because you all know so much more about music now?
No, it sounds exciting and vital. It sounds very energized to me. We were young men and we definitely didn't know as much as we know now, but we had more energy and it was more hard-driving. It was more naive and more innocent.

How so?
Well, we were discovering a lot of our trademark licks. Now, we play them knowing what they are. Before we'd play them and be surprised each time we'd play them. There are things we've built into the music that we use as signposts that we hit every time now. That's the way it should be. And certainly we still come up with new things enough that it stays interesting. There are still surprises.

What was the weakest aspect of the early band?
Vocals, definitely. Otherwise we could pull off most of what we were trying to do then.

What did you gain from the experience in the late Sixties of rehearsing for hours every day?
We were entraining. I learned how to entrain with the band and the band learned how to entrain with itself. That was a major, major thing for the band. It shouldn't be overlooked. That's where we learned to really breathe together and take chances, but still have confidence. The hours had to be put in to do what we do—the Grateful Dead *flex*.

What was the process like when you came back into the band in 1976?
There was no process; we just started playing together again. It was completely natural.

The tapes from that year sound slow to me, as if the engine is just starting to rev up again.
Yeah, everyone was playing slow. The songs had slowed down, and then we started to build up steam again. I was out of shape. Billy and I hadn't really played together for years. This looks easy to some people, but the reason you don't see two drummers playing together very often is because it's not easy. It's not just being good, and it's not just putting two drum sets up on the stage.

What happens when you add a third drummer? We've seen Airto or Sikuru or Olatunji up there with you.
These are great drummers and they instinctively know how to fit in with what we do, and vice versa. You don't breathe the same way. Billy and I have this breath that we don't have to discuss even; it's the way we breathe. When you put anybody else in there, no matter how good they are, you're adding another element, so Bill and I will *give* it to them— we'll give the groove to that person, or listen to that person and let him have some input into the conversation and become a part of the rhy-

Mickey, Billy, and Airto, New Year's Eve 1989–90. *(Photo by Ron Delany)*

thmscape. These guys are all sensitive to what we're doin'; they don't just play crazy. Airto says, "Man, if you don't *listen*, you're just up there bangin' shit around." [Laughs] He's right.

Billy and I really listen well to each other. We don't even have to look at each other. We're hearing it all. Sometimes we'll crack each other up. We have our own little musical conversation going most of the time. Sometimes it lasts the whole evening and we'll never talk about it, but we've talked about it in the drums. We have complete conversations—it's how we move the rhythms, what we do to what, who treats what which way . . . there are a million things that go on every night between us. It can be very satisfying because you're doing it *with* somebody else.

Billy told me he's rarely in the mood to play the cowboy tunes. Are there songs you don't get off on?
Yeah, he hates those! [Laughs] I don't really like them much, either. I don't like "El Paso."

Because there's nothing going on in it for you?
Nothing's happening for me. The song has absolutely no meaning to me. I just don't like that song. But I'll play it. It's no sweat. I might even play it passionately. I like "Mama Tried" all right. "El Paso" is the only song I really don't like. Oh . . . and "Victim or the Crime."

I hated it at first but I've come to like it quite a bit. I'm always surprised how much I like it.
I'm starting to see the grotesque industrial madness behind it, I guess. [Laughs] I've never really warmed to it.

What's the most challenging material? The songs that open up?
It's all a challenge, because it isn't easy to constantly stay on top of everything and dance through a night. Every song is a challenge. Obviously, things like "Help on the Way" and "Slipknot" are very challenging rhythmically. "Terrapin" is another one. "Let It Grow." Those are real heavyweight songs.

They all have so many changes in them.
Right. But even something more straightforward—a great "Sugar Magnolia" or a great "Playin' in the Band"—is just as satisfying. The idea is to snap and then relax, and go through all this passionate interplay; go on a ride together, and at the end of the night feel exhilarated. To be

able to do that after all this time and still be full of energy and spirit—that's the trick.

Do you ever feel like you play a bad show?
Oh, I *know* I do.

You always look like you've got a lot of energy.
Well, I'm a battery—I supply a lot of energy to the band. I like to think that I can kick at the end. I take great pride in that. I don't like to wimp out at the end. But sometimes I spend myself too early or I'm not up to it, and I feel bad about that. In the old days I'd get completely despondent about it. I take music very seriously, and when you don't play it well, it hurts. It hurts, man. I'd get very depressed and withdrawn and sometimes I wouldn't snap out of it for a day or more—or until somebody snapped me out of it. It doesn't affect me like that anymore, but you still want to play well every time. But that's one of the hazards of becoming a musician—you're not going to play well every time. Of course they don't tell you that at the beginning. [Laughs] I guess it depends on where the ante is: If you don't have great expectations about your playing, you won't be disappointed very often. Remember, we're after something invisible—feeling.

*In the early Eighties you exposed us all to so many different exotic percussion instruments. You had a **berimbau** year. A **balafon** year or two... there were the Tibetan bowls of 1983. Now I understand you have most of those sounds electronically sampled as part of your setup. I'd think the aesthetic experience of actually playing the instrument live, as opposed to triggering the sound electronically on a pad, would be more satisfying.*
There's nothing like the real thing, obviously. But to be honest, taking all those delicate instruments around was such a hassle. Now [with the electronic setup], I'm able to call up a lot more exotic sounds a lot quicker, I have more control over the sounds, and I can carry them around in a little case. I have those other instruments rotating around my house, so I play them personally. If I'm alone at home, I'll curl up with a Tibetan bowl or a *berimbau* and just play for an hour or two. They've turned into private instruments for me.

What kind of feedback do you get from people about the Rhythm Devils part of the show?

Oh, everything from "What are you doing to my head?" to "I saw God." [Laughs] It's not for everyone, but you can say that about anything in the Grateful Dead. I don't try to play a normal drum solo because I don't believe that's really relevant anymore. It's not just drums; it's percussion, it's sound, it's *space*. It's not Gene Krupa and Buddy Rich anymore. It's not Ginger Baker. That stuff is history. That was great, too, but my ideas aren't like that. The stuff I do is stuff that's fallen through the cracks—it's alternative; it's new space. I'm not looking for applause. But I want people to like it, sure. I want it to be entertaining to them. But I'm appealing to another region that's not strictly entertainment. When I vibrate the low D on The Beam, it's to tap in to a whole other range of feelings in you. It's not just to play the lowest note in the world. I'm trying to shake your insides and rattle your bones. Sometimes I like it real noisy and sometimes I like it real quiet. Being in the Grateful Dead gives me the range to do both.

Hunter/Garcia Words/Music

▬ ▬ ▬ ▬ ▬ ▬

An Interview About Songwriting and Inspiration

January 31, 1991

In more than two decades of reading everything I could get my hands on about the Grateful Dead, I never encountered an interview with Robert Hunter and Jerry Garcia together. Hunter's memory is that they sat down together with a writer once in 1970, but no one seems to know what came of it. Though I'd wanted to do such an interview for many years, I waited until this issue to see if it could actually happen. To my amazement, the duo readily agreed. We met at the Dead's Marin County office on the afternoon of January 31.

Hunter is the first to arrive, roaring up on his Harley, decked out in a gray leather jacket. One sometimes forgets that the same man who penned "Must've Been the Roses" also wrote rough and tumble tunes like "Easy Wind" and "Mr. Charlie." As we sit in the kitchen of the Dead office waiting for Garcia, Hunter tells me that he's been spending

Hunter and Garcia. *(Photo by Jay Blakesberg)*

Hunter and Garcia. *(Photo by Jay Blakesberg)*

most of his time transfixed by the television coverage of the Persian Gulf war, and pounding out his thoughts on the subject on his trusty word processor. "I've written seventy-one items about the war so far," he says grimly, shaking his head. His VCR was taping CNN as we spoke, so he wouldn't miss a thing. Clearly, this is something that's driving him. "I'm really interested to see how this whole thing is changing us," he adds somewhat cryptically.

Garcia shows up a few minutes later in his BMW and heads straight for the coffee machine. Last night, he and his band had played at the Warfield Theater in San Francisco, but he seems surprisingly alert. "You should get a Harley," Hunter tells him enthusiastically. "They're so . . . *loud*." After more cajoling, Garcia agrees that maybe he should look into it, though he doesn't sound too convincing to me. That boat of a Beamer seems more his style.

The three of us retire to an unused office to rap for a while about their long songwriting partnership and a few of the gems they've crafted together. In the loose chronology that the interview follows, I've deliberately stopped at about 1980, since both have spoken at length about their more recent collaborations. I also steered clear of some of the songs that Hunter discusses in his annotations in *Box of Rain* (his book of lyrics), such as "Terrapin." Our conversation opens with a more general discussion about their influences.

I've been thinking recently that perhaps one of the reasons so many people my age (thirty-seven) or of my generation grew up to be fairly open-minded about music is that we were exposed to so many different kinds of music in school. In elementary school we sang all sorts of great songs— "Swanee," "Funiculi Funicula," "The Happy Wanderer," "Tumbling Tumbleweeds," "Red River Valley," "The Ballad of Jesse James," "When Johnny Comes Marching Home," "Barbara Allen." Folk music was an integral part of my education in this time before pop music had really infiltrated the mainstream.

Garcia: I'm sure that sort of thing would have a big impact on you. Everybody has those songs that they hear when they're young that they love and that stick with 'em through the years and even influence their character in some way, I suppose. Growing up in the Forties, I think it was more hit or miss. I heard a few things in school, but not that much. It seems to me that using folk music in American schoolrooms was probably a fairly radical idea, but I don't really know. What kind of music did they teach in the schoolrooms in the middle 1800s? That would be interesting to find out. Because most of those songs that you're talking about are from the middle of the nineteenth century on; around the turn of the century. Some are much older, of course.

America's one of those places that has such an incredibly rich musical history it's hard to avoid encountering it. But I never felt that school was particularly responsible for me being interested in music. I always thought the fact that my grandmother listened to the Grand Ole Opry on the radio when I was a kid probably had more to do with my appreciation of country and bluegrass and that sort of thing.

Do you agree there wasn't much of a pop music context in the culture at that point?
Garcia: Not in the schools, but certainly in the world, and everybody then, like now, was affected by the movies and radio. I know I was a radio kid before I was a television kid, and on the radio you could hear all sorts of stuff. But this was that tail end of the Forties kind of music—weird stuff like Frankie Laine.

"Lucky Old Sun."
Garcia: Right.
Hunter: Those Frankie Laine songs had a nice tone to them.
Garcia: They did have a nice quality to them, and so did all those Mitch Miller arrangements, and Guy Mitchell—I don't know what you'd call it: popular, ersatz folk-flavored music.

But I also sensed there was a deep connection between children's folk songs and regular traditional folk songs. The distance between "Jimmy Crackcorn" and some Bill Monroe tune was not that great, so it seemed fairly natural to move from one style to the other as you got older.
Garcia: That's true. It's not that far apart.
Hunter: Burl Ives was a good example.
Garcia: Right, he was maybe the main popular folk voice of that time; a guy who did folk and did kids' stuff. The Weavers, too. I remember being really impressed as a kid by their versions of "Goodnight Irene," "So Long It's Been Good to Know You." I don't think of those kinds of songs as direct influences, but they probably were in a way because they were a part of American culture.
Hunter: You know, Jerry, you once said something to me about a lyric that really impressed you when you were young, and it impressed me the same way, and I almost feel that that line is where we took off in

divergent directions. Remember that line, "ten thousand got drowneded—"

Garcia: "—that never was born." That was amazing. That line really scared me.

What's it from?
Garcia: It's from a tune called "The Mummer's Song," that Jean Richie used to sing. It's an a capella song with only two verses, and they're nonsense insofar as that if they have any sense, it's so deeply symbolic we don't know what it's actually about. I don't know what the "Mummers" thing is. It's from the Appalachian tradition; I think it might be another word for players or something. I'm not sure. Not knowing, though, is part of what makes it so evocative. The mystery is part of what makes it interesting to me.

When you say that that's a line you "took off" from, what do you mean?
Garcia: We both loved it for different reasons, and it set us off on the long march, you know what I mean? He on his, and me on mine.
Hunter: The evocative power of that mysterious line is what got to me—the notion of evocativeness rather than pat statements.
Garcia: The lack of specificness. It was the power of the almost-expressed, the resonant. It seemed to speak at some level other than the most obvious one, and it was more moving for that reason, since you don't know what it's about. It has the kind of scary power that the Mass used to have in Latin.
Hunter: You recognize it because it makes the hairs on your arms stand up. That's the test.
Garcia: That's it. The hairs–standing–up test! [Laughs]

Certainly in the old ballads you've covered in the Dead you've gravitated toward the partially told tale.
Garcia: That's a real folk thing.

When we learned "Lord Randal," we learned all these different verses that told a coherent story.
Garcia: I prefer it the other way. See, the versions that made it to Appalachia were like two hundred years after the fact for those English ballads. They got sung from father to son or mother to daughter so much that eventually nobody remembered who Lord Randal was, but

they did remember the guy's head rolling down the stairs in that verse.
[Laughs]

Hunter: There you've got all those incredibly evocative lines like "black
eels and eel broth, mother" and "I fain would lie doon."

Garcia: Right! You get these little hunks of good stuff and you don't
need all twenty-nine verses to get the feeling of it. You only get three
or four verses, but they're so rich in weirdness because they're the ones
that made enough of an impression that they could last through the
telephone game through several generations.

*Was the natural evolution of these kinds of songs stilted by the fact that
the advent of the phonograph record concretized them at a certain point?*

Hunter: Probably, but I decided early on that this wasn't going to be
the case, and that in spite of the phonograph record I was personally
going to try the as-if-by-ear tradition. That's what things like "Dupree"
and "Stagger Lee" are—studied efforts to continue the oral tradition.

Garcia: I think the phonograph record only lifts it out of its locality.
The reason we have all this early folk music on records to begin with is
the standard ploy [in the Twenties and Thirties] was to record local music
so the companies could then sell phonographs to the people in that area.

What a scam!

Garcia: It was. But in the process they inadvertently preserved a huge
amount of American folk music. The "race records" [early black music]
were the same deal. But it allowed someone in Memphis to hear what
a guy in Mississippi was doing, and I think that made a lot of people
better players because they had new influences. At the same time, though,
it confused up a lot of the locally specific stylistic content of the music
you hear in Twenties music. By the Thirties, it had already started to
swim around a lot.

*To what extent did you hear original 78s of old folk and blues songs
before the Folkways and Library of Congress recordings came out in the
late Fifties and early Sixties?*

Garcia: For me, not at all.

Hunter: Me neither, though I guess radio sometimes played the 78s.

Garcia: Once I found out there was such a world, though, I met guys
who were into 78s and collected them. So then I had access to them and
I could mine that resource. But I had no consciousness of it before the
Folkways stuff came out. For me it was the Harry Smith anthology that

showed me that there was this vital, rich, primitive form with these guys sawing away on their fiddles and banjos and singing in these creaky old voices. That was very exciting for me. I knew the blues version of it to an extent, because by then I'd heard Blind Lemon Jefferson and some of those other early guys, but before Folkways I didn't know there was this other white music in America.

Was the traditional music you played in the early Sixties learned mainly from other musicians or from records?
Hunter: I'd say from records mostly.
Garcia: And tapes, too. Getting into that world was like opening a magic door, because I met all these people who had live tapes of bluegrass. That's what really did it for me, because live, the music sounded so energized and so beautifully detailed. That point of view of the one microphone on all those old bluegrass recordings allowed you to hear the depth of it—you'd hear the instruments coming toward the microphone and then moving away. You'd hear them playing the little holes and doing all this wonderful dynamic stuff. It had the feeling of seeming very familiar: "This is something I've been trying to get at."

Bob, did you find that since you've always been literarily inclined you gravitated more toward the British tradition than rawer Appalachian folk music?
Hunter: As a lyricist I would pretty much have to tend that way because it was so articulate compared to a lot of the early country music, which was all very nice—it sang very well—but doesn't look like much on paper.
Garcia: Yeah, it doesn't have the rich poetic power of the English stuff.
Hunter: It's just a different kind of tradition. [The British tradition] sort of reaches its culmination with Alfred Lord Tennyson, things like *Morte d'Arthur*. Certainly I liked that sort of writing.
Garcia: Also, bluegrass owes as much to dance music, which is totally part of the oral tradition; the music side. The fiddle tunes, breakdowns, reels and so forth don't owe much to any verbal tradition. There are really only a handful of outstanding traditional ballads that found their way into bluegrass, and just bits and pieces of them: things like "Down in the Willow Garden," a few murdered-girl songs.
Hunter: "I poisoned the girl who would not be my wife/Now I'm going down to the river and I'm *goyne* to take my life."

Garcia: Right. [Laughs] "I took her to the river and there I *thrun* her in."

Sort of the "Wind and Rain" space.
Garcia: Absolutely.

Where did you guys actually meet?
Hunter: The Commedia Theater in Palo Alto. You were going with an old girlfriend of mine—
Garcia: Diane! Yeah, that's right.

Is this before or after the Army?
Garcia: After. We'd both just gotten out, I guess. Hunter had just gotten out of the National Guard and I'd just been bounced.
Hunter: I was a weekend warrior!

Lucky thing you're not there now. You'd probably be in Saudi Arabia.
Hunter: Hey, I got called down to the Watts riots and got a campaign ribbon for it. I know what it feels like to be a *troop*. [He chuckles]

Judging from tapes I've heard of the Wildwood Boys, you [Hunter] were sort of the guy with the personality in the band, talking between songs and all.
Hunter: I was just more jacked up and nervous than the rest, and I'd open my mouth and spill. [Garcia cracks up]

It seems as though string bands always had somebody in that role.
Hunter: The jokey-boy, yeah. It never occurred to any of us that we could stand onstage with our mouths shut.
Garcia: Yeah, Hunter always had a little more of the entertainer in him than me. But I used to be that guy, too, sometimes, when Hunter wasn't around. We always had a sort of abuse-the-audience attitude. Once they were in there, they were yours and you could do whatever you wanted to them. [Laughs] That was part of the fun of playing those little clubs.

The oldest lyric I see in your book [Hunter's Box of Rain] is "Ariel," from 1964. Had you been writing songs very long at that point?
Hunter: No, I'd only written a few by that point.
Garcia: Some of those things you had, like "China Cat Sunflower," went back pretty far, didn't they?

Hunter: Not quite that far, though. I don't really remember exactly. "China Cat" took a long time to write. I wrote it in different settings and added this and that to it. It was originally inspired by Dame Edith Sitwell, who had a way with words—I liked the idea of quick, clicky assonance and alliteration like "See me dance the polka, said Mr. Wag like a bear, with my top hat and my whiskers, that tra-la-la trapped affair." I just liked the way she put things together. I'd have to admit that before you could trace it back that there was some influence.
Garcia: [Laughs] That's pretty obscure!

I was thinking more Lewis Carroll.
Hunter: Oh sure! I suppose I owe a debt to "Jabberwocky."
Garcia: He's an old Lewis Carroll freak.

Where were you [Hunter] when the Warlocks started?
Hunter: I must've been down in L.A. at that point; I'm not really sure.
Garcia: He was doing other stuff, but he only barely missed it. The first time I saw him after we'd been playing . . . there was a big hole there for a while because he wasn't around for the Acid Test either, except at the very end, were you?
Hunter: No, I was there at the San Jose Acid Test and the Fillmore Acid Test . . .
Garcia: That's right, I remember you at the Fillmore Acid Test.
Hunter: I made most of the local ones.
Garcia: And you and me first talked about writing tunes together sometime after our first record came out.
Hunter: That sounds about right.
Garcia: When we [the band] started working, we were really working hard. I never saw anybody. When we were working the bars, I lost contact with almost all my friends 'cause the Warlocks were playing every night and on Sundays, afternoons and nights. We were booked solid.

Sunday afternoon with the Warlocks. That must have been something.
Garcia: Yeah, it was pretty weird.

When did it first strike you there might be a partnership between you?
Garcia: It was always in the back of my mind, because I knew what he could do.

Hunter: Remember that song we wrote in like 1961 or 1962: "Tell you a story 'bout my old man's cat . . . "?
Garcia: Right! I'd forgotten about that. We did write a song then.
Hunter: And then we didn't write another one for three or four years! [Laughs]

Jerry, at the time of the first album you were writing some stuff alone, like "Cream Puff War."
Garcia: Only by default. I felt my lyric writing was woefully inadequate.
Hunter: [to Jerry] Oh, you could've done it by yourself, man! I didn't want to tell you then—
Garcia: Well, it's too late now! [Laughs]

Who or what inspired your section of "That's It for the Other One"—"The other day they waited," etc.?
Garcia: I don't know really.
Hunter: Whatever would rhyme!
Garcia: Right, because I was that kind of writer. [Laughs] Seriously, I think that's an extension of my own personal symbology for "The Man of Constant Sorrow"—the old folk song—which I always thought of as being a sort of Christ parable. Something fuzzy like that. Fuzzy Christianity.

So Bob, when you started contributing lyrics to the Dead, you literally sent them in the mail and said, "Here, I've written some things, do you want to do anything with them?"
Hunter: Yeah. I was living in New Mexico at the time and I sent Jerry "Alligator," "St. Stephen," and "China Cat." Then somebody—maybe it was Jerry—wrote or called me up and said, "Why don't you come on out and be with us?" So I hitchhiked here and Phil picked me up somewhere, and he drove me over to Ashbury Street.

This was late 1966 or early 1967?
Hunter: Gee, I'm not really good with dates. I think it must've been late 1966. At that point I'd had those three songs for four or five months.

Did you have your own musical settings for them?
Hunter: I had songs, but I didn't have them on tape or anything. I just sent lyrics through the mail at that point. I always wrote my own melodies, but after a few years Jerry got to the point where he said, "Will

you stop giving me melodies, because they just confuse me and I can't get them out of my head."

Garcia: That's true. A lot of times his melodies would be so fucking catchy: "God I can't hear this any way except with his melody!" [Laughs] Sometimes they were perfect, though, and I didn't fool with them—like "Must've Been the Roses" was one. That's totally Hunter's melody.

Hunter: Actually, you stuck a minor chord in there which makes it ever so much more powerful.

So is your original flash of how you envisioned "St. Stephen" lost to the ages?

Hunter: No, I remember it: [he sings the first line in a high, sing-songy tenor] "Sa-aint Stephen with a rose/In and out of the garden he goes."

Garcia: Sort of like that old song, "The hunter would a-hunting go/da-da-da he carried a bow...."

Hunter: Right. It was a nice little thing and then they put this up-against-the-wall-motherfucker arrangement on it! [Garcia laughs] We came up with a hybrid that hit between the eyes!

I've always regretted that there were no really great songwriters in the Haight in its earliest days to capture that energy in songs. There were no mature songwriting voices.

Garcia: Well, everybody was having too much fun.

Hunter: We tried a few things, didn't we? "Cosmic Charlie," "Truckin'."

Those are later, and both of them are pretty heavily laced with cynicism if you ask me. I'm talking about the first bloom in 1966 and early 1967.

Garcia: "Golden Road" was our effort at nailing down some of that feeling, I guess. That was sort of a group writing experience before Hunter was with us. We kept it simple.

But you know, what could you say, really? "We took a bunch of acid and had a lot of fun"?

Hunter: What about "The Other One"? I would think that qualifies.

Garcia: Yeah, that was sort of a serious, hole-in-the-wall psychedelic explosion.

Hunter: Maybe Blair is wrong about this and what was being written *was* the expression of what was happening.

Garcia: There were diverse expressions, because there were so many different ways to perceive it. There were the people who always insisted you be very serious about it, like the Eastern mystic types, and others were just having a good time—

Hunter: And "If you go to San Francisco be sure to wear a flower in your hair" had already been written. You certainly didn't want to write *that* again. [Laughs]

Garcia: That was the lamest version of it I could possibly imagine.

What did you think when you heard all that bogus mainstream psy-chedelia—"Green Tambourine" and "Pictures of Matchstick Men" and things like that? Did you feel co-opted?

Garcia: Not at all. People who knew what was happening could see that stuff for what it was. But beyond that, as a band, the Grateful Dead has never thought of itself as being a psychedelic band. We've always thought of ourselves as a rock 'n' roll band. What we were playing back then was basically a harder, rhythm and blues–oriented rock 'n' roll; especially Pigpen's stuff. We were going for a sort of Chess Records school of R&B—Howlin' Wolf and Muddy Waters. Those are the records we stole a lot of our tunes from. That was our background. Pigpen's father was a rhythm and blues disc jockey, and Pigpen played the blues so naturally. We didn't have that Midwestern authority—we weren't like the Butterfield band, but we were a funky blues band.

Hunter: We didn't know who we were then. We were in the process of becoming what we were going to be, which is why there are no specific reports, in terms that you would recognize, of the psychedelia of that era.

How fully realized was the "Eagle Mall" suite of songs? I know they were intended to be tackled by the Dead around the time of Aoxomoxoa, and I see what seem to be complete versions of the songs in Box of Rain, but did the group ever actually work on any of them?

Garcia: No, we never got to 'em.

Hunter: I started writing that thing when we were down there [in Los Angeles] recording *Anthem of the Sun,* and it was more a personal project. I had eyes for the band doing it, but then I was informed by my colleague here, "Listen, basically we're a dance band and there's no way in the world people will be able to dance to this sort of thing." I saw his point. I finished it off, and I've performed the whole suite myself.

Garcia: I remember we did actually take a few cracks at trying to set some of it, but I couldn't come up with anything that didn't sound very hackneyed.

Hunter: It almost had to have an old English flavor, and that wasn't really where the Grateful Dead was going then.

Garcia: Right. I said, "What we need is the New York Pro Musica [the famous early music ensemble] to make this sound the way it's supposed to go—with the bells and recorders and viola da gambas and all that stuff.

Some of the music you were doing with the Grateful Dead at that time had an almost baroque quality to it.

Garcia: Well, "What's Become of the Baby" was originally baroque. I had this melody worked out that had this counterpoint and a nice little rhythm. The original setting I'd worked out was really like one of those song forms from the New York Pro Musica. [He and Hunter break into a lilting counterpoint melody] Dum-dee-dee-dum-dee-dee-dee-dee-do-dah-dum."

And then a nitrous tank got in the way? What happened?

Garcia: [Laughs] Nah, I just had a desire to make it much weirder than that and I didn't know how to do it. Also, the technology wasn't there to do what I could easily do now. I had something specific in mind but simply couldn't execute it because I didn't have the tools.

Hunter: Either that or you did execute it and it's been overlooked because it's so challenging.

Garcia: Maybe, though personally I was never quite satisfied with it.

Hunter: It could've been the great psychedelic song of that year. It just didn't happen to crack through that way in listeners' ears. If it had, then we'd be sitting here bragging about it rather than excusing ourselves.

Garcia: [Laughs] Right! I had something in mind that was extremely revolutionary. I wanted to use the entire band, but I didn't want to use it in a standard rhythm section and lead instruments way. I wanted something more like the stuff we did in the bridge section of "St. Stephen": "Lady finger dipped in moonlight . . ." That weird scratchy shit. I wanted something more like that, but which also included feedback and other stuff, and it would all be gated through the mouth, the voice.

Sort of early "Seastones."

Garcia: Yeah, it would all be somehow enclosed inside the voice. But, well, you know how it goes. [He chuckles]

The best laid plans . . .

Garcia: It's too bad, because it's an incredible lyric and I feel I threw the song away somewhat.

Hunter: We feel perhaps it sunk the album! [Laughs]

Garcia: I think, "Why the fuck did everybody let me do that?" "Mountains of the Moon" had a little bit of the "Eagle Mall" thing.

Hunter: Maybe that's as much as you needed.

Garcia: Yeah. That song turned out nicely. I had an acoustic setting in mind from the get-go and it turned out pretty much how I envisioned it. I don't know what made me think I could do a song like that, but something at the time made me think I could do it. [Laughs] I like the tune a lot.

Hunter: It's a nice finger-picking tune.

To what degree did your early lyrics shape the direction of the musical settings that were eventually written for them?

Hunter: I don't think very much. I think most of those songs could've worked with different lyrics.

Garcia: That works the other way, too—the lyrics could've worked in lots of different musical settings. When Hunter and I were living together is when we wrote some of the richest stuff. Some of those lyrics were so perfectly beautiful.

This is in Larkspur [in southern Marin county] in 1969 and early 1970? The **Workingman's Dead** *and* **American Beauty** *material?*

Hunter: Yeah. I'd be sitting upstairs banging on my typewriter, picking up my guitar, singin' something, then going back to the typewriter. Jerry would be downstairs practicing guitar, working things out. You could hear fine through the floors there, and by the time I'd come down with a sheet and slap it down in front of him, Jerry already knew how they should go! He probably had to suffer through my incorrect way of doing them. [Laughs]

Garcia: You know, I have almost no recognition of the actual process of writing those songs. I listen to them now and I wonder, "Where the hell did that come from?" [Laughs] Some of them seem to have appeared out of nowhere. Others I can remember the actual moment when they came together. And sometimes it was the thing of Hunter giving me the lyrics and I'd carry them around for a while, then sit down with them in a hotel room or some place and work it out.

Hunter: The best example of that is "Ripple," which I wrote in England

Garcia. *(Photo by Jay Blakesberg)*

and brought back. Then we were on the trans-Canadian train trip [June–July, 1970], Jerry woke up one morning, sat out on the railroad tracks somewhere near Saskatoon, and put it to music.

Garcia: It just seemed to happen automatically. We worked on a lot of stuff together, but I'll be damned if I can remember how we did it.

Dylan said something to the effect that a lot of his early songs seem so distant that they sound like they're "public domain" songs. They don't even feel like "his" songs; they're bigger than that.

Hunter: We've got to give Dylan credit for being the guy who really opened the door to being literate in music. That was his door and we thank him very much for opening it.

Garcia: He sure did. He gave rock 'n' roll the thing I'd wished it had when I was a kid—respectability; some authority. He took it out of the realm of ignorant guys banging away on electric instruments and put it somewhere else altogether. The Beatles, too.

Hunter: Although the Beatles owe the same debt to Dylan.

Garcia: Right. They took their lyric cue from him, too. Dylan is the guy who allowed the music to become what some of us hoped it could be.

Hunter: He's the Picasso of the movement.

So did you make a conscious decision to simplify the lyrics and music around the time of **Workingman's Dead,** *or was it just a natural evolution?*

Hunter: I'll tell you what affected me. I was so impressed by the songwriting of Robbie Robertson [of the Band] I just said, "Oh yeah, this is the direction. This is the way for us, with all our folk roots, our country and bluegrass roots."

Was **Music from Big Pink** *the only Band album out at that point?*

Hunter: No, I think the second one [*The Band*] was out too. The one with "The Night They Drove Old Dixie Down."

Garcia: I met those guys right around that time.

Hunter: The historical consciousness in "The Night They Drove Old Dixie Down" is a real formative moment in directions in American music.

Garcia: Absolutely.

Hunter: You can hang these things up with a nice, languid historical viewpoint. I liked that. Some of those songs are probably the father of "Jack Straw" and things like that.

So when the two of you decided to live together during that period, was it specifically to write songs?
Garcia: It was the basic thing of friendship, economics and all that stuff. We had a nice big house that we could afford to live in together but probably couldn't have afforded separately at that point. It was a nice place to be, and Hunter was kind of floatin' at the time.
Hunter: That's right. I was sleepin' on floors and stuff and he took me in.
Garcia: Right! [Laughs]
Hunter: And it's not easy livin' in the lion's den, let me tell you! This is cheerfulness you're seein' here, but let me tell ya what this guy is like in the morning! [Laughs]
Garcia: Well, everything was fine until [Merry Prankster Ken] Babbs moved in with us. [Laughs]
Hunter: That was a great time, looking back on it.
Garcia: It was funny as hell. He had The Bus out front, him and Gretch [Gretchen Fetchin], and they had a couple of kids at the time; they were just starting out.
Hunter: I wanted to seriously concentrate on the forward thrust of my lyrical bent, but Babbs wouldn't have it.
Garcia: [Laughs] Simply wouldn't allow it!
Hunter: He'd be playin' his tuba, driving us crazy. [Laughs]

I think the saying is "Never trust a Prankster."
Garcia: Yeah, but it was fun.
Hunter: Those were glorious days.

Distractions aside, how prolific were you during this period? The sheer volume of material is immense.
Hunter: I wrote endlessly.
Garcia: He never stopped.
Hunter: I never really stopped until about three years ago, when I came to some kind of halt in my prolixity.
Garcia: The amount we set was nothing compared to the amount we didn't set. There are a lot of songs that still deserve to be set.
Hunter: That's one reason I wanted to put out the *Box of Rain* book. If

Jerry loses that, I can just give him another copy . . . or he can go down
to his bookstore and *buy* another copy. [Laughs]

*There's such a nice simplicity to songs like "Ripple" and "Attics" and
"Brokedown Palace."*
Hunter: They don't seem simple to me.

*I mean in terms of the economy of words and the language. They're not
nearly so florid as the* **Aoxomoxoa** *material, to say the least.*
Hunter: No, that's true. I wrote "Ripple," "Brokedown Palace," and
"To Lay Me Down" all in about a two-hour period the first day I ever
went to England. I sat there with a case of Retsina and I opened up a
bottle of that stuff, and the sun was shining, I was in England, which
I'd always wanted to visit, and for some reason this creative energy started
racing through me and I could do no wrong—write, write, write, write!
Garcia: Excellent!
Hunter: And there's something about being in a foreign country that
makes me more Western than I am here. "Tennessee Jed" was written
in Barcelona, for instance. Maybe it's a hunger for my own identity.
Garcia: Yeah, I set some tunes on our first European trip. "Stella Blue"
was one. There were a couple of others.

Do you remember the genesis of "Uncle John's Band"?
Hunter: That came from a tape that the band made of a tune of Jerry's.
They had the whole tune together, drums and everything—in fact I still
have that tape—and I played it over and over and tried writing to it. I
kept hearing the words "God damn, Uncle John's mad," and it took a
while for that to turn into "Come hear Uncle John's Band," and that's
one of those little things where the sparkles start coming out of your
eyes.
Garcia: And for me, at that time I was listening to records of the Bul-
garian Women's Choir and also this Greek-Macedonian music—these
penny whistlers—and on one of those records there was a song that
featured this little turn of melody that was so lovely that I thought, "Gee,
if I could get this into a song it would be so great." So I stole it. [Laughs]

Ripping off the "public domain" once again.
Garcia: Actually, I only took a little piece of the melody, so I can't say
I plagiarized the whole thing. Of course it became so transmogrified
when Bob and Phil added their harmony parts to it that it really was no

longer the part of the song that was special for me. That was the melodic kicker originally though.

Hunter: Your influences can't help but speak through you. I don't even care where I got this point or that point. I just open up to it. I'm probably one of the world's biggest plagiarists as far as phrases go. But my plagiarization will often go to the thrust of the song—where it's coming from—and the particulars will be completely different. Like with the Robbie Robertson stuff—you probably wouldn't know that those were the parents of this, that, or another song of mine. It's just the flavor was so fine that it had to speak through me in my own words eventually.

Garcia: That's what inspiration is all about.

Hunter: "Inspire" means to take in, doesn't it?

Certainly you took that inspiration and ran it through your own symbology and outlook. You had that whole Western thing going, with the gamblers and all.

Hunter: I liked the way Dylan handled a deck of cards, and it struck me that it was a pretty basic metaphor. Maybe I played a few too many hands, someone suggested at some point. Somebody said, "I think we've had enough of trains, crows, and card games for a while." [Garcia laughs]

Well, it's definitely part of what gives the Grateful Dead its Western feeling, which is a lot of what sets you apart from other bands. "Loser" and "Deal" and those kinds of songs are part of this undefined West.

Garcia: It's sort of frontier music, I guess. It's the frontier: where the laws are falling apart and every person is the sheriff and the outlaw. [Laughs]

Hunter: You are what you eat!

Were you into Wyatt Earp and that sort of stuff?

Garcia: I wasn't.

Hunter: I was. In fact, when I was in junior high school I thought I was going to write a book about Wyatt Earp. I read all the books I could on him.

Garcia: You were a Wyatt Earp nut?

Hunter: Oh yeah, right down to the battle of the OK Corral and all those people—Johnny Rheingold, Curly Bill. I knew all that in detail.

Garcia: For me it was the John Ford westerns. I liked the wide open spaces in those films and the open melancholy—the sentimental West. That's an important key to my emotional interior.

Were you very familiar with the Western balladic tradition?

Garcia: Not really. Unfortunately, there isn't much of one.

Hunter: "I came into Beehive Valley the spring of ninety-two/I was looking for a whorehouse and a damn good one, too/It was there I met old Nell."

Garcia: There were mostly parodies. Like if you try to find music from the Gold Rush, they're mostly parodies of popular songs of the time, with jokey Gold Rush lyrics. "Days of '49" is an example of that. You'd get these songs about miners and stuff—tall tales.

Hunter: It's hard to say how many guitars made it out to the prairies.

Garcia: Not many, I imagine. A few concertinas, but mainly fiddles. So the music is not particularly rich. This is apart from the cowboy music tradition, which is a whole other thing, and actually relatively recent.

Hunter: Tex Ritter, the Sons of the Pioneers . . .

"The Legend of Pecos Bill" . . .

Hunter: Right. It was developing a tradition after the fact. If we wanted a United States Western musical tradition, we knew we were going to have to help build it.

I think it's amazing how comfortably the Dead used to move from the intense psychedelia of "Dark Star" into a song like "Me and My Uncle," or from "The Other One" into "Sing Me Back Home."

Garcia: I never had any problem with that myself. I always felt that there are so many different styles of music you can incorporate using the same instrumentation, there's no reason they should be mutually incompatible.

Crosby and Stills were hanging out at Mickey's ranch a lot in 1969 and 1970. Is that part of what influenced the vocal direction of the band?

Garcia: Sure, a little bit. Hearing those guys sing and how nice they sounded together, we thought, "We can try that. Let's work on it a little."

Hunter: We can double-track vocals, too, dammit!

Garcia: Yeah! Also I'd worked in the studio with them and we spent some time hanging out. So it was like an inspiration: here's a direction we haven't really explored.

Did the fact that you were playing acoustic sets in 1970 influence your writing during that period?

Garcia: It was the other way around. We wrote the songs and then decided to play acoustic sets to play some of those songs, and some other stuff, too.

I notice in **Box of Rain** *the lyrics of "Bird Song" now say "For Janis" next to the title. Was that written specifically in response to Janis' death?*
Garcia: Yes, it sure was. It says that in the book? [Hunter shows him the page.] That's really nice, man. At the time we never made a point to announce it or anything.
Hunter: But it's what we both had in mind for that song from the beginning.

It seems really different from most of the other things you've written.
Garcia: Really? I don't think so.
Hunter: Well, it reminds me a bit of "Blues for Allah" in that it's got that [he sings] da-de-da-da-da-de-da. These long melodic phrases with maybe more than twelve notes.
Garcia: To me it's like another fiddle tune. It isn't that different to me than a lot of other things, and it's got a bridge which is very much like the chorus of "He's Gone"; it's very similar.

That song was ostensibly written around the whole Lenny Hart thing, wasn't it? [Lenny Hart, Mickey's father, managed the Dead in 1969 and 1970 and embezzled thousands of dollars from the band.]
Garcia: It was written after that. My recollection is we wrote it just before we went to Europe in 1972. I remember working on it in a little apartment I had in the city [San Francisco]. It's when I was playing lots and lots of shows with Merl [Saunders] at the Keystone Korner [a now-defunct San Francisco club]. I had an apartment where I could hang out on nights I didn't feel like driving all the way back to Stinson Beach [45 minutes north of San Francisco on the Coast Highway].
Hunter: It was considerations of Lenny in my head that kicked off the whole "Rat in a drain ditch, out on a limb, you know better but I know him." I was telling them [the Dead] all along this was not the right way to go. [To Jerry] I must say, I told you all so!
Garcia: Yeah, you did.
Hunter: So the song started that way, but later on it became an anthem for Pigpen, and it's changed through the years. These songs are amorphous that way. What I intend is not what a thing is in the end.
Garcia: Me neither, for that matter. We don't create the meaning of the

tunes ultimately. They re-create themselves each performance in the minds of everybody there.

Hunter: If we did "Blues for Allah" right now, it would not mean what it would've meant a year ago.

Sometimes "He's Gone" can seem elegiac; other times it has a bitter edge to it.
Garcia: Right, it has that range.

*Were you sorry that all that great original material on **Europe '72** and **Skull and Roses** was never recorded in a studio?*
Garcia: Sure. I would have loved to.
Hunter: To me, all that material was sort of the kicker follow-up album to *American Beauty*. Instead, we put out this three-album package that sounds wonderful but it spread out the material so much we never got to hear what those songs might have sounded like as a package. I personally would've liked to hear those songs on an album of their own.
Garcia: I concur. Instead we dribbled some of that music all the way up through *Wake of the Flood*.

What can you tell me about the writing of "Wharf Rat"?
Garcia: I think that may have been one of those cases where I had an idea for something and you [Hunter] had a literary version of the same idea and we got together and just worked it out over the course of an afternoon. It was one of those quick flashes.
Hunter: Aren't you talkin' about "Terrapin"?
Garcia: No, I'm talking about "Wharf Rat." It was a similar process. Boy, I don't remember that much about writing that.
Hunter: A few years ago I could have told you right off the bat where this stuff came from.

How about "Brown-Eyed Woman"?
Garcia: [Long pause] I don't remember anything about writing that.
Hunter: I don't either. [They both laugh] My hunch is that it was written around the same time we wrote the *Workingman's Dead* and *American Beauty* songs in Larkspur.
Garcia: I'm just drawing a blank on that one.
Hunter: Now you can see why I didn't put the songs in *[Box of Rain]* in chronological order. [Laughs]

I gather "Eyes of the World" was an older lyric when the Dead got around to recording it in 1973.

Hunter: No, I don't think so. I think it was from around that time. I hadn't intended to stay in cowboy space forever. It was a passing . . . well, it was more than just a passing phase certainly.

Garcia: It was just another voice you could use.

Hunter: Actually, now that I think about it, I'm pretty sure "Eyes of the World" was from Larkspur. I remember I'd practice trumpet out there in the shed all the time—blow my brains half-out until I got psychedelic and then I'd go write. [Laughs] I finally had to quit it—I was afraid I'd blow a blood vessel in my brain if I didn't give it up.

Garcia: I don't remember writing "Eyes of the World," but I do remember that basically it wanted a samba feel, which it still sort of has. It was kind of a Brazilian thing.

Hunter: It has so many lyrics it needed a fast tempo to get them all in.

How about "Scarlet Begonias"?

Garcia: Hmmm. Where the hell did that one come from?

England perhaps?

Hunter: Probably. I don't remember specifically.

Garcia: I don't remember when the tune came into existence. It's another one of those tunes: somebody else wrote it, I guess. [Laughs] I don't know where it came from.

Hunter: Yes, who were we before we were taken over by pods? [Laughs] They've left us with just enough memory to get by on: social security number, that sort of thing.

If "Eyes of the World" was a samba, is it fair to say that "Scarlet Begonias" was an attempt at a Caribbean feeling?

Garcia: It definitely has a little Caribbean thing to it, though nothing specific. It's also its own thing. I wasn't thinking in terms of style when I wrote that setting, except that I wanted it to be rhythmic. I think I got a little of it from that Paul Simon "me and Julio down by the schoolyard" thing. A little from Cat Stevens—some of that rhythmic stuff he did on *Tea for the Tillerman* was kind of nice. It's an acoustic feel in a way, but we put it into an electric space, which is part of what made it interesting.

It's got that nice polyrhythmic thing happening.

Garcia: Yeah, we really worked on it a lot. That record [*Mars Hotel*]

Hunter. *(Photo by Jay Blakesberg)*

we rehearsed a lot before we went into the studio. That was done at Columbia's old place, when Roy Hallee [Paul Simon's engineer] used to have a West Coast place. We'd rehearse across the street at S.I.R. [Studio Instrument Rentals] before we'd go into the studio every day. We rehearsed all the tunes for about a month before we recorded them, so we had them pretty fully arranged.

Hunter: I was living in England at that time, I think.

Garcia: No, you weren't around for that, unfortunately. That was a good record.

Am I right in thinking that **Blues for Allah** *was made differently than your other albums in that it was constructed from the ground up, rather than by bringing in a batch of songs and fine-tuning them?*

Garcia: Right. In fact we kind of made a ground rule for that record: Let's make a record where we get together every day and we don't bring anything in. The whole idea was to get back to that band thing, where the band makes the main contribution to the evolution of the material. So we'd go into the studio, we'd jam for a while, and then if something nice turned up we'd say, "Well, let's preserve this little hunk and work with it, see if we can't do something with it." And that's how we did most of that album. What became "Crazy Fingers" originally had a hard rock 'n' roll feel; it was completely different. A lot of it went through metamorphoses that normally would take quite a long time. We sort of forced them through.

Hunter: This was not a terribly good way for a lyricist to work, because they'd say, "Okay, we're ready for the words for this right now." So I'd try something: "How about this? No? How about this?" "Yeah, that'll do." BAM! And on it would go. So I got involved in that immediacy process, too. I must say I prefer to sit back and toy with things a little bit more. So a method that might work nicely with a musical instrument might not work as well with language.

Garcia: Yeah, you're probably right. But I think we were pretty successful with those songs: "Help on the Way," "Franklin's Tower," "Crazy Fingers."

Hunter: "Crazy Fingers" was, in fact, all written beforehand. It was a page or two of haikus I'd been working on in a notebook. Jerry looked at them and said, "Hey, this might fit together as a song."

But "Blues for Allah," specifically, I remember them saying to me, "Dammit, we need the line right now!"

Garcia: Oh, that song was a bitch to do! When we got toward the end of the album we had some time restrictions and we started working pretty fast. But up until then we'd been pretty leisurely about it.

That song was another totally experimental thing I tried to do. In terms of the melody and the phrasing and all, it was not of this world. It's not in any key and it's not in any time. And the line lengths are all different.

Hunter: I remember trying to get a scan for that, the first line I came up with [he sings it to the song's melody] was "Here comes that awful funky bride of Frankenstein." [Laughs] Sometimes you need nonsense just to get it flowing.

Garcia: [Laughs] We should've used that!

What pushed it in its final lyric direction?

Garcia: We were talking about King Faisal [of Saudi Arabia] in the studio, 'cause an article came up about him in *Newsweek* or something. And I remember being blown away when it said that Faisal owned a third of the world's wealth or something shocking like that. One guy?

That line in there—"What good is spilling blood/It will not grow a thing"—certainly resonates on this day, when there's a war on in that region.

Hunter: I find that song holds up well in the current situation, though it also has a basic naivety—sort of "Why can't we just be friends?" But some of the lines in there work still: "The ships of state sail on mirage and drown in sand."

How is it that Reflections *became half a Grateful Dead album and half a Garcia solo record?*

Garcia: Well, it was a continuation of what we were doing with *Blues for Allah*. We were having fun in the studio is what it boils down to, and that's pretty rare for us. The energy was there, and I thought, "I've got a solo album coming up. Let's cut these tracks with the Grateful Dead. I've already taught them the tunes." So we just went ahead and recorded "Might As Well," "They Love Each Other," and "Comes a Time."

Hunter: Wasn't "Mission in the Rain" on there, too?

Garcia: Yeah, but that wasn't the Grateful Dead on the record. That was my band.

You've described that song as being essentially from your point of view.
Garcia: Right, it's autobiographical, though I didn't write it. [Laughs]
Hunter: I often write for Jerry that way. Over the years I've learned what he'll accept and what he'll reject, and what he'll accept is what he can feel speaks for him. Although we did have some problem with "Foolish Heart," where he wasn't sure where it was coming from.
Garcia: I didn't know it was good advice.
Hunter: He trusted me on it. I think it's good advice, but perhaps it's only minimal advice and maybe you don't really need to know this; maybe it's not a world-shaking issue.
Garcia: I trust Hunter. I just need to find something in the song, some kind of reality, that means something to me. In other words, if I don't feel totally comfortable singing it, I feel like an idiot. And if I feel like an idiot, I know I won't be able to deliver the song worth a shit.

Have there been any songs where you've taken it one way and then later discovered that Hunter was, even obliquely, probably writing it at you?
Garcia: Yeah, sometimes I get the weirdest feeling: I'll be singing a song and I'll think, "Jesus Christ, is this about me? Holy cow!" [Laughs]
Hunter: I'll never tell! [Laughs]
Garcia: I don't even think it matters.
Hunter: We are all one. I mean if I was trying to put something over on him like that, it's got to be filtered through me, and I've got to understand it, and in order to understand it I've got to have experienced it—
Garcia: And if he's experienced it, he knows as much about it as I do! [Laughs]
Hunter: [To Jerry] There are a lot of songs I've written for myself that I wouldn't lay on you because maybe they're not the way you think about things.

Is it a requirement of the partnership that you have to keep tabs, in a sense, on each other's emotional terrain?
Garcia: Nah. I think it's intuitive. I don't think we've ever really even discussed it.
Hunter: You don't change much after eighteen, nineteen, except in the details. We don't talk that much. We don't have that much to say to each other besides "How'd you like Hawaii?" and "How's your new word processor working?"
Garcia: [Laughs] Right, regular stuff.

It seems like the next big burst of creativity following **Blues for Allah** *came with* **Terrapin Station** *and all those great songs on* **Cats Under the Stars.**

Garcia: That's some of my favorite stuff. "Reuben and Cherise" started around the time of *Blues for Allah,* but it was completely different. I had a little riff I was fond of—a cute little thing where each time [the riff came around] it got a little shorter. It was a little trick, like a vanishing box; an optical illusion, or musical illusion. "Hey look at this!" So I played it and Hunter studied it, and he came up with some lyrics. And the lyrics were so much better than my musical idea; the melody sounded diddley in comparison. He was already enunciating some of that *Black Orpheus* undercurrent. [*Black Orpheus* is Marcel Camus' 1960 film, which retells the Orpheus myth in a Brazilian *Carnaval* setting.] So I backburnered it for a while. I came back and looked at it, and he'd changed it again, then I changed it, he changed it, and we went back and forth. Then, when I started work on *Cats Under the Stars* it seemed right all of a sudden and it all clicked into place and I wrote that setting for it. It was one of those songs that had to be slammed and banged and adjusted before it was right. Usually if you work that long on something it ends up sounding forced, but in this case all that work became invisible and the result is a nice, sophisticated song that's invisibly complex. It slides right along and has a great narrative drive that exposes the lyrics in a nice way, and it also has some dramatic contour to it that makes it a better storytelling form than some things we've done.

Hunter: I'd just like to add that "Ruby froze and turned to stone" does not mean that Ruby died. It just meant that she was in a state of shock at hearing her rival's voice through a mandolin. If you think she died there you're going to get the whole song wrong. I know there are people who are confused on that point.

Maybe they're confusing it with "Gomorrah."

Garcia: Well, it and "Gomorrah" share that thing of not looking behind; no point in looking back. That ends up being sort of the underside of *Cats Under the Stars,* which as far as I'm concerned, is my most successful record—even though it's my least successful record.

Hunter: That is such a great record!

Garcia: I know. I've always really loved it and it just never went anywhere.

Hunter: You should get a cake every year on the release date of that thing!

Garcia: [Laughs] I'll never understand it!

Why would a song like "Reuben and Cherise" be a solo tune instead of a Grateful Dead tune?

Garcia: No reason. It could've been a Grateful Dead song. In fact, who knows—I certainly enjoy doing it, and it might be perfect for the Grateful Dead. [In fact, the Dead debuted the song a few weeks after this interview.]

Hunter: When I perform, except for things like dyed-in-the-wool favorites like "Ripple," I get the best response for "Reuben and Cherise."

Garcia: Yeah, when I do it with my band they love it, too, though our version is a little raggedy-assed. It's a fun song to do.

Hunter: I get into it so much that I'm down there in hell with Reuben trying to bring Cherise out. I'm wrung out by the time it's over.

Garcia: Me, too. It's tough to do. You have to be at a certain level to even try it. I don't try it that often for that very reason.

I think "Althea" is one of your most interesting songs—

Garcia: [To Hunter] What is she—the anima? The helpful lady, big sister kind of . . .

Hunter: I don't know if it's the anima, I'm not a Jungian.

Garcia: Me neither. [Laughs] I don't know. I see her out there.

Hunter: You evoke her; you don't say what she is.

Garcia: She's beyond description.

Hunter: Minerva.

Garcia: Right. Your helpful god-woman.

Hunter: Or Athena. Sure.

The whole thing is just an evocation of her, in the same way that a song like "She Belongs to Me" just offers these flashes of feeling more than information about the main character. It's more mood than anything else.

Garcia: Well, sometimes the mood is the thing, and it says it better than anything else does.

What can you tell me about the writing of "Shakedown Street"?

Garcia: For the life of me, I can't remember that either. [Laughs]

Hunter: Well, okay, the days were ripe with disco—

Garcia: Right! Disco!

I was pretty horrified the first few times I heard it—the Grateful Dead go disco?

Hunter: It was a case of abusing the audience and their expectations.
Garcia: "This'll throw 'em!" [Laughs]

Are the types of melodies and rhythms you write sometimes dictated by
a desire to investigate a specific kind of musical terrain? I was thinking
that the jam in "Shakedown" has some of the flavor of what you used
to get into on "Hard to Handle."
Garcia: Sure. You think of songs as having different kinds of functions.
We have our version of the "Come all ye"—"Uncle John's Band"; flag-
wavers. I might say to Hunter, "This is a song that happens late in the
second set, and it wants to be . . . " There's enough personal Grateful
Dead material around that we can refer to it stylistically, 'cause we know
how the songs work and what their function is. Luckily we have a lot
of range, all the way from something really sensitive like "Stella Blue"
to something real rowdy. We can get real grand like "Terrapin" or real
simple like some folk song. There are more possibilities than limitations
in that range.
Hunter: There are still holes in the Grateful Dead to fill up. It's mostly
painted right now, but there are still spots on the canvas that aren't filled
in.

Is it something you articulate to each other?
Hunter: What's the point of articulating it? We know. If you can say
it, there isn't much point in writing it. It's what you can't say that you
have to write.

Roots

■ ■ ■ ■ ■ ■

Under the Dead's Covers

People seeing the Grateful Dead for the first time are invariably confused by the incredibly broad range of song styles the band attempts during a given show. Most fans of conventional rock 'n' roll are accustomed to hearing bands stay within certain musical parameters—a band may show hints of blues or country roots, for example, but most groups work hard to develop a distinctive sound that doesn't really show those roots. (And now, of course, there are bands whose roots are the bands who tried to escape their roots. No wonder so many new groups are bland.)

Needless to say, the Grateful Dead are an exception to the above. A country tune like "Big River" might be followed by an obviously blues-inspired original like Garcia's "West L.A. Fadeaway." New Orleans R&B sits side by side with songs that have complicated jazz voicings. Old folk songs are juxtaposed with vintage rock 'n' roll tunes and Dead songs that defy genre classification. For instance, what style is "Playin' in the Band"? Certainly there are heavy country shadings—Garcia's guitar fills sometimes sound like pedal steel—but is it truly a "country song"? And what of songs like "St. Stephen," "Help on the Way," "Let it Grow"? Somewhere along the line, the Dead decided, unlike virtually all of their contemporaries, that almost any musical tradition that moved them was worth incorporating in the ever-expanding group gestalt. Nothing was rejected because "we don't play that kind of music." Instead, the dynamic of the band was shaped around and by the interaction that developed from the stylistically divergent players tackling different kinds of songs. They were unselfconscious eclectics whose music reflected the openness of the late-Sixties youth aesthetic, which was molded by an unending bombardment of old and new ideas. In many ways, the Dead were analogous to the original San Francisco poster artists, who fashioned a startlingly original style by drawing from myriad art traditions—American Indian, oriental, Tantric, European engravings, art nouveau, etc.—and mixing them in a madcap reverie of art and life itself.

The Dead's eclecticism came naturally, given the players' backgrounds in country, blues, jazz, and rock 'n' roll. That they managed to take their disparate influences and forge a style of music that was both cohesive *and* a rich amalgamation of different approaches, is truly miraculous and undoubtedly a major reason why the Dead have not become stale. They are still open to new influences as they continue to reexamine and reinterpret their old ones.

The group's choice of cover songs through the years says a great deal about where their music came from and about the concerns of the individual members. Far from being a motley collection of completely unrelated tunes, the bulk of the Dead's covers have an underlying thematic thrust that is also underscored by the lyrics of many group originals. Over and over again we encounter characters on the run—from the law, bad romantic entanglements, mean bossmen, simple poverty—and looking for a better life in a world that seems to be conspiring against them. The Dead's covers are frequently songs of defiance, but almost as often, of humbling realizations. None of the characters in this cornucopia of old blues, folk, and country songs has any grand answers—only the hopeful knowledge that *somewhere* the grass is greener, the sun is shining, and there's fun to be had. (No doubt many of you occasionally feel, as I do, that Dead shows are that place in today's world.)

The importance of all these songs and music styles goes beyond the choice to cover them. Many songs the Dead themselves have written show traces of music from the various eras represented, and Robert Hunter's lyrics and song themes were heavily influenced by older styles.

"Casey Jones" is, of course, an old story, though the Dead's song is obviously their own. It is based on a real train wreck that occurred on the Illinois Central Railroad's Chicago–New Orleans line April 30, 1900. The engine, driven by a John Luther Jones (known as K.C. or Casey because he hailed from Cayce, Kentucky, and because it differentiated him from other Joneses), did in fact leave Memphis' station at quarter to nine and, after falling behind schedule, tried to make up time by speeding. There was a switching problem at one junction and Jones apparently ignored a signal to stop before he plowed into a stationary freight train's caboose. Jones was killed (he had one arm ripped off and his skull crushed), but his fireman (who probably *did* scream) jumped and saved his own life.

The incident almost instantly became fodder for songwriters of the day, and by 1909, T. Lawrence Siebert and Eddie Newton had written a pop hit about it. Over the years, various people have said that the Casey Jones saga occurred in *their* state (writers in Montana and Oregon claimed the wreck happened in their backyard) and Jones became heavily mythologized. The story crops up in black and white song traditions. A popular black version was recorded by Furry Lewis in 1928 as "Kassie Jones."

Another popular character in early twentieth century black music is the "Candyman," though most of the rural Southern tales about him are considerably more lascivious than Hunter's more involved story (e.g. "He's got a stick of candy nine inches long," etc.). It is also interesting to note that Hunter's opening line, "Come all you pretty women..." mirrors the narrative form of numerous older songs that essentially invite the listener to hear the tale. That sort of opening was very popular in early logging songs, such as "Blue Mountain Lake" and "The Jam on Jenny's Rocks."

"Stagger Lee," who pops up on the *Shakedown* album, is a fabled character who some suggest dates back to the Civil War. Variously called "Stag-O-Lee," "Stack-O-Lee," and other names, the song is about a scoundrel who killed Billy Lyons because he stole Stag's Stetson hat. Stag-O-Lee was upset about the death, though—because he failed to shoot Billy right between the eyes. Songwriters over the years have elaborated on the story, bringing in the bad man's deals with the devil, etc. It's been recorded often, by everyone from Mississippi John Hurt (his 1928 version is one of the first on record) to Professor Longhair and Doc and Merle Watson.

"Dupree's Diamond Blues" has its roots in a song variously called "Betty and Dupree" or just "Dupree." Unlike "Stagger Lee," which is basically American mythology by now, it is based on a well-documented incident: A white man from Abbeville, South Carolina, robbed an Atlanta jewelry store in December of 1921, and killed a policeman while fleeing from the scene. He was apprehended later and thrown into an Atlanta jail. He was hanged September 1, 1922. Even before he was executed, songs about Dupree sprang up in both white and black circles. The white versions tended to be somewhat flowery, but the black ones were more like Hunter's—in the form of conversations, and unromanticized. In Josh White's 1963 "Betty and Dupree," Dupree's mother blames Betty, his girlfriend, for turning her son bad. (After all, "jelly roll will drive you so mad.")

"Hunter and I always had this thing where we liked to muddy the folk tradition by adding our own versions of songs to the tradition," Garcia told me in 1989. "We had our 'Casey Jones' song. We had our 'Stagger Lee' song. 'Dupree's Diamond Blues' is another one of those. It's the thing of taking a well-founded tradition and putting in something that's totally looped. So *that's* Hunter's version of that. Originally, it's one of those cautionary tales; one of those 'Don't take your gun to town'–type tunes. So Hunter elaborated on that in a playful way."

Some titles and phrases in old songs that pop up in Hunter's writing: "Don't Let Your Deal Go Down" was an oft-covered gambling song that was popular with both card and craps players; "Buckdancer's Choice" (mentioned in "Uncle John's Band") is an old white mountain tune; "Truckin' " was a popular dance step, and the word is immortalized in a number of Twenties and Thirties songs, including the blues "Keep on Truckin' " and Blind Boy Fuller's "Truckin' My Blues Away." Sleepy John Estes recorded a song that was regionally popular called "Easin' Back to Tennessee"; "Mojo Hand" (mentioned in "Ramble On Rose") was a common term among rural blacks for a person with extraordinary or seemingly magical abilities, and was the name of a song recorded by Lightnin' Hopkins. Hopkins also recorded a song called "Mr. Charlie" years before Hunter and Pigpen wrote theirs.

And finally, there is "Terrapin," which is a reworked version of an old English ballad called "Lady of Carlisle" (which Hunter has recorded, even). That song begins with a line Hunter uses in his first verse for "Lady With a Fan"—"Down in Carlisle there lived a lady . . ." That

story, for those who might be confused by Hunter's poetic telling, goes
as follows:

A fair lady is approached by two men, a brave lieutenant and a cou-
rageous sea captain. The lady doesn't know how to choose between them
so she sets up a test of sorts. She leads them to a lion's den and throws
her fan into the beast's domain, saying, "Which of you to gain a lady
will return her fan again?" The soldier replies, "I will not give my life
for love," but the sailor says, "I will return her fan or die." And so the
sailor does take the risk . . . "And when she saw her true lover coming/
Seeing no harm had been done to him/She threw herself against his
bosom/Saying, 'Here is the prize that you have won.'"

It is typical of Hunter's genius that he takes that relatively simple story
and turns it into an epic tale, and typical of the Dead that they could
transform a story from a culture seemingly far removed from their own
into an allegory about love, courage, resolve, and much more.

The Grateful Dead have exposed me to countless kinds of music I
probably would not have encountered had I not been curious about the
origins of this or that song. And so, for the benefit of those who hunger
to know more about the Dead's roots—and perhaps hear some great,
great music in the process—I've put together the following compendium
of songs the Dead have covered through the years. There are a few that
have eluded me, but most of them are here.

"Ain't It Crazy" This is one of the few tunes that was played both by
Mother McCree's Uptown Jug Champions and later the Dead (though
very infrequently). It was a humorous Pigpen vehicle, with its raunchy,
suggestive lyrics. The authorship of the song was claimed by Sam "Lightnin' " Hopkins, the Texas blues and folk singer, and it can be found on
an early Sixties live album on the Prestige label called *Hootin' the Blues*.

Hopkins' career was long and colorful, spanning some sixty years. He
quit school early to bum around playing music in the streets of Houston.
There he met and learned from the great Blind Lemon Jefferson. He
worked as a laborer and served a couple of short prison stretches in the
Thirties, and it wasn't until the mid-Forties that he began recording. In
1947 he had two hits, "Short Haired Woman" and "Baby Please Don't
Go," the latter an oft-covered nugget (Muddy Waters had great success
with the tune, too). His career faded in the early Fifties, but he enjoyed
a second wave of popularity beginning in 1959, thanks to his "rediscovery" by blues historian Sam Charters prior to the folk and blues boom.
He died in 1982.

Lightnin' Hopkins, one of Pigpen's big influences and originator of "Ain't It Crazy."
(Photo by Chris Strachwitz)

Incidentally, "Ain't It Crazy" is the song that frequently turns up on Dead tapes identified as "The Rub."

"All Along the Watchtower" One of Dylan's undisputed master-pieces, "Watchtower" originally appeared on 1968's *John Wesley Harding,* the first album he recorded following his famous motorcycle accident, and perhaps his most esoteric record ever. It was *the* radio song from that album, although it didn't get much airplay outside of hip FM sta-tions. The rest of young America learned the song through Jimi Hendrix, whose version on his 1968 *Electric Ladyland* LP is still definitive in my opinion. Not only was *Ladyland* one of the most popular albums of the late Sixties, "Watchtower" was Hendrix's only Top 40 single—it hit number 20 in September 1968.

Dylan had this to say about the song in the liner notes of his five-record *Biograph* album in 1985: "I liked Jimi Hendrix's record of this and ever since he died I've been doing it that way. Funny though, his way of doing it and my way of doing it weren't that dissimilar; I mean the meaning of the song doesn't change like when some artists do other artists' songs. Strange, though, how when I sing it I always feel like it's a tribute to him in some kind of way. . . . I was thinking about him the other night—I really miss him a lot, him and Lennon. 'All Along the Watchtower' probably came to me during a thunder and lightning storm. I'm sure it did."

Three live versions of the song have appeared on records: *Before the Flood,* recorded in 1974 with The Band; *Bob Dylan at Budokan,* recorded in 1978 during what I call his "Elvis period" (white spangled jumpsuit, lounge-rock arrangements, etc.); and 1989's *Dylan and the Dead* LP.

"And We Bid You Goodnight" I first heard this song on the Incredible String Band's wonderful LP, *The Hangman's Beautiful Daughter.* (It was tucked into their epic composition, "A Very Cellular Song.") Simultaneously, the Dead were using the song, sung a capella, to close many of their late-Sixties shows. According to the String Band's Robin Williamson, who has been a successful solo performer since his ISB days, the song likely has its roots in English religious music. He and Heron, though, became interested in the song after hearing it performed by the Pindar family on a 1965 Nonesuch album called *The Real Bahamas,* which was popular in folk circles. Jenny Pindar was the sister of the Bahamas' greatest arranger and interpreter of religious songs, guitarist Joseph Spence. This might explain the slightly Caribbean lilt to the longer Dead versions of the song (the LP version has only a fraction of it), with its arching vocals and internal rhythms.

"Around and Around" Not to be confused with the better-known "Reelin' and Rockin'," this was one of the lesser songs from Chuck Berry's peak years. It became popular in the mid-Sixties because the Rolling Stones covered it on their 1964 smash, *12 x 5.* Berry's version is easily found on any number of hits collections—the definitive LP is probably *Chuck Berry's Golden Decade Vols. 1 & 2.*

"Baby What You Want Me to Do" This Jimmy Reed–penned tune is of relatively recent vintage, hitting the Top Ten of the R&B charts in 1960, the same year his "Big Boss Man" came out. Elvis Presley is among the many musicians who have covered "Baby What You Want Me to Do" over the years.

Reed was born and raised in the Mississippi Delta and, like many Southern blacks, traveled north to Chicago after the Second World War in search of a new life. He didn't begin seriously playing music until he was in his twenties. In one of those classic turns of fate that seem to happen so often, Reed's big break came one day when the singer on a session he was playing guitar on was too ill to play, so Reed sang a few of his own songs. The tapes knocked out Vee Jay Records, and a new career was launched for Reed, who'd been making ends meet working in a Gary, Indiana, foundry. Throughout the late Fifties and early Sixties, Reed scaled the R&B charts with his original blues tunes, which generally retained more of the Delta feeling than most of his Chicago blues contemporaries. Personally, I find his style a little lacking in fire and his arrangements a bit dull, but there is no denying the greatness of his songs. Reed died in Oakland in 1976 at the age of fifty.

"Beat It on Down the Line" The original recording of this one appears on a 1961 album called *The Lone Cat* by the song's author, Jesse Fuller. Fuller was a fixture on the Bay Area blues scene for many years, and the Dead were familiar with his records and local live performances.

Born into extreme poverty in Jonesboro, Georgia, in 1896, Fuller never really knew his natural parents, but was instead brought up by a couple who treated him "worse than a dog" until he managed to get out of the house at age nine and work as a cow grazer outside of Atlanta. Throughout his teens he worked for next to nothing in a lumber camp. He went west in the early Twenties, taking odd jobs and singing along the way. After a stay of several years in Los Angeles (he ran a hot dog stand inside the United Artists film lot and even appeared as an extra in two films) he moved to Oakland, where he lived until he died a few years ago. During those decades, he worked variously as a laborer for Southern-Pacific Railroad (hence the train imagery that fills so many of his songs), a shipbuilder, and farm laborer. He was "discovered" in the mid-Fifties playing in Bay Area clubs and bars, and recorded his first record in 1955. Never particularly well-known, Fuller was nonetheless a fine songwriter and interpreter whose songs vividly spoke of a life of hard times and hard work, while still exhibiting great spirit and even humor.

An interesting aspect of his talent (and Weir even alludes to this before the May 5, 1970, version of Fuller's "The Monkey and the Engineer") was that he made some of his own musical instruments, including a huge stand-up bass called a fotdella, which he would play with his right foot in solo performances.

"Big Boss Man" A relatively contemporary blues, this song was a rhythm and blues hit for Jimmy Reed (1895–1976) in 1961. The song was cowritten by Reed and his manager/producer Al Smith (who was also famous for his work with Memphis Minnie and Tampa Red) and appears on several Reed albums, including *Big Boss Man, The New Jimmy Reed Album,* and *Jimmy Reed at Carnegie Hall.* Mance Lipscomb also cut the song in 1964 for Arhoolie Records (*Mance Lipscomb, Vol. 3*). (See "Baby What You Want Me to Do.")

"Big Boy Pete" This song, which the Dead played a few times from 1966 through 1970, and once in 1985, is about as close to a "novelty" song as the Dead have come. That's not surprising when you consider that it was originally recorded by the Olympics, a Los Angeles–based black quartet who had big hits with tunes such as "Peanut Butter" ("Well it tastes so good but it's so hard to chew . . . peanut, peanut butter"), "Hully Gully" (which the Dead played at least once, in Amsterdam in 1981), "The Bounce," and "Baby, Do the Philly Dog," mainly in the early Sixties. "Big Boy Pete" was originally issued in 1960, then again in 1965 as "Big Boy Pete '65." The first time it clicked with record buyers, the second time it did not. It was also covered in the mid-Sixties by the Tidal Waves (from Detroit) and the Kingsmen (from Portland, Oregon), who altered the lyrics to it to make their "Jolly Green Giant" hit. All of the Olympics' big hits are included on a fine Rhino Records album called *The Official Record Album of the Olympics,* released in 1984. This is great party music!

"Big Railroad Blues" Another classic tale of a loser who didn't listen to good ol' mom's advice (like "Mama Tried"), this was recorded originally as a 78 by Cannon's Jug Stompers (see "New New Minglewood Blues") in 1928 for the Victor label.

"Big River" Johnny Cash became such a popular country music figure in the late Sixties, thanks to a few hits and a popular TV show, that many people forget his best recordings were his work for Sun Records in the middle and late Fifties, when he was regularly hanging out and playing with labelmates Jerry Lee Lewis, Elvis Presley, and Carl Perkins. "Big River" was one of his early classics, and it appears on a Columbia CD box set spanning his entire career. Later, when he moved to Columbia, the song turned up on the *Johnny Cash* LP (out of print), as well as *I Walk the Line*. (The title song of that one was his first Sun single and also available on Sun reissues.)

"C. C. Rider" This is better known as "See See Rider," as the title refers not to someone's name, but to a mistreated lover's command in the first verse: "See, see, rider/see what you have done." The authorship of this traditional blues is unknown and it certainly dates back to pre-recording days. The first successful recorded version was a 1925 Paramount 78 by the great Gertrude "Ma" Rainey and her Georgia Jazz Band. On the record the song is credited to Rainey and Lena Arant, and through the years, others have credited Rainey with the composition.

Rainey was one of the most popular blues and jazz singers of the 1920s, and her bands frequently contained players who were either already well known or who would become famous later, among them: Louis Armstrong, Kid Ory, Don Redman, Coleman Hawkins, Tampa Red, and Fletcher Henderson. Among the multitude of artists who have covered the song in the past sixty years are Armstrong, John Lee Hooker, Chuck Berry, Big Bill Broonzy, Champion Jack Dupree, Mississippi John Hurt, B.B. King, Jerry Lee Lewis, and even Duke Ellington.

"Cocaine Habit Blues" The Dead played this song a few times during their 1970 acoustic sets. The original was recorded in 1930 by Will Shade's Memphis Jug Band, the group responsible for the first recordings of "On the Road Again" and "Stealin'." Four years later, Leadbelly cut the tune under its more popular name, "Take a Whiff on Me." Its whimsical nature pretty much sums up the Twenties' and Thirties' attitude toward cocaine among black musicians. Good ol' "wacky dust"! The Memphis Jug Band recording is easily obtained on Yazoo Records' excellent anthology of their work.

"Cold Rain and Snow" This tune comes from the Eastern mountain music tradition, most likely the Blue Ridge Mountains of North Carolina or Virginia. Rarely recorded, this white blues has long been popular among old timey music groups. Pegging an "original" version is impossible since it dates back (at least) to the nineteenth century and is "folk" music in the truest since. Perhaps the best-known recording of the tune among country aficionados is one by Obray Ramsey on his long-out-of-print album from the late 1950s, *Obray Ramsey Sings Folksongs from Three Laurels*. Ramsey's version is much more akin to the way the Dead currently perform the song than the frenetic reading on the first Dead LP. A Bay Area old timey group called the Arkansas Sheiks recorded the song on their fine *Whiskey Before Breakfast* album in 1976.

"Dancin' in the Streets" One of the best-known tunes of the Motown era, "Dancin' " was a number 2 hit for Martha and the Vandellas in August of 1964 on the Gordy label. A 1966 Dead version appears on the Sunflower disc, *Vintage Dead*. The Dead's "disco" version pops up on *Terrapin Station*.

"Day Tripper" This Beatles classic was cut in the fall of 1965 and released initially as part of the group's first double-A-side single with "We Can Work It Out." It has been alternately interpreted as being about psychedelics (questionable given the date of its writing) and a clandestine love affair. Paul McCartney revealed in *Playboy* that the line that was commonly printed in songbooks as "She's a big teaser/she took me half the way there" is actually "She's a *prick* teaser . . . " Nasty boys, those Beatles.

"Dear Mr. Fantasy" This song was a well-loved staple of Sixties rock radio, and the potency of the Dead's version attests to its staying power. It was originally recorded by the very popular band Traffic on their debut album, titled *Mr. Fantasy,* and cowritten by the three main members of the group, Jim Capaldi, Chris Wood, and Steve Winwood, who sang it. *Mr. Fantasy* was recorded in London's Olympic Studios in the fall of 1967 with Jimmy Miller producing.

"It was quite a weird circumstance that we wrote that song," Capaldi told me by phone from his London home. "It was the summer of 1967 and we were all living in this cottage in Berkshire [in the English countryside]. We were one of the first English bands to live together like that—we thought we'd try it and see if anything came of it. I know people over there [in San Francisco] were doing it, too.

"I remember the day very clearly. A bunch of friends came over early in the day and we had quite a party. It was sunny and the corn was coming up nicely around the cottage and we were *quite* enjoying ourselves," he continues with a knowing chuckle that suggests that various consciousness-altering agents helped make the day memorable. "As things finally wound down in the evening I was sitting around just doodling, as I would often do, drawing this character. It was this little fellow with a spiked sun hat. He was holding some puppeteer's strings, and the puppet hands on the end of the strings were playing a guitar. Under that I just scribbled some words: 'Dear Mr. Fantasy, play us a tune, something to make us all happy'... and on a bit. It was nice, but I didn't think much of it. Certainly it wasn't intended to be a song.

"I crashed out eventually, but I remember hearing Steve and Chris playing around after. The next day I woke up and found that they'd written a song around the words and drawing I'd done. I was completely knocked out by it. Chris wrote that great bass line. We added some more words later and worked out a bigger arrangement, too. Those were very happy days for Traffic."

When the group later went into the studio to record "Dear Mr. Fantasy," "We tried originally to record it regularly, with all of us in little booths and all," Capaldi remembers, "but we weren't *feeling* anything. So we got rid of the booths and all played together in this big room. Eddie [Kramer, who engineered the session] was flicking the lights on and off, and Jimmy [Miller] was running around shaking these maracas. It was quite a scene. We ended up cutting the song very live."

Traffic and the Grateful Dead shared several bills together in the late Sixties, and Garcia and Hart each jammed with Traffic on several occasions. "I quite like the Grateful Dead, their approach," Capaldi says. "If you see them, tell them it was fun..." and he laughs heartily.

"Death Don't Have No Mercy" Reverend Gary Davis' influence on the Dead goes beyond simple song choices. Weir actually took a lesson or two from this deeply religious singer-guitarist-teacher. He didn't write "Death Don't Have No Mercy"—it's a traditional blues—but his version is certainly the best known. Always a devout Baptist, Davis began recording in 1935. Though he is thought of as a blues singer, he actually rejected conventional blues to a degree, instead singing blues-based spirituals, like "Samson and Delilah" and others. In the Forties he moved to New York, where he played the streets of the South Bronx and gave guitar lessons. Like many bluesmen, he was "discovered" in the early Sixties. His version of "Death Don't Have No Mercy" (as well as "Samson and Delilah") can be found on an excellent Fantasy reissue called *When I Die I'll Live Again*. Hot Tuna recorded the song on its first album.

"Death Letter Blues" Since not many songlists from the late Sixties exist, it's difficult to tell whether this song was played more than just a couple of times, or whether it was played at all outside of Mickey and the Hartbeats shows at the Matrix in San Francisco. Whatever the case, it is one of the best-known tunes sung by the great folk-blues singer Leadbelly (a.k.a. Huddie Ledbetter). Though he is commonly credited with writing "Death Letter Blues," it was probably an adaptation of a traditional Texas blues. By the time Leadbelly made his first recordings for the American Record Company in 1935 (following a stretch in prison for attempted murder) he'd already been a street musician for many years, singing popular blues and his own songs. It's quite possible he learned the song from Blind Lemon Jefferson, greatest of the early Texas bluesmen and a big influence on Leadbelly. Leadbelly's original recording of the song can be found on a fine Columbia Records anthology, simply titled *Leadbelly*. It also appears as a cut on one volume of his final, early Sixties sessions for Folkways.

"Deep Elem Blues" The word "Elem" (also spelled "Ellem") is a corruption of "Elm," referring to a street in Dallas that was the center of a lively (and dangerous) red light district that was a hotbed of sin and music until the Thirties. There were hookers, musicians, and singers all over the streets, and a number of fine singers, including Blind Lemon Jefferson, played there. The oldest version I could find of the song was by the Lone Star Cowboys, who cut it as a 78 in 1933. It appears on an excellent CD anthology called *Are You from Dixie?* on RCA. No doubt, though, the song is older and of Negro origin. "Elem" is also mentioned in Henry Thomas' original "Don't Ease Me In."

"Devil with a Blue Dress On"–"Good Golly Miss Molly" The earlier of the two is "Good Golly Miss Molly," which was a Top Ten hit for Little Richard in February 1958. The song was cowritten by Little Richard and Bumps Blackwell, his producer at Specialty Records. The Swinging Bluejeans scored with an ultra-wimpoid version of the song in 1964, and then in 1966 it was fused to "Devil with a Blue Dress On" by those Detroit bad boys, Mitch Ryder and the Detroit Wheels. (Ryder wrote "Devil . . .") More recently, the medley was popularized by Bruce Springsteen, whose live version on the *No Nukes* benefit album a few years ago was a radio staple. His version also included Little Richard's "Jenny Jenny," which Mitch Ryder had combined with "C. C. Rider" a few months before he waxed the "Devil..."–"Good Golly..." combo.

"Don't Ease Me In"   Yet another popular folk and jug band number in the late Fifties and early Sixties, "Don't Ease Me In" was originally recorded in the late Twenties by Henry Thomas, who generally traveled under his hobo moniker, Ragtime Texas. The child of slaves, Thomas lived in East Texas and worked on the Texas-Pacific Railroad. He was middle-age when he made his only recordings, which have been compiled on several anthologies.

The Dead's version is fairly similar to Thomas', although Thomas' vocal is more plaintive, almost sounding like Hank Williams (whom he predated, of course). One lyric difference that's worth noting arose, no doubt, from the song being passed down through the years by players who either didn't understand the original lyrics, or chose to make them less specific. On *Go to Heaven,* the chorus is "Don't ease, don't ease/ Don't ease me in/I've been all night long coming home/Don't ease me in." But on Thomas' original, he sings: "Don't ease, don't you ease/Ah, don't ease me in/It's a long night, *Cunningham,* don't ease me in." The Cunningham in the song was a well-known Texas businessman of the era who would lease convicts to work his sugarcane fields along the Brazos River. According to Mack McCormick's biography of Thomas on a Herwin Records album by Thomas, "Don't Ease Me In" was often heard along the Brazos in various local prison farms. I confess to mild bafflement on what the actual phrase "don't ease me in" means in the context of the song, but a 1929 song called "Easin' In" by Texas blues singer Bobby Cadillac clearly has some sort of sexual implication.

"Down in the Bottom"   Not to be confused with a better-known blues tune called "Meet Me at the Bottom," which has been covered by the likes of Big Joe Williams, Lightnin' Hopkins, and Brownie McGhee, "Down in the Bottom" is yet another Willie Dixon song originally covered by Chester Burnett, better known as Howlin' Wolf. The original version appeared on *Howlin' Wolf* (also known as "The Rocking Chair Album" because of the cover photo), which was released in 1961 by Chess Records. That LP also contains the originals of "Spoonful," "Wang Dang Doodle," and "Little Red Rooster." Fronting a band that featured Dixon himself on bass, guitarist Jimmy Rogers, drummer Sam Lewis, and pianist Johnny Jones, Wolf recorded what must be considered some of the most powerful urban blues ever during the late Fifties and early

Sixties. (I saw him a couple of times in the early Seventies in Chicago and he was still an overpowering presence.)

Wolf's "Down in the Bottom" doesn't quite echo "Minglewood" the way the Dead's few versions did, but Weir and Co. did capture its spirit effectively. Nick Gravenites, a fixture on the Bay Area rock and blues scene (and a frequent musical partner of John Cipollina's) has long included the song in his repertoire, too.

"El Paso" This was one of the biggest country hits of all time and it firmly established its author, Marty Robbins, as a mega-star shortly after it came out in 1959. Story-songs were all the rage in country music in the late Fifties, as the success of musical sagas such as "The Battle of New Orleans," "Long Black Veil," "Ten Thousand Drums," and Robbins' "Hangin' Tree" attest. With its strong Mexican flavor and linear storyline, "El Paso" is reminiscent of the great *corridos* that were sung in old Mexico. The original appears on a still-in-print LP called *Gunfighter Ballads*. Robbins also wrote "Big Iron," which was covered by both Kingfish and Bobby and the Midnites.

"Gimme Some Lovin' " This tune was written by Steve Winwood at the age of 16 when he was the *wunderkind* keyboardist and primary singer of England's Spencer Davis Group (which also included Steve's brother Muff on bass). It was a monster hit in both the United Kingdom and United States in late 1966–early 1967 and became another garage band standard of the late 1960s, with its irresistible beat and famous organ line that, with Procol Harum's "Whiter Shade of Pale," helped put the Hammond B-3 organ on the map. Winwood's version appears on any number of easily obtainable Spencer Davis hits compilations.

"Gloria" A staple of every garage band of the late Sixties (I once saw a thirty-minute version by a Connecticut band called the Other Half that was so dirty it would have made the Fugs blush), "Gloria" was written by Van Morrison when he was still lead singer for Them, the great Belfast-based rock and R&B band. They had a hit in England with the song in 1965, and it was a minor hit in the United States. The Shadows of Knight had the big United States hit with the song shortly after that, though their version is clearly inferior. Van has performed the song on and off over the years.

"Goin' Down the Road Feeling Bad" This is one of those songs that have been a popular part of both black and white musical traditions for many decades. According to noted folk and blues authority Dave Evans of Memphis State, the tune is of Negro origin, but it surfaced as an Appalachian Mountain tune in the Twenties. It became a popular song among Okies during the dustbowl era (for obvious reasons) and as impoverished farmers fled the Southwest, they took the song with them to California's blossoming fruit orchards, the beet farms of Michigan, Oregon's cherry orchards, and a hundred other points scattered around the land. As the song traveled, the verses changed frequently, so that the Dead's version is a hodgepodge of lyric ideas from all over, most likely. For instance, a couple of the verses in the first Okie versions contained such sentiments as "Ain't got but one old lousy dime (three times)/But I'll find me a new dollar some day," and "A two dollar shoe won't fit my feet, (three times)/Ain't gonna be treated this way."

"Good Lovin' " The only musician to come from my hometown of Pelham, New York, who ever amounted to much in the pop world was Felix Cavaliere, leader of the Young Rascals. It was the bucks he made from recording Arthur Resnick and Rudy Clark's "Good Lovin' " on the Rascals' Atlantic debut album of 1966 (*The Young Rascals*), as well as several hits he cowrote, that financed the sports cars we'd see Felix drive around town in. The song has had a couple of very different incarnations in the Dead, from Pigpen's driving soul version (always a great jamming song) to Weir's current reading, which has an almost calypso feel in places. The Olympics (see "Big Boy Pete") had a minor hit with the song before the Rascals did.

"Good Morning Little Schoolgirl" There are a few different tunes with this title; the song the Dead covered in the late Sixties with Pigpen at the helm was originally recorded by blues great Sonny Boy Williamson in 1937, but popularized a decade later by a relatively obscure Texas blues singer named Smokey Hogg. Born in Westconnie, Texas, in 1914, Hogg learned to play guitar at an early age and was part of a wide circuit of musicians who played country dances. He was well-versed in a number of different styles—blues, ballads, pop songs of the day, even cowboy tunes. As a blues singer he was most heavily influenced by such early recording stalwarts as Peetie Wheatstraw, Leroy Carr, and Big Bill Broonzy, but he also forged a distinctive style of his own and he amassed quite a following in central Texas. In 1937 he went to Chicago to record his first sides for Decca. Over the next two decades he made records for more than twenty different labels, occasionally scoring small regional hits. He hit the national R&B top ten twice: in 1948 with a song called "Long Tall Mama," and in 1950 with "Little School Girl," the song the Dead later covered. Both of the tunes featured Hogg backed by the Hadda Brooks Trio. While other Texas blues singers of the Forties and Fifties embraced different styles to keep up with shifting pop music tastes, Hogg—like his cousin, Lightnin' Hopkins—remained true to his blues roots for most of his career. He died of a hemorrhaged ulcer in 1960.

"Good Times" Not to be confused with Brent's "Good Times Blues," or various songs called "Let the Good Times Roll" by everyone from Shirley and Lee to Ray Charles, this song was written and recorded in 1964 by the late, great Sam Cooke (though the debt to Shirley and Lee's 1956 song is obvious).

Cooke was one of the most distinctive and versatile singers of the late Fifties and early Sixties, equally comfortable singing velvety smooth ballads and bright soul-pop. In some ways he's the link between the middle-of-the-road stylings of Nat King Cole and the grittier, gospel-tinged soul of Otis Redding.

Born in Chicago in 1935, Cooke was the son of a Baptist minister, so he grew up singing gospel music exclusively. While still a teenager he became the lead singer of the Soul Stirrers, one of the top gospel groups of the early Fifties. His secular debut came in 1956 with the song "Lovable," but it wasn't until a year later that he scored the lone number one hit of his career, "You Send Me." Over the next seven years he had a whopping twenty-nine singles jump into the *Billboard* Top 40, making him perhaps the most successful black artist of that era. Among his biggest hits were "Chain Gang," "Wonderful World," "Cupid," "Having a Party," "Twistin' the Night Away," "Shake," and "Good Times," which made it all the way up to number eleven in June of 1964. (The flip side of that single, "Tennessee Waltz," was also a hit.) The out-of-print RCA album on which "Good Times" appears is called *Ain't That Good News*. But you can probably find it on a good Cooke anthology.

The Rolling Stones also cut the song on their 1965 album, *Out of Our Heads,* which the Dead were certainly very familiar with. And here's a nice little scoop: Garcia himself wrote the lyrics to the verse he sings: "It might be six o'clock, it might be eight/Don't matter if it's gettin' late/We gonna make the band play one more song/Get in the groove if it takes all night long . . ."

What ever became of Sam Cooke? some of you are no doubt asking. Well, the sad truth is he was shot and killed in a Los Angeles motel room in December of 1964 following a dispute with a jealous lover.

"Green, Green Grass of Home" Thematically, this wistful classic about a condemned man has some of the feeling of Merle Haggard's "Sing Me Back Home." The Dead performed "Green, Green Grass of Home" a few times in 1969, four years after it was a Top Five country hit for Porter Wagoner. It was written by Curly Putman, a 1975 inductee into the Country Songwriters' Hall of Fame who also wrote "D-I-V-O-R-C-E" for Tammy Wynette.

These days, Porter Wagoner is probably best remembered as Dolly Parton's singing partner on TV and records from 1967 to 1974, but actually the Missourian's long career dates back to the mid-Fifties, when "A Satisfied Mind" became his first number one record. Beginning in 1960 he hosted a syndicated country music TV show; by the early Seventies it had an estimated viewership of 45 million!

Unlike many of his contemporaries, Wagoner has remained true to his country roots through the years, resisting the temptation to dilute his style with pop clichés. He has also recorded country gospel music throughout his career. It's been a while since his last hit (1983's "This Cowboy Hat"), but with three decades of TV work, touring, and eighty-one records on the charts, we don't have to worry about the sixty-two-year-old singer's retirement years.

"Hard to Handle" Much to his credit, Pigpen derived his material from the best—in this case the late Otis Redding, who cowrote "Hard to Handle" with Allen Jones and Alvertis Isabell in the mid-Sixties. Born in Macon, Georgia, in 1941, Redding was heavily influenced by fellow Maconite Little Richard and soul master Sam Cooke early in his singing career. He soon developed a distinctive style which in turn was a major influence on numerous black and white singers of the Sixties and Seventies. His hits included "Respect," "I've Been Loving You Too Long," "Try a Little Tenderness," "I Can't Turn You Loose," and "Sittin' On the Dock of the Bay," most of which he had a hand in writing. Arguably the greatest soul singer ever, Redding was killed in a plane crash in Wisconsin in December of 1967, just a few months after his triumphant appearance at the Monterey Pop Festival. No record library should be without a good Otis Redding collection, and fortunately there are many to choose from.

"He Was a Friend of Mine" This is generally attributed to Dylan, since he was the first to record it (for his first album, though it was not used) and publish it. But back in 1962, when that auspicious debut was released, he told a writer that he had learned the song from a Chicago street singer named Blind Arvella Gray, and then rewritten the lyrics. Indeed, the original copyright filed by Dylan indicates it is traditional with supplemental lyrics. At any rate, the first artist to release a record containing the song was folkie Dave Van Ronk. The most famous version, however, was cut by the Byrds in 1966, as a tribute to slain president John F. Kennedy. In fact, for about a year, David Crosby of the Byrds introduced the song with this inflammatory speech:

"We'd like to do a song about this guy who was a friend of ours. And just by way of mentionin' it, he was shot down in the street. As a matter of strict fact, he was shot down in the street by a very professional kind of outfit. Don't it make you sort of wonder? The Warren Report [the controversial "official" investigation of the Kennedy assassination] ain't the truth, that's plain to anybody. And it happened in your country. Don't you wonder why?"

Frankly, I doubt the Dead were thinking so topically. The song turned up in Dead sets from 1966 to 1969, though how often it was performed remains a mystery, since set lists from that period are so rare. Garcia sang lead, with Weir and Lesh struggling along with him on backup vocals.

"Hey Jude" The Dead had performed this song at least twice before they unexpectedly went into the famous "na-na-na" coda at the September 7, 1985, Red Rocks show. With Pigpen singing lead (weakly, I'm afraid), the band played the tune at the Fillmore East February 11, 1969, and the Fillmore West March 1, 1969.

The original was written by Paul McCartney, with some help from John Lennon, in July of 1968. According to McCartney, the song came to him as he was driving over to Lennon's house one day. Originally, he conceived it as "Hey Jules," written for Lennon's son Julian, who was despondent over the breakup of his parents' marriage. McCartney played what he had for John, and then the next day, July 26, they got together at Paul's house and finished the song. A couple of days later, they began recording it at EMI Studios in London, where the Beatles frequently worked. On August 1 they moved over to another big local studio, Trident, where they recorded the version that was eventually released. Augmenting the Beatles on the track was a forty-piece orchestra (Paul had originally wanted a full 100-piece orchestra), many of whom were also enlisted to sing on the four-minute fade. At more than seven minutes, "Hey Jude" is the longest single the Beatles ever released; indeed, it is one of the longest hits *anyone* has had. And what a hit it was: It sold close to eight million copies worldwide between its release, in the summer of 1968, and 1972. (Consider that only one or two singles a year manage to sell one million copies!) "Hey Jude" remains the best-selling Beatles record ever and, amazingly enough, the album on which it later appeared (a compilation of non-LP singles and B-sides called *Hey Jude*) outsold *Sgt. Pepper* and the White Album.

"Hey Pocky Way" Like "Iko-Iko," this song started out as a street chant among the black Mardi Gras "Indians" in New Orleans long before it was actually set to music. That task fell to the fabulous New Orleans rock-funksters, the Meters: Art Neville, Leo Nocentelli, Joseph "Ziga-boo" Modeliste, and George Porter. When Art Neville later formed the Neville Brothers, he brought several Meters tunes into their repertoire, including "Hey Pocky Way." The Nevilles' version appears on their 1981 LP, *Fiyo on the Bayou,* as well as a Rhino Records Nevilles anthology, *Treacherous.*

"Hog For You Baby" Another humorously raunchy Pigpen vehicle in the mid-Sixties, this came from the pens of noted hit-writers Jerry Leiber and Mike Stoller, who wrote it for the Los Angeles band the Coasters. They had a medium-size hit with it in 1959. Though white, Leiber and Stoller wrote scores of hits for numerous R&B sensations, including the aforementioned Coasters ("Searchin'," "Young Blood," "Charlie Brown," "Yakety Yak," "Poison Ivy"), the Drifters ("Fools Fall in Love"), Wilbert Harrison ("Kansas City"), and Ben E. King ("Stand By Me").

"I Ain't Superstitious" You probably won't be surprised to hear that this tune, too, is from the pen of Willie Dixon and was originally recorded by Howlin' Wolf. This is the sort of song that was perfectly suited to Wolf's growl. His version is most easily found on the Wolf reissue *Chess Masters Vol. III.* For my money, though, the definitive "I Ain't Super-stitious" is found on Jeff Beck's *Truth* album, with Rod Stewart on gritty lead vocals and Beck on howlin' *cat* guitar. (That album also includes a version of "Morning Dew.") Dixon's version of the song appears on his Columbia LP, *I Am the Blues,* a title that would seem boastful coming from anyone else *but* Dixon.

"I Know You Rider" This traditional black song has been passed around in different versions (with different verses added and subtracted) for over a century, though it has been recorded relatively few times. The term "rider" comes up often in early blues, usually to talk about a woman, but here is a case where the song has been popular sung from each gender's perspective. One example of a verse from a woman's point of view: "Lovin' you baby, just as easy as rollin off a log/But if I can't be your woman/I sure ain't gonna be your dog." The Dead used to sing a verse (pre-1971) that included a few of the key words from the above— "I'd rather drink muddy water, sleep in a hollow log/Than stay here in Frisco, be treated like a dog."

One more note on the term "rider": According to Bruce Jackson, author of *Wake Up Dead Man,* a book about early Texas prison songs, "rider" was also slang for the guards who would supervise prison laborers on horseback. The term found its way into some prison blues almost as a code word that the guards wouldn't understand. (If this were applied to the song in question, it lends the tune an interesting possible meaning— an inmate escaping prison and taking a guard's girl with him on the run!)

"Iko-Iko" This tune has an interesting and complicated origin. It definitely derives from African call-and-response chants, and it probably came over to the Americas with the first slaves. In Africa, people would put on ceremonial leaves for big celebrations, but initially, white plantation owners who used slaves in the eighteenth and nineteenth centuries prohibited that kind of behavior. Then, in the late-eighteenth century, whites evidently became fascinated with the black tribal chants and music and decided to allow the slaves one day a week to strut their stuff and whoop it up in New Orleans' Congo Square while the gentry watched. Over the years, different groups of blacks formed Mardi Gras "tribes," and the leaves gave way to feathers, most likely because of the influence of the Seminoles and other native Indian tribes (some of whom even owned slaves). The Mardi Gras tribes used their celebration days to fight each other as well as to get crazy, but the white powers that ruled put an end to the fighting in the 1890s and the "wars" evolved into battles of *style* and dressing up.

The song we know as "Iko-Iko" started out as two separate Mardi Gras chants. There is no real translation of the lyrics, but it adds up to gentle mocking of rival tribes, a thumbed nose as it were. "It was just something you grew up saying in the neighborhood," says the great New Orleans songwriter/producer Allen Toussaint." "You'd use it like a cocky argument. It has verses like, 'My spy boy saw your spy boy sittin' by the fi-yo./My spy boy told your spy boy, 'I'm gonna set your flag on fi-yo.'" ("Spy boys" are supposed to alert other tribe members when an "enemy" tribe approaches on Mardi Gras Day.)

Art Neville, of New Orleans' Neville Brothers, is more literal in his speculation about the meaning of "Iko": "I think it's a case where the pronunciation changed over the generations. It was 'Iko' by the time it got to Chief Jolly. It may have come from the word 'hike,' because that's what you'd do on Mardi Gras—hike all over the city, trying to see all the masks and the different parades. It was like you'd 'hike-o, hike-o all day.' I heard a couple of other definitions, too," he adds with a knowing, lascivious laugh, "but I don't know how true they are."

The first recorded version of "Iko-Iko" was "Jock-O-Mo," cut by a young New Orleans singer named James "Sugar Boy" Crawford for Checker Records in 1954. "I didn't really know much about the Indians and all that," he confessed when I reached him by phone at his New Orleans home, "but I'd heard these chants and I liked the sound of them, and so I just put a little tune to them. I can't take credit for the words, obviously, but I guess the tune is mine. I don't know, though. I never got any royalties."

Pianist Professor Longhair was undoubtedly the main influence on "Jock-O-Mo," which was a big regional hit for Sugar Boy Crawford. "I don't think people outside New Orleans knew what it was all about," Crawford says with a laugh. "But then, to be honest, I didn't, and still don't, have any idea what the words mean."

The next version of "Iko" worth noting was by the Dixie Cups, three New Orleans girls who had a fluke Top 20 national hit with the song in 1965. The group hadn't even intended to record the song and were actually just singing it casually in the studio—as any Mardi Gras–loving daughters of New Orleans might—when their producer, Phil Spector, surreptitiously turned on the tape machines. The trio, who still perform around New Orleans, are best remembered for the title tune of the album on which "Iko-Iko" appeared, "Chapel of Love."

In the late Sixties, an accomplished singer and instrumentalist named Mac Rebennack burst out of New Orleans as Dr. John the Night Tripper and was an immediate hit with fans of psychedelic music. Though his image—complete with feathered gowns and singers and dancers who seemed born of both Mardi Gras and Caribbean voodoo traditions—was somewhat contrived, his music was pure, based in Creole folk and New Orleans R&B. (Indeed, Rebennack did session work for Professor Longhair, Lee Allen, and other Crescent City greats in the Fifties and early Sixties.) As his career went on, he dropped the *gris-gris* trappings and instead helped pioneer modern New Orleans funk along with Allen Toussaint, his sometime collaborator and producer, and musical colleagues such as the Meters, who later evolved into the Neville Brothers. This triumvirate exerted considerable influence on music in the mid-Seventies, touching the Rolling Stones (who had the Meters open shows for them on one tour), Paul Simon, Paul McCartney, LaBelle, and numerous others. Dr. John's own recording of "Iko-Iko," which he says he recorded at the urging of J. Geils' Peter Wolf, strangely enough, appeared on his 1972 album *Gumbo*.

It was up to the Meters, and now the Nevilles, to really bring the Mardi Gras into contemporary pop music. Art Neville had played on local records for more than a decade before he formed the Meters in 1967. (He led a group called the Hawketts, who had a local hit with "Mardi Gras Mambo" in 1954.) In conjunction with the other members of the Meters, including Joseph "Zigaboo" Modeliste, a world-class drummer, Art successfully integrated traditional Mardi Gras tunes and chants into the band's otherwise funk-oriented repertoire. In 1975, the Meters joined forces with Art's uncle Chief Jolly and the Wild Tchoupitoulas to record their one eponymously titled LP for Antilles Records. (It's a classic and still available.) The Meters eventually broke up in an ugly dispute over the ownership of the band's name, and in 1977, Art and three of his brothers formed the Neville Brothers. *Their* version of "Iko-Iko" appears on the album *Fiyo on the Bayou* joined with "Brother John," written by Cyril Neville.

The Grateful Dead first played "Iko-Iko" in St. Louis on May 15, 1977, out of "St. Stephen," of all things. The song, which was played only rarely until 1987, is a natural for the Dead, both because of its interesting rhythm—so well suited to the two-drummer format—and because of its *attitude* and lyric ambiguity. Like Allen Toussaint says, you *know* what it's saying. It's a call to party *down* and strut your stuff, and, to paraphrase, "If you don't like what the GD say, jockomo feena nay!"

"I Second That Emotion" The Dead performed this song only a few times in the early Seventies, but it remains a part of the Jerry Garcia Band's repertoire to this day. The song was originally recorded by Smokey Robinson and the Miracles for Motown in 1967. It was an instant smash, reaching number one on the R&B charts, number four on the pop charts. Robinson cowrote the tune with Al Cleveland. It appears on Motown's excellent Miracles *Anthology,* an earlier Tamla hits package, and, no doubt, other Motown compilations.

"I'm a King Bee" This is perhaps the best-known tune of Louisiana-born blues great Slim Harpo, whose real name was James Moore. Moore was born in rural Louisiana in 1924 and moved to Baton Rouge when he was eighteen to help make money to support his younger brothers and sisters. While working various construction and other physical jobs, he began playing Baton Rouge and New Orleans clubs under the name Harmonica Slim, which he later changed to Slim Harpo. Though he never attained the fame of many of his blues contemporaries, for my money he is one of the most compelling singers and songwriters in the genre.

"I'm a King Bee" was the A-side of his first single, recorded in Crawley, Louisiana, in 1957 for Excello Records. According to Harpo's wife, the song was written on the highway when the two of them were driving to Virginia. "We passed a bunch of beehives and he started singin' 'I'm a King Bee, buzzin' around your hive.' I always carried a legal pad with me, and when he'd think of something or I'd think of something, I'd write it down. Then when we got home we'd compile it." "King Bee" was regionally popular, but it wasn't until 1961, with the song "Raining in My Heart," that he had his first real chart success.

In 1964, the Rolling Stones cut "King Bee," which further put Harpo on the map; then in 1966 he had a huge hit with "Baby Scratch My Back" (which is quoted obliquely in the Stones' "Stray Cat Blues"). The Stones also recorded Harpo's "Shake Your Hips" virtually note for note on their 1972 album, *Exile on Main Street*. "I'm a King Bee" was a showcase for Pigpen's blues vocals and harmonica and Garcia's slide guitar, mainly in 1970, the year Harpo died. There are several good Slim Harpo anthologies; the best is probably *The Best of Slim Harpo—The Original King Bee* on Rhino.

"It Hurts Me, Too" Elmore James, author of this song, was perhaps the first great electric blues slide guitarist, and his style influenced everyone from Al Wilson to Lowell George to George Thorogood. He was born in Mississippi in 1918 and played in one of Sonny Boy Williamson's bands early on. His first record didn't come until 1952, but it was a smash that has become a bona fide blues classic—"Dust My Broom." Like Williamson, he didn't make albums per se, cutting 78s instead. "It Hurts Me, Too" appears on most of the posthumous James collections (he died in 1963), including *The Great Elmore James* and *History of Elmore James* (both on Phoenix), and *One Way Out* (on the English Charly label).

His blues is highly accessible to most rock fans, and he's another I'd recommend checking out.

"It's a Man's, Man's, Man's World" With all due respect to Pigpen and the Dead, James Brown's under-three-minute original (which he cowrote with Burt Jones) has more passion than any of the ten-plus-minute jams the Dead did on the song in 1970. This is not to say the Dead didn't take the song some interesting places, but as recorded by Brown in 1966 (when it was a Top Ten smash), the tune was lean and charged—a blues in soulman's clothing. As Phil Lesh noted in a 1967 radio interview (on which he and Garcia played some of their favorite records), "It's a Man's, Man's, Man's World" was a very influential record in its day, with a string arrangement that helped shape much of the soul music that followed it.

The Dead added some vocal flourishes and opened up the arrangement to make it an instrumental showcase, but their readings suffered from strained vocals—a problem J.B. never had, of course.

James Brown versions are available on several albums, including a reissue called *It's a Man's, Man's, Man's World,* and Rhino Records' re-release of the legendary *Live at the Apollo, Vol. II.* If you want to put some slip in your hip, by all means investigate the early work of The Godfather of Soul.

"It's All Over Now" This is another tune commonly associated with the Stones, who had a hit with it in June 1964. Actually, though, the tune was penned and originally recorded by Bobby Womack, a Cleveland native who became part of the Memphis scene in the Sixties. Championed by soul singer Sam Cooke, Womack recorded both with his brother and as front man for the Valentinos, with whom he cut the original of "It's All Over Now." The song was the first tune the Stones recorded in America—they cut it at Chess Studios in Chicago, where the likes of Muddy Waters, Howlin' Wolf, Bo Diddley, and others had worked. Ironically, it became the first Stones song to hit number one in England. The song has been covered often since then. My favorite version is probably the R&B-gospel-reggae reading by Ry Cooder on his magnificent *Paradise & Lunch* LP.

"It's All Over Now, Baby Blue" This has been a part of the Dead's repertoire during two different periods: from the mid-Sixties (you can hear it on the Sunflower LP, *Vintage Dead,* recorded at the Avalon in 1966) until 1972, and from 1981 to the present (during which time it's been used exclusively as an encore). The song is one of Bob Dylan's best—and best-known—compositions, a masterful opus that has been variously interpreted as being about mortality, the death of innocence, the end of a relationship, and, no doubt, hundreds of other things. Dylan's original version appeared on his half-electric, half-acoustic 1965 LP, *Bringing It All Back Home,* the bridge between Dylan's folk days and the inspired rock and blues of *Highway 61 Revisited.*

"Johnny B. Goode" Chuck Berry is unquestionably one of the most important figures in the history of rock, and "Johnny B. Goode" is perhaps the first great song *about* rock and roll stardom.

Born in St. Louis in 1926, Berry formed his first group in the early Fifties, and was signed to Chicago-based Chess Records on the recommendation of Muddy Waters (who used him as a musician) in 1955. His first single, "Maybellene," sold close to a million copies, a phenomenal number for a record by a black singer, and Berry was on his way to mass stardom that was to evaporate a few years later when he was busted and jailed for violating a puritanical sex law known as the Mann Act, which makes it illegal to take a minor across state lines. While he made a fortune from having his numerous hits ("Rock and Roll Music," "Sweet Little Sixteen," "Roll Over Beethoven," *et al.*) covered by white rockers in the Sixties and Seventies, he never recaptured his early popularity.

"Johnny B. Goode" became a hit for Berry (reaching number eight in *Billboard*) in 1958. There must be a dozen Berry compilations albums, and most contain the song. Like "Not Fade Away," it has been covered by *everyone.* Two versions that stand out in my mind are Johnny Winter's breakneck version on *Johnny Winter And Live* and a dynamic reggae version by Peter Tosh (on *Mama Africa*).

"Jackaroe" Since it was introduced in the spring of 1977, "Jackaroe" has been among my favorite Dead cover tunes. However, only in the past few years has it become common in the Dead's sets; maybe that's why it's on my mind. It always gives a nice kick to a first set, though my favorite version is probably the one time it was played in the second: November 20, 1978, Cleveland Music Hall, where it materialized out of a very abstract space jam. Normally I am immediately drawn to a song's lyrics, but for some reason it took me a few years before the particulars of the "Jackaroe" story seeped into my consciousness. Knowing that folk songs evolve over time, I decided to search for antecedents of the Dead's version in hopes of putting a little more flesh on the bones of this intriguing tale.

First, a retelling of the story as it appears in the Dead's song: A wealthy merchant in London has a daughter who has many worthy suitors, but she is in love with a sailor named Jack. Jack sails off to war. In an attempt to be with her darlin', the girl dresses up like a man and tries to enlist in the war. At first there is some skepticism: "I see your waist is slender, your fingers they are small/Your cheeks too red and rosy to face the cannon ball." But she allays their fears: "I know my waist is slender, my fingers they are small/But it would not make me tremble to see 10,000 fall." She gives her name as Jackaroe. After a big battle, she succeeds in finding Jack "among the dead and wounded," and takes him to a doctor. The couple marries and presumably lives happily ever after.

Pinpointing the origins of the story is impossible. Historians note that tales of what is sometimes called "The Maiden Warrior" date all the way back to ancient Greece, though our "Jackaroe" probably derives from the folk balladry of the British Isles of the past two or three centuries. (How's that for vague?) It also has a long and rich history in the United States, with variations on the story turning up in the nineteenth- and twentieth-century folk traditions of many states—most notably Missouri, Kentucky, North Carolina, and Virginia. It's known variously as "The Wealthy Merchant," "Jack the Sailor," "Jack the Farmer," "Jack's Gone A-Sailing," "Jack Munro," "Jackaro," "Jack-A-Roe," "Jackaroe," etc., depending on the region. Most of the American versions collected by musicologists early in this century share similar plot points and language, but there are regional differences and some have more story than others. And typical of songs in the oral tradition, some versions are localized— "There was a wealthy merchant, in *Louisville* he did dwell"—to make them more immediate to the listener.

In the expanded readings of the song, there is usually a fair amount of intrigue involving the heroine's family, which is horrified that she would eschew the "men of high degree" for a sailor. In a Missouri version called "Jack the Sailor" dug up from a turn-of-the-century ballad book, the girl, Mollie, is betrayed by her maid-in-waiting, who snitches to the parents that Mollie is in love with Jack. Her parents fly into a rage at this revelation and confront Mollie, but she won't back down. At this, the parents go to an enlisting officer and offer him 5,000 guilders "If you'll press young Jack the sailor to the wars of Germany." Now *that* is *cold*. Money talks, of course, so it's off to England and then, eventually, Germany for poor Jack.

The next part is familiar: Mollie goes to the tailor shop, "and dressed in men's array" succeeds in convincing a sea captain to take her to England. "She rose early the next morning, a battle was to be/And in the ranks astanding, her darling boy did see/She marched straight up to him, but her he did not know/'Til a smile lit up her countenance. You're an English boy, I know.'" She pledges to stand by his side in battle, and indeed they march into the fray together. Jack is wounded but she takes him to a doctor, "and next they found a parson and in marriage they were bound." They sail back to "French London" (?) and reveal the marriage to the parents. The moral of the story appears in the last verse: "Now this young couple's married and living at their ease/Kind people, let your children get married when they please."

In another version the father gives the newlyweds all his money because "my children's all I crave." A third version has "Polly" (who masquerades as "Jack Munroe") living a full life with Jack the sailor, until he dies and "she drew out her broadsword and bid this world adieu/Saying, 'There's an end of Jack the sailor, Likewise of Jack Munroe.'" Holy pathos, Batman!

The Dead's "Jackaroe" is essentially a slightly speeded up variation of the version popularized by Joan Baez on her 1962 album *In Concert, Volume 2*. (That album contains a version of "Peggy-O," too.) The song also appears on a 1961 Folkways album by Peggy Seeger and Ewan MacColl called *Two-Way Trip*. Joan, Peggy, and Ewan were giants in the genre in those days and had an incalculable influence on aspiring folkies coast to coast, the future members of the Grateful Dead included.

"Jordan" Often called "Cold Jordan" on Dead tapes, this country gospel number turned up occasionally in the group's 1970 acoustic sets. It was popularized in the late Fifties or very early Sixties by the Stanley Brothers. The song was in the repertoire of the Black Mountain Boys (with Garcia, Sandy Rothman, and David Nelson), and Rothman speculates they learned it from a Stanley Brothers gospel album called *For the Good People*.

"Just Like Tom Thumb's Blues" It's really hard for me to believe that this Dylan song is more than twenty years old, because I'm still getting new things from it; indeed, from the entire album on which it appears, *Highway 61 Revisited*. If you don't already own this record, you really owe it to yourself to pick it up: It is Dylan at his peak, in my opinion (before his lyrics went totally "outside" on his 1966 epic, *Blonde on Blonde*), truly one of the great rock albums of all time. In addition to "Tom Thumb's" and the title track, it also contains the classics "Like a Rolling Stone" and "Desolation Row." The songs on *Highway 61 Revisited* paint a bitingly cynical picture of Dylan's world—the bleak urban landscapes are populated by a strange assortment of desperate and lonely figures who, for the most part, are sinking or have sunk into a miasma of angst and hopelessness. In its imagery of a loser on a binge in a sleazy Mexican town, "Just Like Tom Thumb's Blues" has an almost cinematic quality: I see it as a scene from Orson Welles' great film *A Touch of Evil*, with dark shadows that still can't hide the inevitable doom facing the main protagonist. The song is more than just a portrait of stoned desolation, however. It is both visual and cryptic, two words that also describe many of Robert Hunter's songs.

"We recorded that song in New York City," Al Kooper, keyboardist on the Dylan session, told me. "I played Hohner Pianette, which was like a forerunner of the clavinet that sounded almost like a guitar; and tack piano, which is the dominant instrument there. We all worked on the arrangements on those songs. Dylan brought the song in basically finished and he played it to us on electric guitar and gave a few ideas of what he heard, as far as the arrangement went. From there, we just played along a couple of times, and he recorded them all. We almost never did more than a few takes of any songs, though I remember that on a lot of the songs during that period, we'd record them, and then a few days later we'd record them again in completely different arrangements—different tempos, maybe a different time signature—just to see if anything new came out. He still does that pretty often, I understand. I think on 'Tom Thumb's' we only did the one arrangement, and the one on the album is like a second or third take."

Besides appearing on that landmark album, "Just Like Tom Thumb's Blues" was also released in a live version (with the Band backing Dylan at London's Royal Albert Hall) on the B-side of "I Want You" in early 1966. (That entire concert turned into one of the best known of the many Dylan bootlegs that have been released through the years.) It was covered by Judy Collins on her hit 1967 LP, *In My Life,* on Elektra.

"Katie Mae" This tune was written in the mid-Forties by Texas bluesman Sam "Lightnin' " Hopkins, one of many great blues singers who were rediscovered in the late Fifties and early Sixties and whose influence was more far-reaching than his fame. It appears on several different Hopkins collections, including a fine French reissue called *Lightnin' Hopkins Strums the Blues.*

"Keep On Growing" Cowritten by Eric Clapton and Bobby Whitlock, this song appears on the *Layla* album, recorded in the fall of 1970 by Derek and the Dominoes—which included Clapton, Whitlock, Carl Radle, Jim Gordon, and, on the album, Duane Allman—at Criteria Studios in Miami. This LP was arguably the zenith of Clapton's career, though it was made during one of the lowest periods in his life—when he was addicted to heroin and still reeling from the deification that weighed him down in the late days of Cream and on into his brief involvement with Blind Faith. The songs on the record are brimming with passion, and while most are tinged with sadness—this truly is *the blues,* though expressed in some nontraditional ways—there is a life-affirming optimism that ultimately makes the record uplifting. Clapton asks "Why Does Love Got to Be So Sad?" at the same time his playing and singing speak of love's sheer exhilaration. "Keep On Growing" is among the most upbeat songs on the album, and its introduction to the Dead's repertoire in 1985, at the beginning of their third decade, seemed quite apropos. If you don't own *Layla* already, by all means take the plunge.

"Knockin' on Heaven's Door" You couldn't turn on a radio in the summer of 1973 without hearing this song. On the surface it seems like an unlikely candidate for hit-singledom, yet it went all the way to number twelve in September of that year. And it wasn't even on a regular Dylan album. It was written for the soundtrack of the marginally popular Western *Pat Garrett & Billy the Kid,* directed by Sam Peckinpah and starring Kris Kristofferson and James Coburn. Dylan had a cameo role (his first) as one of Billy the Kid's followers, and not surprisingly his presence became the focus of the media's interest in the film. And the success of "Knockin' on Heaven's Door" undoubtedly brought more than a few viewers into theaters. In the context of the life-and-death Western story, the song seemed downright topical, whereas in recent years, and with Garcia singing, it's become more metaphoric. (Garcia has played the song for several years with his own band, and recorded it on his 1982 *Run for the Roses* LP). Two live Dylan versions are on record—on *Before the Flood* and *Dylan at Budokan.*

"The Last Time" Have you ever noticed that many of the cover songs the Dead perform come from their first couple of years, 1964–1965? That was a magical era in the history of both rock 'n' roll and R&B, but, more important, that was the period when the band was cutting its musical chops playing popular tunes of the day. They weren't writing many songs of their own, and in the places they played nobody wanted to hear original tunes anyway. People wanted to hear the hot stuff they were gettin' on their radios. Any garage band worth its salt played a bunch of Rolling Stones covers—usually things like "Satisfaction," "Get Off My Cloud," and "The Last Time." Although there's no record of the Warlocks or the early Dead playing "The Last Time" (set lists are virtually nonexistent from that time), the writer of a 1967 interview with Garcia mentioned hearing the Warlocks play it in 1965. That said, I suppose we must recognize the version from the February 27, 1990, show at Oakland Coliseum as the Dead's first.

"The Last Time" holds the distinction of being the first Mick Jagger–Keith Richards composition to make it to the top of the charts in England; all the Stones' previous number one's had been cover tunes. Strictly speaking it wasn't a Jagger-Richards song, however. The Stones' "The Last Time" was based, in part, on an early Sixties gospel song of the same name by the Staples Singers. The main similarity is in the chorus: "This may be the last time . . ." etc. The Stones' verses are completely original, however, and the main riff is definitely a Keith Richards creation.

Released in December 1964 in England, the A-side single (backed by "Play With Fire") made its assault on the American pop charts in the winter of 1965, climbing all the way to number nine. Three months after it peaked, "Satisfaction" became the group's first U.S. number one. Both songs appeared on the album *Out of Our Heads* in America.

"Little Red Rooster" One of the most frequently covered tunes to come out of the Chicago blues scene, "Little Red Rooster" was penned by perhaps the greatest of all blues writer, Willie Dixon, who is also responsible for such tunes as "Spoonful," "The Same Thing" (both of which the Dead have played live), "Back Door Man," "Hoochie Coochie Man," and others. Before migrating to Chicago, Dixon lived in Mississippi, growing up in rural Vicksburg. It was farm life, he says, that inspired him to write "Little Red Rooster."

"On farms," he told me in 1983, "there always seems to be an animal that has the spotlight on it—it makes trouble, chases everything, messes around, but also in a way keeps life going. In this particular instance, it was a rooster that kept everything upset. One day, the red rooster comes up missing, nobody can find him, and they learn that the barnyard is too quiet without him. I wrote it as a barnyard song really, and some people even take it that way!" He laughs heartily, knowing full well that every version ever made of his song has had lusty overtones. "People try to pretend that the blues have a lot of sexual things involved, and they say that's bad. I say the blues is about the facts of life. If there are things about sex, well, everything that fly, crawl, walk, or swim is involved in sex one way or another. But with a lot of songs, it's just the way people think that makes 'em see sex in everything."

The original recording of "Little Red Rooster" was by that consummate interpreter of Dixon's work, Howlin' Wolf. (Fellow Mississippian Muddy Waters also frequently covered Dixon's material.) "The Red Rooster" (as it was called) appears on an out-of-print Chess LP simply called *Howlin' Wolf,* but any good anthology of the Wolf's work will include the tune. Other good versions of the tune were recorded by the Rolling Stones, and a personal favorite is the one by The Doors on the album *Alive She Cried.*

"La Bamba" When was the last time the Grateful Dead had a current hit by another band in their repertoire? Of course "current" isn't the most accurate description of this venerable Mexican folk song, but the fact is Los Lobos' version was nestled securely in the number one slot on *Billboard*'s Hot 100 chart when the Dead debuted "La Bamba" in Providence September 7, 1987. Of course, Garcia's affection for Los Lobos is well known, and musically it made great sense to insert the song in the middle of "Good Lovin'," since the rhythm and chord progressions are nearly identical.

The exact origins of the tune are unknown, but it was first popularized in the Vera Cruz region of Mexico just after the Second World War. It wasn't until the Pacoima, California, teen idol Ritchie Valens recorded the song in the late Fifties (shortly before his death in a plane crash in February 1959) that the song became well known outside the Latino community. Valens' version went as far as number two on the charts, and a few years later Trini Lopez also enjoyed moderate success with the song, both in the United States and in various Spanish-speaking countries. We have Valens' producer, Bob Keane, to thank for the first rock recording of the song:

"I heard Ritchie strumming this Latin thing one day and he was just singing 'La, la, la, la,'" Keane recalled. "I said, 'What's that?' and he said, 'A Mexican folk song.' He didn't know the words so we found his aunt, who did, and she wrote them out for Ritchie and he learned them. I said, 'Let's do it as a rock and roll song.' He didn't want to do that, but finally agreed to it."

Valens' recording is on a couple of different anthologies of his work (the best is on Rhino Records). Los Lobos appears on the soundtrack for the film *La Bamba,* directed by Luis Valdez, of *Zoot Suit* fame.

And what, you may wonder, does the song mean? Basically, it is about a dance called La Bamba, and about the flirtation that goes on between young men and women. Following the Mexican folk tradition, versions differ depending on the region or country where the song is sung, with local references and verses added.

"Louie Louie" Whether you love or hate this garage-rock classic (it's never been a favorite of mine), you have to admit that the Dead's late-1980s versions—led by the group's resident trashman, Brent—put a new spin on it, turning a truly dumb anthem into a sinewy, sexy little shaker.

Written by Richard Berry, the song was originally recorded by the Portland, Oregon, band the Kingsmen for the Jerden label in mid-1963. When it became regionally popular, Wand Records picked it up and the song eventually rocketed all the way to number two on the national charts. At least part of its mystique derived from the tremendous amount of controversy stirred up by lead singer Jack Ely's slurred, unintelligible vocals. It was commonly believed that the song had "dirty" lyrics; in fact, both the FBI and the Federal Communications Commission investigated the song extensively—even slowing it down to try to decipher the words—and called on Ely and Berry to testify. There was such an outcry that some radio stations refused to play it, which only helped sales, of course. In all, it sold some twelve million copies worldwide.

The Kingsmen had a few minor hits following "Louie Louie," including the similarly trashy "Little Latin Lupe Lu" and "The Jolly Green Giant," which "Roots" trivia buffs know is the old Olympics tune "Big Boy Pete" with different lyrics. By 1968 the group had disbanded. In 1973 original lead guitarist Mike Mitchell formed a new version of the band, but it bombed.

But this is truly the song that wouldn't die, and its popularity has actually increased through the years. In the late 1970s it became the staple of every fraternity party band thanks to its appearance in the film *Animal House* (with John Belushi on lead vocals no less). In 1984, KALX, the

University of California at Berkeley's student station, aired the first "Louie Louie" marathon, playing twenty-four consecutive hours of versions of the song, many of them cut by local bands for the occasion. That, in turn, inspired John DeBella, a DJ at Philadelphia radio station WMMR, to start that city's now-annual "Louie Louie" parade, which features thousands of marchers, on many odd floats, playing the song over and over on everything from kazoos to oboes.

The Kingsmen's version of the tune is available on a slew of 1960s hits packages and soundtracks. However, more deranged collectors will accept nothing less than Rhino Records' compilation album, *The Best of Louie Louie,* featuring versions by Black Flag, the Sandpipers (who had a hit with it in 1966), and the Rice University Marching Band. *C'est bizarre!*

"Mama Tried" This one comes straight out of the life of the song's author, Merle Haggard. Haggard is a native of Bakersfield and has been one of the most popular singers in country music since the 1960s (though his roots go back even earlier). Like the character in the song, Haggard had troubles with the law when he was young, though obviously he never served "life without parole." For a few years, Garcia sang another of Haggard's prison songs, "Sing Me Back Home." Most of Haggard's best early sides were recorded for Capitol, and that label's hits anthology, *The Best of the Best of Merle Haggard,* contains "Mama Tried" and a slew of his other classics. Haggard still performs the song live from time to time.

"Man Smart, Woman Smarter" If you've ever thought this song sounded slightly calypso, you're dead-on—it was popularized by Mr. Carribbean himself, Harry Belafonte, on one of his early RCA albums, *Calypso* (1956). Belafonte was not the first to cut the tune, however, as several recorded antecedents exist, including the Brute Force Steelband of Antigua's peppy instrumental version of the mid-Fifties on their Cook Records album, *Music to Awaken the Ballroom Beast.* Belafonte's version differs quite a bit from the Dead's musically and, even more, lyrically. He sings it with a thick, almost exaggerated accent, and his includes entire verses not found in most contemporary versions by white artists— particularly the final verse in which the woman in the song has a baby and its eyes are *blue,* implying it isn't the child of the black singer!

There seems to be some confusion over the authorship of the song. On the Belafonte version, it is credited to Norman Span and King Radio.

At least two other versions credit a "D. Klieber," the pseudonym of a writer named David Miller, who does get royalties for some versions. There have been several rock and roll readings of the tune in recent years, most notably by Robert Palmer (who nearly had a hit with it), Rosanne Cash, and Carlene Carter.

"Me and Bobby McGee" By now, this song is virtually a "standard," quite a feat for a song that is just twenty years old. When Texas-born, Yale-educated songwriter Kris Kristofferson moved to Nashville in 1965, he initially worked as a janitor for Columbia Records. He held several jobs as he pursued his songwriting, and he got his big break in 1969 when Roger Miller had a hit with "Me and Bobby McGee." Kristofferson's own version of the tune appeared on his debut LP, *Kristofferson,* recorded for Monument Records in 1970. The following year, Columbia picked up the album and released it as *Me and Bobby McGee.* The song was a posthumous smash for Janis Joplin in 1971 (it's on *Pearl*), the year *Skull and Roses* was recorded and released. Since then, numerous artists have covered the song, from Waylon Jennings (*Lonesome*) to Willie Nelson, who recorded a great album of Kristofferson songs in 1979.

"Me and My Uncle" According to Bob Weir, he learned this John Phillips–penned tune from "a hippie named Curly Jim," who I can only assume is Curly Jim Cook, onetime member of the Bay Area band A.B. Skhy. Phillips is best known as the leader and chief songwriter for the L.A.-based Mamas and Papas, but I can find no evidence that he ever recorded the song. Judy Collins recorded a slower version of the song on a mid-Sixties live album, and that may well be where Weir got it from.

"The Monkey and the Engineer" This whimsical song came from the fanciful pen of Jesse Fuller (see "Beat It on Down the Line") and appears on the LP, *The Lone Cat.* It was a staple of the Dead's acoustic shows both in 1970 and 1980.

"Morning Dew" Long before Weir and Barlow wrote their powerful condemnation of the arms race, "Throwing Stones," the Dead were regularly performing one of the most moving songs ever written about nuclear madness, "Morning Dew." There is an interesting story behind this song, which was written by Canadian singer-songwriter Bonnie Dobson in the very early Sixties. On the three Dead albums where it appears, the song is credited to Dobson and Tim Rose, but in fact Rose had no hand in writing the song. After months of searching, I finally tracked Dobson down at an address in London. What follows are comments about "Morning Dew" that she put down in a thoughtful, handwritten, seven-page letter she wrote in reply to a query I sent to her.

"I wrote 'Morning Dew' during my second or third engagement at the Ash Grove [the famous L.A. folk club] in 1961. When I'd go to Los Angeles I'd usually stay with my friend Joyce Naftulin, and it was in her apartment that I wrote 'Morning Dew.' I can't give you specific dates, but I do remember the circumstances. There had been a gathering of friends, and towards the end of the evening a discussion had ensued about the possibilities and the outcome of a nuclear war. It was all very depressing and upsetting. The following day I sat down and started putting together the song. I had never written or even attempted to write a song before.

"It took the form of a conversation between the last man and woman—postapocalypse—one trying to comfort the other while knowing there's absolutely nothing left. When I'd finished, I recall phoning another friend and singing it to her over the phone. She said it was good, but maybe that's just ancient fancy at work. I think I sang it in public for the first time at the first Mariposa Folk Festival in Ontario. Anyway, I recall that the critic from the Toronto *Globe and Mail* described it as a 'mournful dirge.' I have that clipping, amongst others, stored away in a large trunk in Toronto.

"In February of 1962 I recorded an album at Gerde's Folk City in New York [*Bonnie Dobson at Folk City* on Prestige International] and 'Morning Dew' was the last track on side B. [The two songs that preceded it on the record were also anti-nuke tunes, grouped together as "Two Carols for a Nuclear Age."]

"In 1964 I was contacted by Jac Holzman of Elektra Records, who told me that Fred Neil wanted to record 'Morning Dew' and that as I'd not published it, would I like to do so with his company, Nina music. I signed a contract and Neil recorded the song. His is the original cover, on *Tear Down the Walls* by Vince Martin and Fred Neil. His singing of it differed from mine in that he altered the lyric slightly, changing 'Take me for a walk in the morning dew' to 'Walk me out in the morning dew.' He was also the first person to rock it. [Dobson's versions are definitely folk.]

"Among others who have recorded it are Jeff Beck, Lee Hazelwood, Lulu, Tim Rose, Nova, the Highwaymen, and most recently, Nazareth.

I'm probably leaving out a good many. I recorded it again on an album [*Bonnie Dobson*] for RCA in 1969.

"Now I must tell you about my involvement with Tim Rose. In 1967 while I was living in Toronto (from 1960 to 1965 I lived in the States), I had a call from Manny Greenhill, my agent, saying that Tim Rose wanted to record 'Morning Dew,' but that he wanted to change the lyric. I duly signed a new contract and Rose was written in as colyricist on the basis of his new lyric. Unfortunately, it wasn't till after the signing that I heard his 'changed' version. You can imagine that I was somewhat dismayed to discover that his new lyric was precisely the one that Fred Neil had recorded in 1964. So if anyone is entitled to be the colyricist, it is Neil and not Rose. You may be wondering why I signed the contract in the first place—some mistakes are only made once, and I guess I was pretty naive.

"In 1968, when Lulu released her single of 'Morning Dew,' a full-page ad was placed in *Billboard* referring to it as 'Tim Rose's Great Hit'— no mention of Ms. Dobson at all. From that time till now—particularly here in England—people have never believed that I had anything to do with the writing of 'Morning Dew.' Rose never gave me any credit. Even Nazareth's single from 1981 has only him listed as composer. It has caused me a lot of aggravation and unhappiness. Even though I have and still do receive substantial royalties (75 percent as opposed to his 25 percent), it doesn't make up for the man's behavior."

And lest you believe that Dobson sits around in the English rain being bitter about this, I should add that she is happily married to an architect and has two children. She still sings—mainly for the BBC, but also in concerts and occasional small tours of Europe.

She closed her letter with this:

"I always liked the Dead's version of 'Morning Dew.' My one regret is that when they first appeared in Toronto—was it 1967 or 1968 at the O'Keefe Centre?—they didn't sing 'Morning Dew' in the concert I attended. I also regret that I was too shy to go backstage and meet them."

"New New Minglewood Blues" Here's a great example of a song that has been passed from player to player through the years and changed so much that it bears almost no relation to its original antecedent, a song called "Minglewood Blues" that was recorded back in January of 1928 by a black group called Cannon's Jug Stompers. Consisting of banjo and jug player Gus Cannon, guitarist Ashley Thompson, and harmonica player Noah Lewis, the Jug Stompers was one of a number of popular black jug bands that sprang up in the mid-South (particularly Memphis) between about 1915 and the beginning of the Depression. "Minglewood Blues" was written primarily by Lewis, who is also credited as the primary writer of "Viola Lee Blues," which was recorded about nine months after the session that yielded both "Minglewood Blues" and another staple of the Dead's, "Big Railroad Blues."

Strangely enough, though, "Minglewood Blues" is not at all similar to the Dead's "Minglewood." For the germ of the Dead's song we have to jump forward two years to 1930 and a song by the Noah Lewis Jug Band (yes, Noah went solo!) called "*New* Minglewood Blues" (which can be found on an Origin Jazz LP called *The Great Jug Bands*). The first verse is virtually identical to the one Weir sings, but after that the song is largely dissimilar lyrically. Clearly the doubling of the word "New" in the Dead's version is a clever joke on Lewis' own updating of his tune. Weir, who rearranged it (twice) for the Dead, has taken substantial liberties with the song, which, though seldom recorded, was popular among jug bands during their early Sixties revival. And what exactly is Minglewood? Well, according to noted Memphis blues authority Bengt Olsson, who interviewed old-timers from the early Memphis jug and blues scene, Minglewood was a sawmill/box factory in Ashport, North of Memphis, that was torn down early in the Fifties. Noah Lewis and Eddie Green (who played guitar with Lewis for a brief period) were both employees at Minglewood, which also became the name for the small region near the factory.

"New Orleans" You loved it at the 1984 Toronto SEVA benefit, and you may have a tape of it from the Capitol Theatre, Portchester, New York, November 8, 1970. It's amazing that the Dead have done this song so infrequently, because it's a natural for Weir. It was written in 1960 by writer/producer/manager Frank Guida and his friend Joe Royster for a little-known Norfolk, Virginia, singer named Gary Anderson. When Guida put out the record on his own Legrand Records label, though, he changed Anderson's name to U.S. Bonds and scored a major national hit with it. The following year, another Bonds hit, "Quarter to Three" (cowritten by Guida, Royster, and Bonds) hit number one, and the Bonds-Guida team earned its niche in rock history.

Bonds' first Legrand album, *Dance Till Quarter to Three with U.S. Bonds* (which contains "New Orleans" and the title track) was rereleased by a German label a few years ago and should be available at better record stores. In addition, Guida put out an album about five years ago called

Rock's Revolution: The Roots that contains several Bonds hits, as well as tracks by other artists in the Guida stable such as the Church Street Five (immortalized in "Quarter to Three"), Jimmy Soul, Tommy Facenda, and Lenis Guess.

"Next Time You See Me" I've frequently seen this on tape lists as "You Lied and Cheated," which is incorrect. A Pigpen-sung staple of the Dead's live shows in the early Seventies, it is a relatively recent blues, originally recorded by Junior Parker (1927–1971) in 1957, when it hit number seven on the R&B charts for Houston-based Duke Records.

Parker is a frequently overlooked figure in the history of R&B. Born in Arkansas, he was "discovered" by Sonny Boy Williamson and toured with him for a brief time. In the early Fifties he recorded for Sam Phillips' Sun Records label, for whom he cut one of his original tunes, "Mystery Train." That song became one of Elvis Presley's first hits shortly after that, but Parker remained in the shadows. He recorded for Duke in the late Fifties and had several popular songs, including "Driving Wheel." Penned by William Harvey and Earl Forest, "Next Time You See Me" has been recorded by several different blues and R&B artists, including Jimmy Cotton (who now goes by James Cotton) and Memphis Slim.

"Nobody's Fault but Mine" The original version of "Nobody's Fault" was recorded in Dallas on December 3, 1927, by a Texas street singer known as Blind Willie Johnson. Johnson only recorded thirty songs in his career, almost all of them (like "Nobody's Fault") spirituals from the Baptist church. His output included "If I Had My Way I'd Tear That Building Down," which Reverend Gary Davis heard and rearranged as "Samson and Delilah"; and "Keep Your Lamps Trimmed and Burning," recorded by Hot Tuna in the early Seventies.

Though several of Johnson's records for Columbia sold well, he never saw a penny for his efforts, and he remained a street singer until his death of pneumonia in 1949 (at the age of forty-nine). Blind Willie's soulful version of "Nobody's Fault but Mine" can be found on an excellent Folkways album simply called *Blind Willie Johnson* that was put together by Sam Charters in the late Fifties. Besides containing tracks by Johnson, Blind Lemon Jefferson, and Blind Boy Fuller, it features a side-long audio documentary tracing Charters' search for Blind Willie, with the singer's friends and, ultimately, his widow, filling in some of the sketchy details about his life and music. Interesting stuff. Yazoo Records put out a more comprehensive, all-music anthology of his songs, as well.

"Not Fade Away" A true rock classic, this was cowritten by Buddy Holly and his producer/manager Norman Petty in 1957 as the flip side of "Oh Boy" for the Coral label. Holly died in a plane crash less than two years later, but his songs continue to be covered by countless rock artists. "Not Fade Away" was the Stones' first American chart hit in 1964, and it appeared on two Stones albums during that era. (I've always been partial to the hyped-up version on *Got Live If You Want It*.) The original appears on any number of Holly "hits" packages.

"Oh Babe It Ain't No Lie" When I tracked down this song's author, Elizabeth Cotten, in early 1984, she was in the midst of helping prepare dinner for some of her children, grandchildren, great-grandchildren and great-*great*-grandchildren in her home in Syracuse, New York. "Young man," she said, "I hope that someday you're blessed with as good a family as mine." Heartwarming words from a woman who led a long, good life after a childhood spent in relative poverty in North Carolina. She played music most of her life, and she wrote "Oh Babe It Ain't No Lie" when she was a little girl living in Chapel Hill, North Carolina.

"We had this woman named Miss Mary who used to take care of us kids, and once I got punished for something she said I did that I didn't

Elizabeth Cotten, writer of "Oh Babe It Ain't No Lie." *(Photo by Richard McCaffrey)*

do. The song came to me when I was laying in bed one night. The words did, then I made up the tune. I'd sit out on the porch and sing it so she could hear it. She'd say, 'I sure do like that song, Little Sis.' That's what she'd call me. I wouldn't tell her it was about her, because I might get another punch!" She cackled at the reminiscence.

Cotten didn't record until she was middle-age, but she made several albums that were well received in folk circles. "Oh Babe It Ain't No Lie" appears on a 1958 Folkways album (as does her version of "Goin' Down the Road Feeling Bad") called *Folksongs and Instrumentals with Guitar.* (Cotten was an excellent guitarist in her time.) She is best known as the composer of the classic tune "Freight Train." Cotten died in 1987.

"On the Road Again" We go back to the original jug band scene for the first recording of this tune. Will Shade and his Memphis Jug Band cut the song as a 78 in 1928, and it has been recorded several times since. The Memphis Jug Band also was one of the first groups to record "Stealin'," which was the B-side of the Dead's first single on Scorpio Records. (The other side was "Don't Ease Me In." Both were credited to "J. Garcia," no doubt for his arranging work.) An interesting feature of the Memphis Jug Band version—which is actually remarkably similar to the Dead's, down to the jive talk in the background—is the use of the word "nigger" in two instances (for example, "big black nigger in my foldin' bed"). The late Twenties were not far removed from the age of what were called "coon songs," so evidently vestiges of that sort of entertainment were still influential then.

"Peggy-O" Often called "Fennario," this song has a very long lineage. According to the *Joan Baez Songbook,* Joan recorded it on her 1962 LP, *In Concert Vol. 2.* "Cecil Sharp discovered several versions of this ballad in the Southern Appalachians on his collecting trips during the first World War, though it seems to have disappeared from American tradition since that time. It is still extremely popular in Scotland as 'The Bonnie Lass o' Fyvie-O' and was earlier known in England as 'Pretty Peggy of Derby.'"

There *are* precedents for calling the tune "Peggy-O," however: Simon and Garfunkel recorded it under that title; Bob Dylan's first album calls it "Pretty Peggy-O"; and one of the most respected volumes of folk song lyrics, *The Folksinger's Wordbook,* by Irwin and Fred Silber, lists the song as "Peggy-O."

"Not Fade Away" author Buddy Holly.

"The Promised Land" One of Chuck Berry's great strengths as a writer was that he was able to transcend the regionalism that kept most R&B artists from mass popularity, by devising a sound that couldn't be identified with a certain area. Beyond that, though, he literally brought cities from all over America into his lyrics, effectively unifying different regions under his new rock 'n' roll banner. "The Promised Land" is a good example of his expansive American consciousness—a portrait of a restless soul discovering the U.S. of A. while trying to find some (mythical) promised land. Obviously Berry's tale struck a chord with the American public, because the song was a minor hit for him in 1964, the year he ended his stint in prison. Berry had two other hits that year, "Nadine" and "No Particular Place to Go," his last high-charting songs until his early Seventies fluke hit, "My Ding-a-Ling." Elvis Presley had a hit with "Promised Land" in 1974.

"Quinn the Eskimo" (also known as "The Mighty Quinn") This is another nugget from the catalog of Garcia's favorite outside writer, Bob Dylan. Dylan wrote it in the late Sixties and recorded it as part of the infamous "Basement Tapes" sessions with the Band in the summer of 1967. Although those recordings were heavily bootlegged, the world at large first heard "Quinn the Eskimo" through the British band Manfred Mann, whose spunky, melodic version hit number ten on the American pop charts in March of 1968. (Manfred Mann also covered "Million Dollar Bash" from the same Dylan-Band sessions.) Dylan's recording of the tune first came out on the generally dismal *Self-Portrait* (1970), though it wasn't until 1985's five-album retrospective/rarities LP, *Biograph,* that the original "Quinn" became readily available. It is considerably more subdued than either the Manfred Mann or Dead versions.

Dylanologists can't seem to agree on either the song's meaning or its significance in the Dylan canon. Michael Gray, author of *Song and Dance Man,* calls it "possibly Dylan's most trivial song"; while John Herdman writes in *Voice Without Restraint* that it is one of Dylan's most powerful songs, filled with messianic overtones. Dylan's own comment on the song: " 'Quinn the Eskimo,' I don't know. I don't know what it was about. I guess it was some kind of nursery rhyme."

"The Race Is On" This song is well known to most hardcore country fans, as it was a big hit for George Jones early in his career. The Don Rollins song appeared on Jones' *I Get Lonely in a Hurry* album for Liberty, recently reissued in its original cover (love the crewcut, George) by Capitol Records. "The Race Is On" can also be found on Jones' *All Time Greatest Hits* LP on Epic, a great anthology of this distinctive stylist's work. British rocker Dave Edmunds has a nifty version of the song, too, on his *Twangin'* album (on Swan Song Records).

"Revolution" Written by John Lennon when the Beatles were in India, this song was originally recorded in June of 1968. It first appeared as the flip side of the Beatles' best-selling single ever, "Hey Jude." A slower version—which is closer to the way the Dead perform it—was included on their next album, *The Beatles* (a.k.a. the White Album). Younger fans might be unaware that when the song was originally released it was very controversial, particularly with the radical Left, who thought the politics in the song were soft and the "it's gonna be all right" thrust of the song a cop-out.

"Rockin' Pneumonia" Let's put in a good word for Huey "Piano" Smith, who wrote and first recorded this rock chestnut, which the Dead performed a couple of times in 1972 (London, May 23–24). Like Fats Domino, Smith grew up steeped in the black music of New Orleans and was heavily influenced by Professor Longhair. Smith, too, was an in-demand session pianist, and his work appears on innumerable records that came out of New Orleans in the 1950s, including hits by Lloyd Price, Earl King, Smiley Lewis, Little Richard, and Sugarboy Crawford. As a solo artist—first fronting a group called the Rhythm Aces, and later the Clowns—he recorded for several different R&B labels in the early and mid-Fifties. It wasn't until he recorded "Rockin' Pneumonia and the Boogie Woogie Flu" (its full title) for Ace Records in 1957 that he gained any national attention, though the song never cracked the Top 40. In the late Fifties and early Sixties he recorded a string of marginally popular rock 'n' roll songs, many of them with funny titles like "Little Chicken Wah Wah," "Don't You Know Yockomo," "Well I'll Be John Brown," and "Tu-ber-cu-lucas and Sinus Blues" (which was covered by David Lindley on his debut solo LP, *El Rayo-X*).

A very limited singer and songwriter, Smith was nonetheless a great entertainer and a popular fixture in New Orleans for many years. He retired from music in the late Sixties and became a Jehovah's Witness. His version of "Rockin' Pneumonia" is available on several compilations of his work. This is good-time party music all the way.

"Rosalie McFall" This was originally recorded in the late Thirties by the Monroe Brothers, who are generally credited with popularizing blue-grass. Charlie and Bill Monroe played together for only a few years, but both went on to great fame leading their own groups; in fact Bill, by far the better known of the two, continues to tour. "Rosalie McFall" appeared on an early Sixties album culled from vintage Monroe Brothers 78s called *Early Bluegrass Music* on the RCA/Camden label.

Muddy Waters wrote and recorded "The Same Thing." *(Photo by Blair Jackson)*

"Run Rudolph Run" This is, to my knowledge, the only holiday tune the Dead ever performed. "Run Rudolph Run" was a little novelty song written and recorded by Chuck Berry at the peak of his popularity in the late Fifties. It came out in early December 1958, on Chess Records, and was a mild success. (The flip side was a version of the great yule blues "Merry Christmas Baby," a much stronger song in my opinion.) With Pigpen on lead vocals, the Dead performed "Run Rudolph Run" at least three times that we know of in December of 1971—at the Felt Forum in New York City (December 4); at the Fox Theater in St. Louis (December 9); and the following week at Hill Auditorium in Ann Arbor, Michigan (December 15). Chuck Berry's version of his song appears on *Rarities,* a fine album of unusual tracks and alternate takes of his hits on MCA.

"The Same Thing" One of Willie Dixon's major strengths as a blues writer was his uncanny ability to say a lot while being purposely vague. This slow blues was a perfect example: "What makes you feel so good, when your baby get an evenin' gown?/Must be the same old thing that made the preacher lay his Bible down/That old same thing/Tell me who's to blame, the whole world's fightin' 'bout that same thing." My favorite Muddy Waters version of this appears on his live/studio *Father and Sons* LP, recorded in Chicago in the late Sixties with a band including Duck Dunn, Michael Bloomfield, Otis Spann, and others. The song was part of the Dead's repertoire in the mid-Sixties, sung by Pigpen in a style not too far removed from the original. A version of the song is found on the Sunflower *Historic Dead* LP. It was revived by the Dead in December 1991, with Weir singing lead.

"Samson and Delilah" This was a popular Negro spiritual, usually sung a capella until it was put on record in the late Twenties by Texas bluesman Blind Willie Johnson. (See "Nobody's Fault but Mine.") His version (titled "If I Had My Way I'd Tear the Building Down") appears on *Let Your Light Shine on Me,* an Earl Records compilation of Johnson's 78s. That version inspired Reverend Gary Davis to work out his own arrangement, and it is his recording of the tune that prompted people like Peter, Paul, and Mary, Dave Van Ronk, and, later, the Dead to record it. The song, of course, derives from the Bible story in the book of Judges: 13–16. A sample verse from a Negro spiritual transcription shows that it has changed little over the years: "They bound him with ropes and while walking along/He looked on the ground, he saw an old jawbone/He moved his arms, the rope popped like threads/When he got through killin', 3,000 was dead." The out-of-print Davis album on which it appeared originally is *Pure Religion,* on the Prestige label.

"Satisfaction" Opinions about so-called "classic" rock 'n' roll tunes vary pretty dramatically from one rock historian to another, but one thing virtually *everyone* agrees on is that "(I Can't Get No) Satisfaction" is one of the most powerful and expressive rock tunes ever written. It's got a great hook, lyrics that deal with sex and alienation, and that attitude of frustrated rebelliousness that the Stones expressed better than anyone. The original riff for the song was written by Rolling Stone Keith Richards during the band's tour of America in April of 1965. As he and Mick Jagger worked on the song throughout the tour, it metamorphosed from what Jagger characterized a "folk song" *à la* Bob Dylan to the steamy, fuzzed rocker it became. The group recorded it in May at RCA studios in Hollywood. Shortly after its release, it became the Stones' first American number one hit. It appeared on their *Out of Our Heads* LP.

"She Belongs to Me" Who but Dylan could write a tune about a mysterious, almost diabolical woman who leaves broken men in her wake, and then ironically title it "She Belongs to Me"? The song dates back to what many consider Dylan's peak period—1965, the year the Dead formed, and well before anyone in the band was an accomplished songwriter. (This far down the line it's easy to forget just how influential Dylan and the Beatles were and how advanced their songwriting was compared with the work of other people on the scene.) "She Belongs to Me" is one of many bona fide classics on Dylan's *Bringing It All Back Home,* which contains Dylan's first tentative forays into electric rock 'n' roll. Other songs on the record include "Subterranean Homesick Blues," "Maggie's Farm," "Mr. Tambourine Man," "It's Alright Ma," and "It's All Over Now, Baby Blue." No analysis of "She Belongs to Me" is needed; its moods are easily discerned. I like Dylan's observation about his writing on the album's liner notes: "my poems are written in a rhythm of unpoetic distortion/divided by pierced ears. false eyelashes/subtracted by people constantly torturing each other. with a melodic purring line of descriptive hollowness—seen at times thru dark sunglasses an other forms of psychic explosion."

"Sing Me Back Home" Though this tune didn't usually translate very well to tape because of ragged harmonies, for many of us, "Sing Me Back Home" was a real highlight of the Dead's early Seventies concerts. Sung plaintively by Garcia, it occupied a position in the set somewhat analogous to current late-second-set ballads like "Black Peter" and "Stella Blue." The song was written by Merle Haggard (who also wrote "Mama Tried") in the late Sixties, based loosely on an actual incident.

Born in 1937 to a family of poor Oklahomans who lived in a converted boxcar, Haggard quit school at a young age and hopped a train headed to California, where he got into petty crime of various kinds. In 1958, Haggard was sentenced to prison for burglary and shipped to San Quentin ("He turned twenty-one in prison"), across the bay from San Francisco. There he befriended an inmate named James Hendricks, a.k.a. "Rabbit," who strongly encouraged young Merle to hone his developing skills as a singer and musician. Hendricks also cooked up an escape scheme that Merle wisely decided to ignore. Hendricks did escape for a while, but was eventually cornered by police and captured. Before being nabbed, however, he killed an officer, and for that he was sentenced to die in San Quentin's infamous gas chamber. It is Hendricks' last night before his execution that some years later inspired "Sing Me Back Home."

Haggard wrote in his autobiography, *Sing Me Back Home:* " 'You've got talent,' Hendricks had said. 'You can be somebody someday.' Rabbit's words roared through my head. Years later, when I wrote 'Sing

Me Back Home,' it was because I believe I know exactly how he felt
that night. Even now when I sing that song, it's still for Rabbit and all
those like him."

Haggard originally recorded the song in the late Sixties on a now-out-
of-print Capitol LP called *Sing Me Back Home*. It appears on a few different Haggard hits collections that are available.

"Silver Threads and Golden Needles" Bobby warbled this one a few
times in 1969 and early 1970, with the Dead and with his infamous short-
lived country band, Bobby Ace and the Cards from the Bottom of the
Deck. The first hit recording of the Dick Reynolds–Jack Rhodes composition was cut by the Springfields, an early Sixties British folk trio led
by Mary O'Brien, who became known during this period as Dusty
Springfield. "Silver Threads" hit the American Top 20 in 1962. Springfield went solo shortly after that hit, and enjoyed several more, mainly
middle-of-the-road successes over the next two decades, including
"Goin' Back" and "Wishin' and Hopin'." Linda Ronstadt had a hit with
"Silver Threads" in 1974.

"Sittin' on Top of the World" According to a 1967 interview, Garcia
was inspired to play this song by Carl Perkins' rockin' version, which
appears on his out-of-print 1958 debut album for Columbia, *Whole Lot
of Shakin'*. (This, of course, was after his stint with Sam Phillips' Sun
label.) His uptempo version likely owes much to Texas Swing king Bob
Wills' take of the tune. The song was first a hit, though, in 1930, when
the Mississippi Sheiks recorded it in a slow, bluesy vein for the Okeh
label. That then became the inspiration for what remains the best-known
version, Howlin' Wolf's early Sixties Chess recording of the song. And
taking it one more step, Cream's 1969 version was adapted from Wolf's.

"Smokestack Lightning" Another song from the repertoire of Howlin' Wolf, though like much of his material, it is a traditional blues tune
of unknown origin. It was a hit for Wolf in the early Sixties and appears
on his first album for the Chess label, *Moanin' at Midnight* (out of print).
It is available on several anthologies, including a comprehensive package
of his best-known material released in the late Eighties on Chess/Sugar
Hill.

"Spoonful" This tune was written in the Fifties by the prolific
Mississippi-born Willie Dixon, author of many of the best-known songs

in the Chicago blues tradition. (He moved there in the late Thirties.) It was originally recorded by the great Howlin' Wolf, who also recorded such Dixon classics as "Back Door Man," "Little Red Rooster," and "Wang Dang Doodle." The song got a major revival in the late Sixties when Cream made it a centerpiece of their live shows, often extending the tune to "Dark Star" lengths. A vintage performance of the song by Cream appears on their 1968 double-album, *Wheels of Fire*.

As original and interesting as Dixon's somewhat cryptic composition may be, it does have a precedent, thematically. Earlier in the century, a tune called "All I Want Is a Spoonful" was a popular part of the black vaudeville tradition. That song, which bears no real musical similarity to Dixon's (it's closer to ragtime than blues), has lyrics that are as mysteriously suggestive and ambiguous. It was first recorded in 1925 by a relatively obscure Louisiana blues and vaudeville singer named Papa Charlie Jackson. Over the years, the tune was cut by the likes of Mance Lipscomb and Charlie Patton.

"Stealin' " The B-side of the Dead's first Scorpio Records single back in 1965, the tune was a regular part of Dead shows during 1965 and 1966. An old Southern blues that dates back to prerecording days, it was first waxed by the Memphis Jug Band, one of the most successful of the many black jug bands that sprouted in the middle South from about 1910 until the Depression. Led by a charismatic singer/guitarist named Will Shade, the Memphis Jug Band recorded dozens of songs between 1927 and 1930, and a few more in 1934. "Stealin' " was cut in 1928. One line in the song, "Put your arms around me like a circle 'round the sun" appears altered in one of the first songs the Dead ever wrote themselves, "The Golden Road (to Unlimited Devotion)," as "Everybody's dancing in a ring around the sun . . ." The Memphis Jug Band version appears on an excellent Yazoo Records anthology of their work.

"That's All Right" One of the best-known numbers of the early rock era, this was the A-side of Elvis Presley's first single on Sam Phillips' Sun label. Cut in early July of 1954, the song was an instant success in the South and helped put Presley on the map. "That's All Right" was written by a Mississippi bluesman named Arthur "Big Boy" Crudup, who was one of Presley's acknowledged influences. (Crudup's own versions of the song don't have nearly the zip that Elvis' did.) It's one of those tunes that every rock band coming up in the mid-Sixties could play in its sleep, though now, with the passage of time, it has become somewhat obscure.

"Tomorrow Is Forever" Donna sang this one a handful of times in 1972. The original was a Top Ten hit for Porter Wagoner and Dolly Parton just two years earlier.

"Turn on Your Love Light" One of the most popular of the Dead's late-Sixties R&B rave-ups, "Love Light" was originally recorded by blues singer Bobby "Blue" Bland, who certainly must be considered among the most popular and influential singers of the Fifties and early Sixties. Bland first came to prominence as part of the Memphis blues scene of the early Fifties. He recorded a few sides for Sam Phillips' Sun label, and appeared on Howlin' Wolf's radio program before the latter went on to greater fame in Chicago. His biggest successes, though, were in the early Sixties, when he recorded for the Texas-based Duke label. With that company he had a number of R&B hits, including "Cry, Cry, Cry," "I Pity the Fool," "Stormy Monday Blues," "That's the Way Love Is," and "Turn on Your Love Light," which hit number two on the *Billboard* R&B charts in 1961. Besides influencing Pigpen, Bland was a definite influence on other rock singers, too, such as Van Morrison, who cut "Love Light" with his group, Them.

"Viola Lee Blues" A classic prison blues by Noah Lewis of Cannon's Jug Stompers, it most likely filtered down to the Dead through the Jim Kweskin Jug Band's version on their *See Reverse Side for Title* album on Vanguard in the early Sixties. (Garcia and Weir have often acknowledged that unit's influence on their own jug band.) Kweskin band member Geoff Muldaur was familiar with the tune from rare 78s. Two fairly different takes of the song, done in a style similar to the Dead's, appear on a Herwin Records collection of Cannon's Jug Stompers' complete works, which I strongly recommend to blues enthusiasts. Apparently the song was purloined many times after the Stompers recorded it, popping up in 1936 as "Prison Blues" by George Clarke, and as "Texas Tommy" in Yank Rachel's 1938 recording. Accept no substitutes.

"Wake Up Little Susie" Popularized by the Everly Brothers, who had a number one hit with it on the Cadence label in 1957, the song was written by the immensely talented husband and wife writing team of Felice and Boudleaux Bryant, who also wrote "Bye Bye Love," "All I

Have to Do Is Dream" (by Boudleaux alone), and "Poor Jenny," all smashes for the Everlys, perhaps *the* most popular duo of the Fifties. (The Beatles cited the Everlys as one of their major influences.) A good starter collection of Everly hits is *The Very Best of the Everly Brothers* on Warner Bros. The song has been recorded by many groups over the years, including the Flying Burrito Brothers (on *Close Up the Honky Tonks*) and Simon and Garfunkel, whose version on their *Concert in Central Park* is one of the few that do the song justice. The Dead's certainly does not.

"Walkin' Blues" Robert Johnson, long hailed as King of the Delta Blues Singers, cut "Walking Blues" in the mid-Thirties, and there is little doubt that he performed it when he was a street musician in the late 1920s. The song was also performed by one of Johnson's contemporaries (and influences), Son House, among the most popular figures on the late-Twenties Mississippi Delta party circuit. (Most of the Delta's "race recordings," as they were called, came after 1930.) Musicologist Alan Lomax recorded Son House playing "Walkin' Blues" on the singer's front porch in 1942 for the Library of Congress, but chances are that version differed considerably from what the revelers at Twenties backwoods hoedowns might have heard. In his book *Early Downhome Blues* (1977, University of Illinois Press), Jeff Titon describes the party blues that was played by small groups this way:

"Because of the continuous, intense activity, it was desirable for the music to keep going and going. House said that he and Charley [Patton, perhaps the most influential Delta singer of the generation that eventually went on to make records: House, Johnson, Skip James, and, down the line, Muddy Waters and Howlin' Wolf] used to play dance pieces that went on for up to half an hour without stopping. . . . As lyrics could be improvised, and songs built of stanzas whose order need not have been memorized beforehand, singers could string together whatever stanzas came in their minds, reaching into their stanza storehouses or creating stanzas spontaneously. Singers were especially prized if they could keep feeding one stanza after the next; but when more than one singer was present, they sometimes took turns, one looking over at the next as a cueing device when he was through with his string."

Alas, there are no recordings capturing these "jams," and when blues records started being made with any sort of regularity, it was the shorter songs of the street tradition that made their way to wax. So we can only speculate what changes a song like "Walkin' Blues" might have undergone from its probable origin among black tenant farmers, up through Willie Dixon's oft-covered version. (Interestingly enough, Dixon also played bass on a different "Walkin' Blues" recorded by Big Joe Williams in 1961.) Muddy Waters' version is available on many reissues, the best of which is probably the Chess *Original Master Recordings* album.

"Walking the Dog" Few performers have had as many ups and downs as the author of this song, Rufus Thomas. In the late Thirties, the Memphis native was a fixture in what would be the last generation of Southern minstrel shows. He performed in tent shows around the South during the Forties, all the while holding a succession of odd jobs, including working as a DJ on Memphis' famous station, WDIA, "Mother Station of the Negroes." (B.B. King was a DJ there at the same time.) In the early Fifties he recorded for Sam Phillips' Memphis-based Sun Records, earning a number three R&B hit in 1953 with "Bear Cat," a rocked-up version of Big Mama Thornton's "Hound Dog" done well before Elvis'. He had another hit with "Ain't Gonna Be Your Dog."

He had faded by 1960, when he hit the charts again with " 'Cause I Love You," sung as a duet with his daughter Carla, who went on to have a string of hits on her own. In 1964, both "The Dog" and "Walking the Dog" became hits for Thomas on the then-new Stax label. Like most Stax performers, Thomas used the label's red-hot studio players, including Steve Cropper and Duck Dunn. Then, after a few more relatively fallow years, he had another string of dance hits with "Do the Funky Chicken," "Do the Push and Pull," and "The Breakdown," all Top Five R&B hits. His career didn't really survive the collapse of Stax Records in the mid-Seventies, though he is no doubt anticipating the next great R&B dance trend and will have a song about it when it happens.

"Wang Dang Doodle" "Wang Dang Doodle" is yet another tune by the talented and prolific blues writer Willie Dixon. It was originally covered by Howlin' Wolf for Chess Records in the early Sixties, and it appears on several anthologies of his work in a hot, almost manic version (especially compared to the Dead's often sedate reading of it).

"In the South, everybody knew that when you said you were going to 'pitch a wang dang doodle,' that meant you were going to have a ball, have a party," Dixon told me. " 'Wang dang doodle' just means havin' a good time.

"I knew guys who had every name in that song," he continued. "Automatic Slim was a guy who was supposedly great with a pistol. Razor

Totin' Jim and a whole lot of people carried razors. You see, years ago in the South, in Mississippi where I grew up, people had nicknames according to what they were involved in. People used nicknames and slang to talk around other people mainly. The blues was able to talk around, sing around, the message they didn't want other folks understandin'. These languages were all to themselves. From the beginning, there were songs they didn't want the boss to know about what was really goin' on. The blues has always given a message to the people who understood the blues, and the people that don't have to make up what they think we meant."

I asked Dixon if *he* had ever attended parties that qualified as "wang dang doodles." "Oh, all the time," he laughed. "There was a place called the Rock House north of Vicksburg [Mississippi] in a place called Watersville. All the old-timers knew about the Rock House. It was built out of rocks, but that's not how it got its name. People would go out there and have these dances. Tom Jones and a bunch of the guys would be playin', and everybody'd be stompin' their feet, dancin', jumpin' up and down, and this house would actually rock!

"One night we was out there singin' and dancin' and carryin' on—having a *real* wang dang doodle—and BAM! The floor fell in! The front part of the floor collapsed so everybody just went to the back and then *that fell in!* Nobody paid it no mind. Everybody just kept playin' and dancin'."

"The Weight" When we polled our readers about a variety of Dead-related topics in 1986, we asked them to list a few songs by other artists that the Dead should cover. "The Weight," perhaps *the* best-known song by the Band, was the fourth-largest vote getter of some 350 songs listed. In the spring of 1990 the band finally got around to playing the song.

The original version of this enigmatic song was recorded at A&R Studios in New York City in late 1967, with producer John Simon overseeing the four-track sessions. It appeared on the Band's first LP, *Music from Big Pink,* released in 1968, and it became an instant staple on FM radio. (It also made it to number sixty-eight on the *Billboard* singles chart.) In the extensive liner notes that accompany the 1989 Band double-CD anthology, *To Kingdom Come,* Robbie Robertson, author of the song, explains that his songwriting during this period was influenced a lot by the Band's association with Bob Dylan, but "I was just as much influenced by [film directors] Luis Buñuel or John Ford or [Akira] Kurosawa . . . [Buñuel, the Spanish neosurrealist] did so many films on the impossibility of sainthood—in *Viridiana* and *Nazarin* . . . there were these people trying to be good, and it's impossible to be good. In 'The Weight' it was a very simple thing. Someone says, 'Listen, would you do me this favor? When you get there will you say hello to somebody, or will you give somebody this, or will you pick up one of these for me? Oh, you're going to Nazareth; that's where the Martin guitar factory is. Do me a favor when you get there.' This is what it's all about. So the guy goes and one thing leads to another and it's like, 'Holy shit, what has this turned into? I've only come here to say hello for somebody and I've got myself in this incredible predicament.' It was very Buñuelish to me at the time."

The band rerecorded "The Weight" in early 1977 for the album and film *The Last Waltz,* and what a version—the Staples Singers handle the verses, backed by the Band! Other artists who have covered the song include Diana Ross and the Temptations.

"Werewolves of London" This certainly has to rank among the strangest songs the Dead have ever covered, yet the tune was a Top Ten hit for its author, Warren Zevon. Also unusual is the fact that the Dead performed it *while* it was a national hit—that's about as close as the Dead ever got to being a Top 40 cover band! Zevon wrote his twisted tale in 1975 but didn't record it until 1978, on his third album, *Excitable Boy,* a record filled with violent imagery and very dark humor.

"I can't disagree that there's a violent quality in my work," Zevon said in 1979, "and it may not be something that's familiar in pop songs. But in any other art form, it's the artist's prerogative to inject the adrenaline. Restraint has never been one of my virtues."

"When I Paint My Masterpiece" This Dylan song first appeared on the Band's fourth album, *Cahoots,* sung effectively by drummer Levon Helm. Dylan's own version popped up a little later on *Greatest Hits, Vol. II,* and he performed the tune regularly during his tenure fronting the Rolling Thunder Review in the mid-Seventies. Garcia sang it with his band for a while, so it was somewhat surprising that Weir took on the tune when the Dead started performing it (at Ventura, June 11, 1987, for the first time).

"Willie and the Hand Jive" This song, which was played by the Dead a few times in 1986, is one of the true classics of rock's first golden era, with its infectious "Bo Diddley beat" and colorful characters. It was written and first recorded by one of rock's most interesting and influential early practitioners, Johnny Otis, who scored a number one hit with it in June of 1958.

Though he is hardly a household name, Otis' impact on the history of rock should not be underestimated. Born Johnny Veliotes to Greek-American parents in the San Francisco Bay Area town of Vallejo in 1921, he grew up among working-class and poor blacks in Berkeley. He played music with blacks from a very early age, and by the time he was in his early twenties, he fronted his own big band.

After World War II he moved to Los Angeles, where he continued his work fronting bands and operated a nightclub in the predominantly black Watts area. He had a number of R&B hits as a bandleader, but he is better known for putting others in the spotlight through his R&B revues, The Johnny Otis Show and the Johnny Otis Rhythm and Blues Caravan. He was instrumental in the careers of such greats as Hank Ballard, Little Willie John, Big Mama Thornton, Etta James, and Gladys Knight and the Pips, for whom he wrote "Every Beat of My Heart," their first hit.

When we asked about the origins of "Willie and the Hand Jive," Otis unraveled quite a tale:

"My partner Hal Zeiger and I had a hit in England in 1957 called 'Ma, He's Making Eyes at Me.' It was a rock and roll version of an old standard, and it became number one in Britain. I couldn't figure out why until I learned that it had been a morale-boosting song for the British during the War. When people went into the bomb shelters, they used to sing that tune.

"Anyway, Hal went over that year to set up a tour for us, and when he came back he said, 'You know, I saw kids sitting in these theaters where they weren't allowed to dance, and they were doing this thing that you guys in the black bands in the old days used to do—the hand jive. You see, when the trumpets would be doing a solo in the old black jazz bands, the saxophonists would be waving their hands in time to the music—that was the hand jive. So Hal said, 'Why don't you write a song called "Hand Jive"? It'll probably be a hit in England.' So I put a little ditty together, and my partner hated it! But the guy at Capitol Records loved it and so did my four year old, and I always listen to the four year old!"

Otis' "Willie and the Hand Jive" was recorded at Bunny Robine's little studio on Fairfax Avenue in Los Angeles. "They wanted me to do it at Capitol at one of the big studios, but it didn't seem right for the kind of music I was doin'," he remembers. "My guys couldn't get relaxed in there. So we went to this funky place and of course we made a hit. Little Richard and Fats Domino used to record at Bunny's, too."

The song was cut live with a three-piece band and Otis' wife and a couple of friends supplying hand claps and backing vocals. It was an instant smash, and Otis says it was also one of the first rock songs to generate a marketing craze: "Capitol put out diagrams of how to do the hand jive, and then there was a wave of products like Hand Jive Shoes, Hand Jive Blouses for women. There was even a hat that was red with the white outline of a hand on it!"

The song has been covered frequently through the years. Eric Clapton's is probably the best-known modern version (Otis says he hasn't heard it), and no doubt many Deadheads recall that it was on the New Riders' second album, *Powerglide,* and was a frequent showstopper for the band in concert.

To what does Otis attribute the song's durability? "I don't have any idea," he says with a laugh, "but let's cover it up so it don't get cold!"

"Why Don't We Do It in the Road?" The original of this tune appears on the Beatles' White Album, released in November of 1968. It was recorded just a month earlier, on October 10, at EMI studios in London. It began as an improvisation by Paul McCartney and, in fact, McCartney is the only player and singer on the track.

"You Ain't Woman Enough" This Donna Godchaux showcase was played thirteen times by the Dead in 1973. It was originally recorded by Loretta Lynn, the country music great whose life was immortalized in the film *Coal Miner's Daughter,* starring Sissy Spacek. The Butcher's Hollow, Kentucky, native began a string of country hits in 1962 that has continued up to the present. "You Ain't Woman Enough (To Take My Man)" was Lynn's tenth charting record—it hit number two in mid-1966—and it paved the way for her first number one a few months later, "Don't Come Home A-Drinkin' (With Lovin' on Your Mind)." Since "You Ain't Woman Enough," Lynn has hit the Top Ten twenty-nine times on her own with such tunes as "Coal Miner's Daughter," "Trouble in Paradise," "The Pill," and "She's Got You," and another twelve times singing duets with Conway "Love the Hair Helmet" Twitty.

"You Win Again" Though he is often considered the "father of modern country music," Hank Williams' roots were as much in black blues as white mountain music. Born King Hiram Williams in 1923 on a tenant

Marquee at the Warfield Theater, San Francisco, for the Dead's fifteen-night run in 1980. *(Photo by Richard McCaffrey)*

farm in Mount Olive, Alabama, he grew up poor and worked at a succession of menial jobs (selling peanuts and newspapers, shining shoes) as a youth. He listened to rural black blues and was also influenced by the gospel music he heard in his local Baptist church. At fourteen, he hit the road with his guitar and tried to crack the hillbilly music circuit. He was only a minor success until the late Forties when he started recording for the Sterling label. (Later he switched to MGM.) His first hit came in 1949 with "Lovesick Blues," and from 1950 until his death in 1952 (of a heart attack brought on by his conscientious misuse of pills and alcohol) he had a number of hits, including "You Win Again."

Like most singers whose work was popular in rural markets, he was recorded almost exclusively on 78s, but a number of LP compilations of his work exist. His impact on Nashville is incalculable, and many of his songs remain in the repertoires of currently popular country artists, much as rock bands pay tribute to Chuck Berry by playing his songs.

The Best of
the Dead

■■ ■■ ■■ ■■ ■■ ■■

A Guide for Tape Collectors

Sooner or later, just about everyone who loves the Grateful Dead
begins collecting tapes of the band's live performances. Some people are
completely casual about it, picking up tapes here and there through the
years from close friends. Others are part of huge networks of traders. I
have friends who own several thousand tapes, and friends who own just a
handful. There are Heads who collect only pre-1972 shows, Heads who
try to collect every show, and Heads who collect only the shows they at-
tend. If you're well connected with experienced (and generous) traders,
building a good collection can be relatively simple. If you're just starting
out, it can be very frustrating. But hang in there—this isn't a competition;
it's supposed to be fun!

With literally thousands of shows to choose from, it's difficult to know
which ones are worth the trouble to seek out from other collectors. Most

of you have probably had the experience of reading a set list on a tape cover, assumed it's a great show because of the songs played, and then being disappointed by the music on the tape. With any luck, what follows will help beginning and intermediate tape collectors shoot for the crème de la crème of Dead shows.

In 1987, *The Golden Road* published the results of a survey in which tape collectors were asked to list their ten favorite Dead tapes from each year. Hundreds of hardcore collectors responded, and those results represent the first real consensus on the subject. Subsequently, the authoritative GD set-list guide, *DeadBase,* polled its readership, too. The lists below were drawn from those surveys, along with a dose of my own opinions. A few caveats: The best shows are not necessarily the best-quality tapes (although the polls tend to favor soundboard and FM radio broadcast tapes). For instance, a show like 6/24/70 belongs in any collection, yet is generally available only as a hissy, low-fidelity audience tape. Because the higher-quality recordings are more popular trade items, they are in more collections and thus score better in these sorts of polls, further skewing the results. And, of course, there are hundreds of shows (mainly in the Sixties and very early Seventies) that simply don't exist on tape, even in the Dead's archives.

There are as many opinions about what tapes are the "best" as there are collectors, and no doubt you'll disagree with some inclusions and exclusions. (Plus, as new tapes become available, opinions about which are "best" change.) A few of my favorites aren't on here, either. But this isn't intended to be The Word From On High. It's just a guide; a starting point, really (with each year's ten recommendations listed in chronological order). But one thing I can guarantee: there's a lifetime of good listening in the lists below.

Using *DeadBase* as my guide, I've listed a few highlights from each of the shows, and also tried to offer a little historical context for each year. Serious collectors should definitely consider purchasing *DeadBase,* which contains the complete set lists for all these shows, as well as thousands of others and all sorts of useful lists and statistics. For info on this invaluable reference, send an SASE (Self-Addressed Stamped Envelope) to DeadBase, P.O. Box 499, Hanover, NH 03755.

1966–1967

Not many tapes from this era are in circulation, and that's a shame, because the ones that are out there show us a lot about the band's development from what was essentially a good-time dance band that played mainly cover tunes to the psychedelic warriors we came to know and love. The music gets progressively weirder as the months pass, and in the fall of 1967 the band starts playing in earnest the material that would become *Anthem of the Sun* (released the following year): "That's It for the Other One," "New Potato Caboose," "Born Cross-Eyed," "Alligator," and "Caution." These songs represent the band's first serious forays into original songwriting. The first versions of "Dark Star" and "Lovelight" occur that fall, too.

1/7/66, The Matrix (San Francisco)—Material from Warlocks demo; "Death Don't Have No Mercy"; "She Belongs to Me"; "Midnight Hour."

3/25, Trouper's Hall (Los Angeles)—The classic early GD-as-danceband show. "Hog for You Baby"; "Hey Little One"; "Cold Rain and Snow."

7/3, Fillmore Auditorium (San Francisco)—"Viola Lee Blues"; "Dancin' in the Streets"; "I Know You Rider"; "He Was a Friend of Mine."

11/29, The Matrix—Three sets. "Viola Lee Blues"; rare "Cream Puff War"; "Good Morning Little Schoolgirl."

1/14/67, Golden Gate Park (San Francisco)—The Human Be-In. "Morning Dew"; "Viola Lee Blues"; long, interesting "Good Morning Little Schoolgirl" with jazz flautist Charles Lloyd.

5/5, Fillmore Auditorium—"He Was a Friend of Mine"; "The Golden Road"; "New Potato Caboose" into "Alligator."

6/18, Monterey Pop Festival (California)—Only two songs on most tapes: "Viola Lee Blues" and "Cold Rain and Snow."

9/29, Straight Theater (San Francisco)—Mickey Hart's first show "China Cat-Rider"; lengthy "Alligator"; "That's It for the Other One."

11/10, Shrine Auditorium (Los Angeles)—"Alligator" into "Caution"; "Viola Lee Blues"; "Morning Dew."

11/11, Shrine Auditorium—"That's It for the Other One"; "Alligator" into "Caution"; "New Potato Caboose."

1968

Again, tapes from this year are fairly scarce, though most of what's in circulation is pretty hot. The first few months of the year find the band still concentrating heavily on the *Anthem* material. "China Cat," introduced in the fall of 1967, pops up more often, and the first versions of "The Eleven" appear. In June, "St. Stephen" is introduced and it becomes an instant favorite with both the band and fans. The rest of the year is one incredible show after another, most featuring "Dark Star" and/or "St. Stephen," the songs from *Anthem*, and nuggets like "Death Don't Have Mercy" and "Lovelight." Tom Constanten (T. C.) begins playing with the band in November, adding a totally new dimension with his organ. The band is clearly spreading its wings at most of these shows, testing the sonic limits of electric instruments (feedback fun!) and the elasticity of the song form. Various members of the band (usually at least Garcia, Lesh, and Hart, plus occasional outside guests) play occasional very loose dates in San Francisco as Mickey and the Hartbeats.

2/14/68, Carousel Ballroom (San Francisco)—"Schoolgirl"; all of what would become *Anthem of the Sun* in very spacey versions; "Midnight Hour."

3/3, Haight Street (San Francisco)—Free concert featuring "Viola Lee Blues," "Smokestack Lightning."

3/17, Carousel Ballroom—"Dark Star"; *Anthem* material; "China Cat" into "The Eleven."

6/14, Fillmore East (New York City)—"The Eleven" into "St. Stephen"; "Caution."

9/2, Sky River Festival (Sultan, Washington)—"Dark Star"; "That's It for the Other One"; "Alligator."

10/9, The Matrix (San Francisco)—(Actually Mickey and the Hartbeats plus Airplane bassist Jack Casady) "Lovelight"; "The Other One"; "Dark Star."

10/13, Avalon Ballroom (San Francisco)—"Morning Dew," "That's It for the Other One"; "Dark Star."

10/19, The Matrix—(Mickey and the Hartbeats plus harmonica ace Paul Butterfield) "Cosmic Charlie"; three different "Dark Star" jams; "The Eleven."

10/30, The Matrix—(Mickey and the Hartbeats plus guitarist Elvin Bishop) "Dark Star"; "Death Letter Blues."

12/31 Winterland (San Francisco)—"Dark Star" into "St. Stephen"; "Midnight Hour."

1969

Live Dead, released at the end of 1969, beautifully captures what this year was all about for the Dead—long, exploratory jams; fascinating rhythm exercises; and Pigpen at his peak on "Lovelight," "Hard to Handle," "Good Morning Little Schoolgirl," and "Alligator." Early in the year, the band frequently opens sets with acoustic versions of two songs that would appear on *Aoxomoxoa:* "Dupree's Diamond Blues" and "Mountains of the Moon." New tunes introduced in the second half of 1969 include a number of songs that would appear on *Workingman's Dead* the following spring: "High Time," "Dire Wolf," "Casey Jones," "Easy Wind," "Black Peter," "Uncle John's Band," "New Speedway Boogie," and "Cumberland Blues." During this period the pairing of "China Cat Sunflower" and "I Know You Rider" gels into permanence, and Weir's increasing infatuation with country music is reflected by the frequent appearance of "Mama Tried" and "Me and My Uncle" in the Dead's sets. The short-lived but fondly remembered rarity "Mason's Children" first turns up in December; it's gone by the end of February 1970.

2/27/69, Fillmore West (San Francisco)—First-set "That's It for the Other One"; second-set with *Live Dead* sequence ("Dark Star→St. Stephen→The Eleven→Lovelight").

3/1, Fillmore West—"New Potato Caboose" into "Doin' That Rag"; acoustic "Mountains of the Moon"; *Live Dead* sequence.

4/5, Avalon Ballroom (San Francisco)—*Live Dead* sequence; "Alligator"; "Doin' That Rag."

4/6, Avalon Ballroom—"Schoolgirl"; "That's It for the Other One"; "Viola Lee Blues."

4/22, The Ark (Boston)—"That's It for the Other One" into "Death Don't Have No Mercy"; *Live Dead* sequence.

6/7, Fillmore West—"St. Stephen"; "Cold Rain and Snow"; "Lovelight" with Janis Joplin.

6/14, Monterey (California) Performing Arts Center—"Lovelight" to open and close the show; "He Was a Friend of Mine"; "Dark Star."

7/12, New York State Pavilion (Flushing)—"Hard to Handle"; "Death Don't Have No Mercy"; "Lovelight."

12/12, Thelma Theater (Los Angeles)—Very early "Uncle John's Band"; "He Was a Friend of Mine"; wiggy "Alligator" jam.

12/28, Hollywood Pop Festival (Florida)—"Good Lovin' "; "Mason's Children"; "China Cat."

1970

The Dead's renewed interest in folk and country music really explodes in this year. T. C. leaves the band in January. The next month they begin incorporating acoustic sets into some of their shows, and the sound of the two records they release in 1970—*Workingman's Dead* and *American Beauty*—show the influence of the softer, harmony-laden music of their friends Crosby, Stills, and Nash. The New Riders of the Purple Sage, a country-rock band whose original lineup included Garcia on pedal steel guitar, Lesh on bass, and Mickey on drums, opens many shows this year and next. A fistful of Dead classics are introduced in 1970, including "Friend of the Devil," "Brokedown Palace," "Ripple," Candyman," "Sugar Magnolia," "Truckin'," "Attics of My Life," "To Lay Me Down." Among the cover tunes that first appear in this year are "Goin' Down the Road Feeling Bad" (usually sandwiched between sections of "Not Fade Away"), "El Paso," and "Around and Around." *Live Dead* material is still common, though "The Eleven" vanishes by midyear. The acoustic set is history by year's end, as well. Quite a year, all in all.

1/16/70, Springer's Ballroom (Portland, Oregon)—"That's It for the Other One" into "Cosmic Charlie"; "The Eleven" into "Death Don't Have No Mercy"; "Alligator."

2/11, Fillmore East (New York City)—Wild jamming with Fleetwood Mac's Peter Green plus Duane and Gregg Allman on "Dark Star," "Lovelight"; "Not Fade Away" set opener.

2/13, Fillmore East—Many people's all-time favorite. "Dark Star"; "Lovelight"; "Smokestack Lightning"; acoustic set.

2/14, Fillmore East—Killer "Not Fade Away" into "Mason's Children"; "Dancin' in the Streets"; "Caution"; acoustic set.

5/2, Harpur College (Binghamton, New York)—One of the best. "That's It for the Other One" into "Cosmic Charlie"; excellent acoustic set; "Viola Lee Blues"; "It's a Man's World."

5/15, Fillmore East (actually an early and late show)—"Easy Wind"; "Attics of My Life"; "That's It for the Other One"; "Dark Star"; acoustic set.

6/24, Capitol Theater (Port Chester, New York)—Amazing sequence of "Dark Star"→"Attics"→"Dark Star"→the second version of "Sugar Magnolia"→"Dark Star"→"St. Stephen"→"China Cat-Rider."

9/20, Fillmore East—Acoustic set with "New Speedway Boogie"; "Easy Wind"; "Not Fade Away" into "Caution"; "Attics of My Life."

10/31, SUNY-Stonybrook Gym (New York) (actually early and late show)—"Viola Lee Blues" into "Cumberland Blues"; "That's It for the Other One" into "Cosmic Charlie"; "St. Stephen."

11/8, Capitol Theater—"Dark Star"; oldies night with "Searchin'," "Mystery Train," "New Orleans," "My Babe"; acoustic set.

1971

Mickey Hart's departure from the band at the beginning of the year changes the band's sound fairly dramatically, though Bill Kreutzmann quickly makes it clear that his loose, airy style is fluid enough to carry the band rhythmically. With Pigpen not much of a factor on keyboards, the band plays as a de facto quartet much of the time—until pianist Keith Godchaux joins the group in October. The beginning of the year sees a burst of great new songs introduced: "Bird Song," "Greatest Story Ever Told" (sans its current chorus), "Bertha," "Loser," "Wharf Rat," and "Deal." In the second half of 1970, new tunes hatched include "Tennessee Jed," "Sugaree," "Mr. Charlie," "Jack Straw," "Mexicali Blues," "One More Saturday Night," "Ramble On Rose," "Brown-Eyed Woman," and "Comes a Time." Among the new covers are "Big River" and "Sing Me Back Home." There is some grumbling among the faithful that the band's new concentration on songs means the band is jamming less, and there is some validity to that complaint. But you'll still find excellent versions of "Dark Star" and "That's It for the Other One," and the sequence of "Not Fade Away" into "Goin' Down the Road" back into "Not Fade Away" matures this year; in fact, they play it most shows. "St. Stephen" doesn't survive the year.

2/18/71, Capitol Theater (Port Chester, New York)—First versions of "Bertha," "Greatest Story Ever Told," "Playin' in the Band," "Wharf Rat," "Loser"; fine "Dark Star," "Hard to Handle."

4/5, Manhattan Center (New York City)—"China Cat-Rider"; "The Other One"; "Sing Me Back Home."

4/17, Dillon Gym, Princeton University (New Jersey)—Pigpen lover's delight with hilarious "Lovelight," "Good Lovin'," "Hard to Handle"; also "Goin' Down the Road."

4/26, Fillmore East (New York City)—"Dark Star" in first set; Duane Allman on fiery versions of "Sugar Magnolia" and "It Hurts Me Too"; "Good Lovin'."

4/27, Fillmore East—The Beach Boys join the Dead for "Help Me

Rhonda," "Riot in Cell Block Number 9," "Okie from Muskogee," and others; "Uncle John's"; "Lovelight."

4/28, Fillmore East—T. C. returns to help out on "Dark Star"→"St. Stephen"→"Not Fade Away," and more; "That's It for the Other One."

4/29, Fillmore East—The band's final Fillmore East show. Tremendously varied jam after hot "Alligator"; "Goin' Down the Road" into "Cold Rain and Snow"; "Morning Dew"; electric "Ripple." Not to be missed!

7/2, Fillmore West (San Francisco)—The group's last Fillmore West show—acidy from beginning to end. "That's It for the Other One" dedicated to Owsley in jail; "China Cat-Rider"; "Good Lovin'."

8/6, Hollywood Palladium (California)—Funky, chunky "Hard to Handle"; "St. Stephen" opens second set; "The Other One" split by "Me and My Uncle."

11/7, Harding Theater (San Francisco)—"Dark Star"; "The Other One" split by "Me and My Uncle"; "Comes a Time."

1972

The momentum the band started building in the fall of 1971 with the addition of Keith Godchaux reaches an incredible peak in the first half of 1972. The band plays its first extensive tour of Europe in April and May, and I'm sure most Heads will agree it stands as one of the group's strongest tours ever. (The superb live album culled from the tour, *Europe '72*, is released in November 1972.) Several new songs appear: "Looks Like Rain," "Black-Throated Wind" (both from Weir's 1972 solo LP, *Ace*), "Mississippi Half-Step," "Stella Blue," and "He's Gone." "Playin' in the Band," "Truckin'," and "Bird Song" mature into red-hot jamming tunes, and some of the versions of "Dark Star" are as spacey as Dead music gets. Donna Godchaux, Keith's wife, joins the band as a singer in March. Pigpen's health continues to decline; his last show with the band is in June of 1972.

4/14/72, Tivoli Theater (Copenhagen)—Mind-bending "Dark Star" into "Sugar Magnolia"; "Good Lovin' " into "Caution" into "Who Do You Love."

5/4, Olympia Theater (Paris)—Another weird "Dark Star"→ "Sugar Mag" combo; "Not Fade Away"→"Goin' Down the Road"→"Not Fade Away."

5/11, Civic Hall (Rotterdam, Holland)—Same highlights as 4/14 (page 299), plus "Morning Dew" to open the second set; "Uncle John's."

5/18, Deutsches Museum Halle (Munich)—"Dark Star" into "Morning Dew"; "Sittin' on Top of the World" second-set opener; "Playin'."

5/23, The Strand Lyceum (London)—"Dark Star"→"Morning Dew"; "Not Fade Away" split by "Hey Bo Diddley"; "Rockin' Pneumonia" in nineteen-song first set.

5/26, The Strand Lyceum—"The Other One" split by "Morning Dew"; hot "Truckin' " jam; "Not Fade Away"→"Goin' Down the Road" in first set.

8/21, Berkeley Community Theater (California)—"Dark Star" into "El Paso"; "Uncle John's" into "Saturday Night."

8/27, Renaissance Faire Ground (Veneta, Oregon)—Three incredible sets with definitive versions of "Dark Star," "Playin'," "Bird Song." One of the best ever.

9/28, Stanley Theater (Jersey City, New Jersey)—Wild and woolly "Other One" split by "Me and Bobby McGee"; "Playin' "; impressive "Not Fade Away" closer.

11/19, Hofheinz Pavilion (Houston)—Colossally out there "Dark Star" into the first "Weather Report Suite Prelude"; "Sugar Magnolia" into "Goin' Down the Road" closer.

1973

The year gets off to an auspicious start with the introduction in the very first show of "Eyes of the World," "China Doll," "Row Jimmy," "Here Comes Sunshine," and more. If any song symbolizes what makes 1973 shows special, it's probably "Eyes," which stretched the band in a new, jazzy direction. "Let It Grow," which pops up in November, usually as the last part of the "Weather Report Suite," also takes the band to some interesting new jamming spaces. Some of the vocal harmonies on songs like "Here Comes Sunshine" and "Eyes" are pretty painful to listen to on some tapes, but the playing all year is fantastic—it really swings in a way it never had before; and again, some of the spacey passages are so far out there it's easy to forget you're listening to a rock 'n' roll band— or music, for that matter. Eight shows in September feature a horn section on several songs; mercifully this was just a temporary aberration in the GD force field. *Wake of the Flood* is released on the band's own Grateful Dead Records label in October. Some of the shows the band played in

1973 and 1974 are among the longest they ever played, with first sets frequently around sixteen songs (the current per-show average), and second sets occasionally approaching two hours in length. There are even a few three-set wonders in there.

2/9/73, Maples Pavilion, Stanford University (Palo Alto, California)—First versions of "Eyes of the World," "Here Comes Sunshine," "China Doll," "Loose Lucy," "They Love Each Other," "Row Jimmy," "Wave That Flag" (precursor of "U.S. Blues").

2/15, Dane County Coliseum (Madison, Wisconsin)—"Here Comes Sunshine"; "Dark Star" into "Eyes of the World" into "China Doll"; first "You Ain't Woman Enough."

2/17, St. Paul Auditorium (St. Paul, Minneapolis)—"Sunshine" into "China Cat"; "Bird Song" and "Playin' " in first set; "Not Fade"→"Goin' Down the Road."

3/21, Memorial Auditorium (Utica, New York)—Seventeen-song first set ("China Cat," "Playin' "); "Dark Star"→"Eyes."

6/10, RFK Stadium (Washington, D.C.)—Three long sets with most *Wake of the Flood* material; "Dark Star"; third set with members of the Allman Brothers. A classic.

8/1, Roosevelt Stadium (Jersey City, New Jersey)—"Bird Song"; "Dark Star"→"El Paso"→"Eyes"→"Morning Dew."

9/24, Pittsburgh Civic Arena—Horn section on "Eyes" and "Weather Report Suite"; "Truckin' " with "Nobody's Fault" jam.

11/10, Winterland (San Francisco)—Knockout sequence of "Playin' "→"Uncle John's"→"Morning Dew"→"Uncle John's" reprise→"Playin' " reprise; "Weather Report Suite."

11/11, Winterland—"Dark Star"→"Eyes of the World"; "Weather Report Suite"; "To Lay Me Down."

Pauley Pavilion, UCLA—Same "Playin' "→"Uncle John's," etc. sequence as 11/10 above. "Eyes" into "Sugar Magnolia."

1974

I've always viewed the Dead's 1974 shows as being part of the same fabric as the 1973 shows. There are several excellent new songs—"Scarlet Begonias," "U.S. Blues" (evolved from 1973's "Wave That Flag"), "Must've Been the Roses," "Ship of Fools," "Cassidy"—but I don't hear much that's really *new* in 1974 tapes, with the exception of the very strange minisets of electronic weirdness provided by Lesh and Ned Lagin at some shows. That's not a criticism, just an observation. Weary from years on the road and lugging around their mammoth "Wall of Sound" during 1974, the band calls it quits for a while after a spectacular five-night run at Winterland in October. The magic of those shows is nicely captured in *The Grateful Dead* movie, released in 1977. A world with no Grateful Dead? Could this really be the end? Nobody knew for sure.

2/24/74, Winterland (San Francisco)—"Dark Star" into "Morning Dew"; "Weather Report Suite"; "China Cat."

3/23, The Cow Palace (Brisbane, California)—Debut of the "Wall of Sound." First "Cassidy" and "Scarlet Begonias"; "Playin' "→"Uncle John's"→"Morning Dew" sequence similar to 11/10/73.

5/19, Memorial Coliseum (Portland, Oregon)—"Weather Report Suite"; "Truckin' " with long jam; one of only three versions of "Money Money."

6/16, State Fairgrounds (Des Moines, Iowa)—Stretched "Playin' "; superb "Eyes of the World"; "Truckin'."

6/18, Freedom Hall (Louisville, Kentucky)—"Eyes" into "China Doll" in first set; "Weather Report Suite"; "Morning Dew" encore.

6/23, Jai-Alai Fronton (Miami)—"Weather Report Suite" into

Dancin' to the Dead, June 1986. *(Photo by Ron Delany)*

"China Doll" to end first set; "Dark Star" into wild "Spanish Jam" into "U.S. Blues"; only version of "Let It Rock."

8/6, Roosevelt Stadium (Jersey City, New Jersey)—"Playin' "→"Scarlet"→"Playin' " in first set; Ned and Phil miniset; fine Spanish jam into "The Other One."

10/18, Winterland (San Francisco)—One of the all-time spacey shows, with Phil and Ned's segment into "Dark Star" into "Morning Dew"; "Weather Report Suite."

10/19, Winterland—Fantastic "Eyes of the World" into "China Doll" in first set; "Truckin' " with "Caution" jam; "Uncle John's."

10/20, Winterland—Last show before the "retirement." Three hot sets. "Playin' "; "Not Fade Away"; "Eyes" into "Stella Blue." Mickey Hart plays on much of the show.

1975

Though the band was officially on hiatus during 1975 to work on assorted solo projects and a new album (*Blues for Allah*), there were four gigs, each one very different from the others. The new songs showcased for the first time at these shows included some of their most challenging material: "Blues for Allah," "Stronger Than Dirt," "Sage and Spirit," "Crazy Fingers," "The Music Never Stopped," and the linked triumvirate of "Help on the Way," "Slipknot," and "Franklin's Tower."

3/23/75, Kezar Stadium (San Francisco)—One short set with ultra-spacey "Blues for Allah," "Stronger Than Dirt"; "Johnny B. Goode."

6/17, Winterland (San Francisco)—The famous "Bob Fried Benefit." First "Help on the Way"→"Slipknot"→"Franklin's Tower" sequence; first "Crazy Fingers"; "Stronger Than Dirt."

8/13, Great American Music Hall (San Francisco)—"Help on the Way"–"Slipknot"–"Franklin's Tower"; first versions of "The Music Never Stopped" and "Sage and Spirit"; "Blues for Allah."

9/28, Golden Gate Park (San Francisco)—One set with "Help on the Way"→"Slipknot" opener; "Truckin' "; "Goin' Down the Road."

1976

This is a major transitional year for the group. The "retirement" from live performing officially ends in June, and Mickey Hart returns to the fold after a five-year absence. A passel of old Dead tunes are revived, including "St. Stephen," "Cosmic Charlie," "High Time," and "Comes a Time." "Dancin' in the Streets" reemerges in a new disco arrangement, and "The Wheel," from Garcia's 1972 solo album, is brought into the repertoire for the first time. "Might as Well" and the band's arrangement of "Samson and Delilah" also debut. "Lazy Lightning," which Weir played with Kingfish earlier, also joins the rotation. To me, the band sounds radically different from the 1974 version of the group. Garcia's guitar tone is rounder, and many of the arrangements sound awfully slow, at least in retrospect. Vocal harmonies are ragged at best, and though there's lots of interesting jamming, there's very little real "space." I think one reason some of these shows seem a tad laid back is that the band decided to play smaller theaters instead of giant arenas and stadiums, so the dynamics weren't stretched the same way they had been in 1973 and 1974. Beyond that, though, the long layoff and Mickey's return meant there was going to be a period of readjustment.

6/3/76, Paramount Theater (Seattle)—The "official" return after the retirement. First versions of "Lazy Lightning," "The Wheel," "Might as Well"; "Samson and Delilah"; new disco "Dancin' in the Streets."

6/12, Boston Music Hall—First "Comes a Time" since 1972; "Let It Grow" split by "drums"; encore of "Sugar Mag" split by "U.S. Blues."

6/15, Beacon Theater (New York City)—"St. Stephen" opens second set; "Sugar Mag" split by "Scarlet Begonias"; "Dancin'."

7/12, Orpheum Theater (San Francisco)—"Help on the Way"–"Slipknot"–"Franklin's Tower"; "Lazy Lightning"; "Dancin'."

7/18, Orpheum Theater—"Supplication" into "Let It Grow"; "St. Stephen" split by "Not Fade Away"; "The Other One."

8/4, Roosevelt Stadium (Jersey City, New Jersey)—"Help on the Way"; "Dancin' " into "The Wheel"; "The Other One."

9/25, Capital Centre (Landover, Maryland)—"Dancin' " into "Cosmic Charlie"; "St. Stephen" split by "Not Fade Away" and "drums"; "Lazy Lightning."

10/9, Oakland Stadium (California)—"St. Stephen" second set opener; "Help on the Way"→"Slipknot"→drums→"Samson"→"Slipknot"→"Franklin's Tower."

10/15, Shrine Auditorium (Los Angeles)—"Eyes of the World" into "The Music Never Stopped" second-set opener; "Comes a Time" into "Franklin's Tower"; "The Other One."

12/31, Cow Palace (Brisbane, California)—"Sugar Magnolia" into

"Eyes"; "Help on the Way"–"Slipknot"–"Not Fade Away"; "Morning Dew."

1977

I know several people who feel that 1977 was the Dead's best year ever. I'll steer clear of that sort of absolute (after all, 1969, 1977, and 1985—three great years—are different bands in so many ways it's like comparing apples and oranges), but clearly 1977 is brimming with spectacular shows and consistently stellar playing. The April-May East Coast tour is easily among the group's finest. Tunes like "Dancin' in the Streets" and "Help on the Way" really blossom in 1977, and then there are the new songs: "Terrapin" (which even turns up as an encore a few times), "Estimated Prophet," "Fire on the Mountain" (paired with "Scarlet Begonias"), "Passenger"—incredible! My favorite versions of "Not Fade Away" come from this year, and "St. Stephen" is greatly improved over most of the 1976 ones. A newly arranged "Good Lovin' " (played twice near the end of 1976) becomes one of Weir's showstoppers. "Jackaroe" and "Iko-Iko" are among the new cover tunes introduced, and a few pre-retirement favorites come back: "Brokedown Palace," "Jack Straw," "China Doll," "Black Peter," and, during the last week of the year, "China Cat-Rider." I've never met a 1977 show I didn't like, and most of them are certifiably great.

2/26/77, Swing Auditorium (San Bernardino, California)—Opens with the first "Terrapin"; first "Estimated Prophet"; "Help on the Way"; "Dancin' " into "Eyes."

3/18, Winterland (San Francisco)—First "Fire on the Mountain" (and first "Scarlet-Fire" combo); only "Terrapin" with "At a Siding" section; blazing "Not Fade Away."

5/4, The Palladium (New York City)—"Dancin' in the Streets"; "Scarlet-Fire"; beautiful "Comes a Time."

5/8, Barton Hall, Cornell University (Ithaca, New York)—Monster show with spectacular "Scarlet-Fire"; "St. Stephen" split by "Not Fade Away" into one of the all-time versions of "Morning Dew."

5/9, Buffalo War Memorial—Awesome "Help on the Way"–"Slipknot"–"Franklin's Tower" opener; "Other One"; "Comes a Time."

5/15, St. Louis Arena—First versions of "Iko-Iko" and "Passenger"; "St. Stephen"; "Eyes of the World."

5/19, Fox Theater (Atlanta, Georgia)—"Terrapin"→"Playin' "→ "Uncle John's"; first "China Doll" since 1974.

6/9, Winterland—Another great "Help on the Way"; "St. Stephen" into "Terrapin"; "Not Fade Away."

9/3, Raceway Park (Englishtown, New Jersey)—"Eyes of the World"; extended jams on "He's Gone," "Truckin' "; "Terrapin" encore.

12/29, Winterland—"Playin' " into first "China Cat" since 1974; more "Playin' " jams; "Terrapin" encore.

1978

It's hard to distinguish between the best of 1977 and 1978; they're definitely part of the same animal. Though Keith and Donna were going through rough times this year—Keith was sufficiently out of it much of the time that he was practically a nonpresence at some shows—the strain in their relationship to each other and to the other members of the band isn't particularly evident on tapes. The band records the album *Shakedown Street* with Little Feat's Lowell George producing, and the new originals introduced in 1978 are all from that record: the title cut, "Stagger Lee," "I Need a Miracle," "If I Had the World to Give," and Donna's "From the Heart of Me." The combo of "I Need a Miracle" into "Bertha" into "Good Lovin' " turns up often. "Help on the Way" and "Slipknot" are put in mothballs, and "Franklin's Tower" shows up paired more often than not with "Mississippi Half-Step." The most interesting new cover tune is Warren Zevon's "Werewolves of London," which gets repeated plays during the group's spring and summer tours. This year has other curiosities, as well: During the first three shows of the year (January 6–8) Garcia was unable to sing, so the song lists are filled with Weir's repertoire. In September the band plays its legendary stand in the shadow of the Sphynx and the Great Pyramid in Cairo.

1/22/78, MacArthur Court (Eugene, Oregon)—Legendary "Close Encounters space" into "St. Stephen"; "Terrapin"; "The Other One."

4/15, William and Mary College (Williamsburg, Virginia)—"Let It Grow"; "Not Fade Away" into "Morning Dew"; "Playin'."

7/8, Red Rocks Amphitheater (Morrison, Colorado)—"The Other One" into "Eyes"; "Wharf Rat" into "Franklin's Tower"; triple encore with "Terrapin," "Saturday Night," and "Werewolves."

8/30, Red Rocks Amphitheater—Another "Other One" into

"Eyes"; first versions of "I Need a Miracle," "Stagger Lee," and "If I Had the World to Give."

9/16, Gizeh Sound and Light Theater (Cairo, Egypt)—Best of the Egypt shows. Second set opens with Hamza El-Din, leading Egyptian musicians, who are joined by the Dead, who eventually go into "Fire on the Mountain," then "Iko-Iko"; "Shakedown."

10/21, Winterland (San Francisco)—Hamza El-Din leads Egyptian-flavored Dead jam to open, into "Promised Land"; incredible jam with harmonica ace Lee Oskar on "Got My Mojo Working"; "The Other One."

10/22, Winterland—Hamza and Dead jam into "Deal" to open; "Scarlet-Fire"; good post-"drums" jams with John Cipollina.

11/20, Cleveland Music Hall—Trippy second set with excellent "Playin'," "Shakedown," "If I Had the World to Give."

12/30, Pauley Pavilion, UCLA—"Scarlet-Fire"; Hamza jam into "St. Stephen"; "Playin' " into "Shakedown."

12/31, Winterland—One of the all-time greats! You name it, it's here: "Scarlet-Fire," "Dark Star," "The Other One," "Terrapin," "Playin'." Three-plus sets.

1979

After a pair of tours in January and February, Keith and Donna are dismissed from the group. Brent Mydland, who'd been playing in Weir's solo group, joins in April, giving the band their best vocal blend ever. He also brings new keyboard colors into the group's sound—synthesizer and Hammond organ. He fits in quickly and easily; the band's playing is surprisingly confident all year. The Dead get another new family member at the same time: "The Beast," the massive ring of giant drums Mickey Hart had put together to work on the soundtrack of *Apocalypse Now*. From this point on, the Hart-Kreutzmann drum solos take on new life—not just because of the big drums, but also the increasing use of exotic percussion from around the world. The Rhythm Devils are born! In August, four new songs appear: "Althea," "Easy to Love You," "Lost Sailor," and "Saint of Circumstance." "Alabama Getaway" premieres in November. "St. Stephen" disappears again.

1/10/79, Nassau Coliseum (Uniondale, New York)—"Shakedown"; "Dark Star"; "St. Stephen."

1/20, Shea's Buffalo Theater (New York)—"Other One" into last "Dark Star" for three years; "Not Fade Away."

2/17, Oakland Coliseum (California)—Keith and Donna's last show with first "Big Railroad Blues" and "Greatest Story" since 1974; "The Wheel" into "Shakedown"; "High Time."

4/22, Spartan Stadium (San Jose, California)—Brent's first show. "Scarlet-Fire"; "Passenger"; "Shakedown" second encore.

10/27, Cape Cod Coliseum—Amazing "Dancin' " into "Franklin's Tower" combo; "Caution" jam into "The Other One."

11/6, The Spectrum (Philadelphia)—Jam-filled, four-song second set highlighted by "Terrapin" opener and lengthy "Playin'."

12/1, Stanley Theater (Pittsburgh)—"China Cat"; "Gloria" jam after "He's Gone"; "Not Fade Away."

12/26, Oakland Auditorium (California)—"Uncle John's" opens second set; first "Brokedown" in two years (and last time it was played not as an encore); "Shakedown"→"Uncle John's" encore.

12/28, Oakland Auditorium—"High Time"; "Bertha"→"Good Lovin' " closer; "Playin'."

12/31, Oakland Auditorium—Three sets; "Sugar Mag" into "China Cat"; "Not Fade Away" with John Cipollina; "Good Lovin' " encore.

1980

The new lineup solidifies as Brent becomes more comfortable in the band. The material from *Go to Heaven* gets a heavy workout, particularly "Alabama Getaway" and "Lost Sailor"–"Saint of Circumstance." For the first time in their fifteen-year history, no Grateful Dead originals are introduced. In the fall of 1980, the band plays its first acoustic sets (in addition to their usual two electric sets) since 1970—fifteen nights at the Warfield Theater in San Francisco, eight nights at New York's Radio City Music Hall, and a pair in New Orleans. In addition to songs from the 1970 acoustic repertoire, tunes added for the sets include "To Lay Me Down," "Bird Song" (both absent since the retirement), "Ripple" (missing since 1971), an instrumental version of Weir's "Heaven Help the Fool," "Oh Babe It Ain't No Lie," and "On the Road Again." The double-album *Reckoning,* released the following year, captures the acoustic sets well. *Dead Set,* culled from the electric sets that fall, is less successful in my view.

5/10/80, Hartford Civic Center (Connecticut)—Seven songs before "drums," including "Stranger" into "Comes a Time," "Uncle John's"; double encore.

6/8, Folsom Field (Boulder, Colorado)—The first fifteenth-anniversary show, opens with "Uncle John's"→"Playin' "→"Uncle John's"; "drums" into "Saint of Circumstance."

6/20, West High Auditorium (Anchorage, Alaska)—"Jack Straw" into "Franklin's Tower"; "Let It Grow"; "The Other One."

8/31, Capital Centre (Landover, Maryland)—"Uncle John's" into "Lost Sailor"; "Comes a Time"; "Lazy Lightning."

9/2, Rochester War Memorial (New York)—"Terrapin" into "Playin' "; "space" into "Iko-Iko"; "China Cat" in mid–first set.

9/6, State Fairgrounds (Lewiston, Maine)—Long second set with "Shakedown" split "Uncle John's," killer "Playin'."

10/10, Warfield Theater (San Francisco)—Acoustic set with "Bird Song," "Heaven Help the Fool," "To Lay Me Down"; "Scarlet-Fire"; "Nobody's Fault" jam.

10/14, Warfield Theater—Acoustic set with "China Doll"; first electric set "Let It Grow" into "The Wheel"; "Morning Dew"; "Scarlet-Fire"; "Terrapin."

10/31, Radio City Music Hall (New York City)—Fine acoustic set; "space" into "Fire on the Mountain" into "Not Fade Away"; encore of "Uncle John's."

12/31, Oakland Auditorium (California)—Acoustic set; "Sugar Mag" into "Scarlet-Fire"; guest appearance by John Cipollina.

1981

Plenty of good shows in 1981, but no earthshaking changes in the format. Brent's bluesy "Good Times Blues" is the only new Dead tune. "Man Smart, Woman Smarter" is the only important new cover tune. "It's All Over Now, Baby Blue" and "Cumberland Blues" turn up for the first time since 1974. The band plays two short tours of Europe (March and October). During the December New Year's run, the Dead back Joan Baez (who was dating Mickey Hart at the time) a couple of nights. An album they recorded with her during this period remains unreleased.

3/28/81, Gruga Halle (Essen, Germany)—Pete Townshend on "Not Fade Away" and others; pre-drums "Other One."

5/6, Nassau Coliseum (Uniondale, New York)—"High Time"; long, completely psychedelic jam after "He's Gone"; "The Other One."

5/16, Cornell University (Ithaca, New York)—"High Time"; "Nobody's Fault" jam; "Uncle John's" encore.

7/10, St. Paul Arena (Minnesota)—"Uncle John's" split by "Playin' " and "China Doll"; "Good Lovin'."

8/28, Long Beach Arena (California)—"Let It Grow" into "China Cat-Rider" in first set; "Shakedown"; pre-"drums" "Wheel."

8/31, Aladdin Theater (Las Vegas)—"Scarlet-Fire"; "Playin' "; "Morning Dew."

9/12, Greek Theater (Berkeley, California)—"Shakedown," "Bird Song," and "China Cat" in first set; fab "Scarlet-Fire"; "Good Lovin' " second encore.

9/26, Buffalo War Memorial (New York)—"Shakedown"; "Playin' " to open second set; "Estimated Prophet" into "Goin' Down the Road."

10/16, Melk Weg Club (Amsterdam)—Bizarre song list includes "Hully Gully," "Gloria," and first post-Pigpen "Lovelight." Also acoustic set.

12/31, Oakland Auditorium (California)—Best New Year's show of the Eighties. Acoustic first set has Dead backing Joan Baez; second

Berkeley's Greek Theater, 1985. *(Photo by Ron Delany)*

electric set with classics galore (and guest John Cipollina); third set opens with "Dark Star."

1982

There are no major changes in the repertoire during the first half of 1982. In July, "Crazy Fingers" appears for the first time since 1976. August and September see the introduction of several new songs: "West L.A. Fadeaway," "Keep Your Day Job," "Touch of Grey," and "Throwing Stones." The band plays its two biggest concerts of the Eighties during this year: the Us Festival in Southern California (September 5) and the Jamaica World Music Festival (October 26).

4/6/82, The Spectrum (Philadelphia)—Hot twelve-song first set; "Shakedown"; "Other One"→"Morning Dew"→"Sugar Magnolia."

4/18, Hartford Civic Center (Connecticut)—Phil's "Earthquake Space" rap into "The Other One"; "Sugar Magnolia" into "Playin'" reprise into "Sunshine Daydream."

4/19, Baltimore Civic Center—"The Raven"; rockin' "Stranger"→"Franklin's Tower"; first set "Cumberland" into "Man Smart."

The band at San Francisco's Warfield Theater, 1982. *(Photo by Clayton Call)*

7/18, Ventura County Fairgrounds (California)—"Samson" into "Franklin's Tower"; first "Crazy Fingers" since 1976; "Satisfaction" encore.

7/31, Manor Downs (Austin, Texas)—"Scarlet-Fire"; "Uncle John's"; "Morning Dew."

8/3, Starlight Theater (Kansas City)—Superb eleven-song first set (long for 1982); "To Lay Me Down" and "Let It Grow" in second set; post-"drums" "He's Gone."

8/7, Alpine Valley Music Theater (East Troy, Wisconsin)—Twelve-song first set with "Music Never Stopped" joined to "Sugaree," "On the Road Again," and more; "Playin' "; "Morning Dew."

9/17, Cumberland County Civic Center (Augusta, Maine)—First "Throwing Stones"; "High Time"; Spanish jam into "The Other One"; "Goin' Down the Road."

10/10, Frost Amphitheater (Palo Alto, California)—First-set "China Cat"; exquisite "Playin' " into "Crazy Fingers" to open second set; "Lost Sailor"–"Saint" into "Touch of Grey" before "drums."

12/31, Oakland Auditorium (California)—Third set with Etta James leading the Dead and the Tower of Power horns through "Hard to Handle," "Lovelight," "Tell Mama." John Cipollina is featured as a second-set guest.

1983

Weir introduces two new songs: "My Brother Esau" and "Hell in a Bucket." Notable revivals include "Help on the Way" and "Slipknot" (the first since 1977) and, in October, three stabs at the original late-Sixties arrangement of "St. Stephen." New covers include "Wang Dang Doodle" and "Revolution," neither of which becomes very common. For a few shows, Weir plugs a silly new verse into "The Other One," but fortunately it doesn't catch on. Otherwise it's business as usual in 1983, with both first and second sets averaging about eight songs each.

4/12/83, Broome County Arena (Binghamton, New York)— "Help on the Way"; "Lost Sailor"–"Saint of Circumstance"; "Other One."

4/17, Brendan Byrne Arena (East Rutherford, New Jersey)— Stephen Stills sings "Love the One You're With"; "Help on the Way"; "Playin'."

5/14, Greek Theater (Berkeley, California)—"Shakedown"; "Playin' "; "Morning Dew."

6/18, Saratoga Performing Arts Center (New York)—"Scarlet-Fire"; "Playin' "; "Not Fade Away" into "Touch of Grey."

8/29, Hult Center (Eugene, Oregon)—"China Cat"; "The Other One"; "Goin' Down the Road."

9/6, Red Rocks Amphitheater (Morrison, Colorado)—"Lazy Lightning"; "Help on the Way"; long "Playin'."

9/11, Santa Fe Downs—Tremendous "Help on the Way"; second-set "Let It Grow"; gnarly "Wang Dang Doodle."

10/11, Madison Square Garden (New York City)—First "St. Stephen" in nearly five years; "Wang Dang" opener; "Bertha" into "China Doll"(?!)

10/15, Hartford Civic Center (Connecticut)—Best of the three 1983 versions of "St. Stephen"; "Playin' "; "Let It Grow."

10/31, Marin Veterans Auditorium (San Rafael, California)— "Help on the Way"; Airto on "drums"; final "St. Stephen" of the Eighties.

1984

No new Garcia or Weir tunes, but Brent has a few: the depressing "Don't Need Love," "Only a Fool," and "Tons of Steel." Two of the new covers indicate Phil's reemergence as a singer in the band: "Gimme Some Lovin' " and "Why Don't We Do It in the Road?" Brent brings in "Dear Mr. Fantasy," and Bob tackles the Beatles' "Day Tripper" and a pair of old Pigpen chestnuts, "Lovelight" and "Smokestack Lightning." He also revives "Dancin' in the Streets" in its pre-disco arrangement. Generally a strong year.

4/1/84, Marin Veterans Auditorium (San Rafael, California)— "Help on the Way"; "Terrapin"; "Morning Dew."

6/14, Red Rocks Amphitheater (Morrison, Colorado)—First "Dear Mr. Fantasy"; "Shakedown"; "Playin' " reprise.

6/27, Merriweather Post Pavilion (Columbia, Maryland)—"Let It Grow"; "Help on the Way"; first "Why Don't We Do It in the Road?"

7/6, Alpine Valley Music Center (East Troy, Wisconsin)—"Dear Mr. Fantasy" into "The Other One"; "Bird Song"; "Let It Grow."

7/13, Greek Theater (Berkeley, California)—First "Dark Star" since 1981; "Scarlet" into "Touch of Grey" into "Fire."

7/15, Greek Theater—"Dancin' in the Streets" into "Bird Song" opens first set; "Do It in the Road" into "China Cat" opens second set; "China Doll."

10/9, The Centrum (Worcester, Massachusetts)—"Help on the Way"; second set "Jack Straw"; "Revolution" encore.

10/12, Augusta Civic Center (Maine)—Zippy first set; "Uncle John's" split by "drums" and "space" and "Playin' " reprise; epic "Morning Dew."

11/2, Berkeley Community Theater (California)—"Smokestack Lightning" and "Spoonful" in first set; first "Gimme Some Lovin' "; "Wharf Rat" before "drums." Show of the year?

11/3, Berkeley Community Theater—Second set "Stranger" into "Cumberland"; gritty "Gloria"; "Uncle John's."

1985

The Dead's twentieth-anniversary year is probably my favorite of the Eighties, with nearly every show from June until New Year's a knockout. The most interesting revival is the "Cryptical Envelopment" section of "That's It for the Other One," played for the first time since 1972. Paired with "The Other One," it appears in several shows during the summer before being retired again. There are also many outstanding versions of "Comes a Time" (dormant since 1980) beginning in June. The Phil-Brent team offers a few workouts on "Keep On Growing," and Garcia hits pay dirt with several spine-tingling readings of Dylan's "She Belongs to Me." At year's end he introduces his version of Dylan's "The Mighty Quinn." The final "Help on the Way" for four years occurs in September. "Werewolves of London" is a one-shot on Halloween (though the Garcia Band has played it several times since, also on Halloween). "Big Boy Pete" is played for the only time since 1970.

3/28/85, Nassau Coliseum (Uniondale, New York)—"Truckin'," "High Time," and "China Cat" in first set; "Scarlet-Fire," "The Other One."

6/14, Greek Theater (Berkeley, California)—First of the twentieth-anniversary shows, with the debut of "Keep On Growing," "Morning Dew" to open the second set, and first "Comes a Time" in five years.

6/16, Greek Theater—First "That's It for the Other One" since 1972; spectacular "Scarlet-Fire."

6/27, Saratoga Performing Arts Center (New York)—"Crazy Fingers," "Supplication" jam and "High Time" in first set; "Stranger"→"Eyes of the World" combo in second.

7/1, Merriweather Post Pavilion (Columbia, Maryland)—"Dancin' " and "Let It Grow" in first set; "Scarlet-Fire"; "Dear Mr. Fantasy"→ "Goin' Down the Road."

9/3, Starlight Theater (Kansas City)—Complete "That's It for the Other One" to open second set; rare "Nobody's Fault"; "Comes a Time."

9/7, Red Rocks Amphitheater (Morrison, Colorado)—"Shakedown"; "Uncle John's"; first "Hey Jude" coda after "Dear Mr. Fantasy."

9/12, Kaiser Convention Center (formerly the Oakland Auditorium)—Incredible "Help on the Way"; "Playin' in the Band"; "The Other One."

9/15, Devore Field (Chula Vista, California)—"Scarlet-Fire"; "She Belongs to Me"; "U.S. Blues" out of "space"; "Satisfaction."

11/1, Richmond Coliseum (Virginia)—"Lost Sailor"–"Saint of Circumstance" split by "drums"; "High Time"; "Gloria."

1986

An uneven year, with both great peaks and a fair amount of sloppy playing. The big event of the spring is the return of "Box of Rain" for the first time since 1973. Garcia plays just two versions of "Visions of Johanna" before abandoning it. Weir drops "Lost Sailor," though its partner, "Saint of Circumstance," continues to show up occasionally the next couple of years. In the early summer, the band plays a few dates in stadiums on the same bill as Bob Dylan and Tom Petty and the Heartbreakers, and Dylan even joins the Dead onstage for a few songs. A few days after the tour ends, Garcia slips into a diabetic coma and nearly dies. Summer and fall shows are canceled, but the band triumphantly returns in mid-December with the slimmer, fitter Garcia sounding better than ever vocally. At the "comeback" shows he even introduces two new songs: "When Push Comes to Shove" and "Black Muddy River."

2/8/86, Kaiser Convention Center (Oakland, California)—"Half-Step" into "Franklin's Tower"; "China Doll"; classic "Gimme Some Lovin' " out of "space."

3/24, The Spectrum (Philadelphia)—Second-set "High Time"; final "Lost Sailor"; "Morning Dew."

3/27, Cumberland County Civic Center (Augusta, Maine)—Only

"Revolutionary Hamstrung Blues"; "Supplication" jam in first set; "Bertha" into "Wang Dang Doodle"; space into "Spanish jam."

3/28, Cumberland County Civic Center—"Box of Rain" to close first set; "Playin' " into "Franklin's" to open the second set; two more "Playin' " jams.

5/4, Cal Expo Amphitheater (Sacramento, California)—First-set "China Cat"; "Uncle John's"; "Box of Rain" encore.

7/4, Rich Stadium (Buffalo)—"Cold Rain" into "Fire on the Mountain"; rare pre-drums "Wheel"; "Uncle John's Band."

12/15, Oakland Coliseum (California)—The triumphant return after Garcia's illness, opening with (of course) "Touch of Grey"; first "Black Muddy River"; "Wharf Rat."

12/16, Oakland Coliseum—Jammin' "Estimated Prophet"–"Eyes of the World"; Neville Brothers on "space," "Iko," "Willie and the Hand Jive."

12/28, Kaiser Convention Center—"Scarlet-Fire"; very heavy "Black Peter"; "Baby Blue."

12/31, Kaiser Convention Center—"U.S. Blues" as first-set closer; second-set "Let It Grow"; third set with "Gimme Some Lovin'," "Box of Rain," and more.

1987

During the first few months of the year, the band is still finding its footing again after Garcia's return. Still, there are a number of excellent, high-energy shows, particularly on the spring East Coast tour. In the summer, the Dead and Dylan tour together again, only this time the six shows include a long set of the Dead backing Dylan, in addition to Dead sets sans Dylan. While the Dylan-Dead collaboration isn't fully successful in my view (another few shows might have really made a difference), their shows together are still fascinating, and it is easily the most melodic music Dylan has made since the Seventies. An album from the tour is released in 1989. There are no original Dead tunes this year, but new covers include Weir's versions of two Dylan classics, "When I Paint My Masterpiece" and "All Along the Watchtower"; Brent rockin' on the Neville Brothers' "Hey Pocky Way" and Mitch Ryder's "Devil With a Blue Dress On"; Garcia's spirited workout on "La Bamba," which he inserts into "Good Lovin' " for a few shows on the fall East Coast tour; and "Knockin' on Heaven's Door." *In the Dark,* the band's first studio album in eight years, is released and nearly hits the top of the charts.

Grateful Dead stadium rock—Rich Stadium in Buffalo. *(Photo by Ron Delany)*

"Touch of Grey" becomes the band's first (and only) Top 10 single. Many of the fall 1987 shows are killers, though there isn't much real jamming, and transitions between songs in the second sets are usually short.

4/4/87, The Centrum (Worcester, Massachusetts)—"Comes a Time"; "Willie and the Hand Jive"; "Playin' " reprise into "Morning Dew."

6/13, Ventura County Fairgrounds (California)—First "When I Paint My Masterpiece"; "Shakedown"; "Saint of Circumstance; "The Other One."

6/21, Greek Theater (Berkeley, California)—"Cumberland" into "Mexicali"; "Saint of Circumstance" into "China Doll" into "Playin'."

7/6, Pittsburgh Civic Center—"Shakedown"; members of the Neville Brothers help out on "Iko," "Day-O," "Knockin' on Heaven's Door" (out of "space"!), and other second-set tunes.

7/8, Roanoke Civic Center (Virginia)—"Scarlet-Fire"; hilarious "Truckin' "; last "Comes a Time" of the Eighties.

7/12, Giants Stadium (East Rutherford, New Jersey)—Second set opens with "Morning Dew"; third set backing Dylan is probably best of the Dead-Dylan pairings.

7/24, Oakland Stadium (California)—Rockin' second set ends with

"Miracle"–"Bertha"–"Sugar Mag"; another excellent Dead-Dylan set.→→→.

8/23, Mountain Aire Festival (Calaveras, California)—Carlos Santana jams on first-set versions of "Iko" and "Watchtower"; second set has great "Scarlet-Fire," "Morning Dew."

9/18, Madison Square Garden (New York City)—"Shakedown"; stupendous "Morning Dew"; "Good Lovin' " into "La Bamba."

11/14, Long Beach Arena (California)—"Hey Pocky Way"; one of only two pairings of "Maggie's Farm" and "Cumberland"; great false ending on "Lovelight."

1988

A very strong year, with more spacey playing all the way around and slightly less predictable song choices than 1987. Half of the songs that would make up the 1989 album *Built to Last* are debuted during June of 1988, including "Foolish Heart," "Victim or the Crime," "Blow Away," and "I Will Take You Home." Another Garcia song introduced at the same time, "Believe It or Not," remains unrecorded. The song "Built to Last" has its maiden voyage in October. In the spring, Weir sings a few versions of Dylan's "Ballad of a Thin Man," and Brent unveils a slinky rendition of "Louie Louie." "To Lay Me Down" returns after a five-year absence. Popular pairings this year include "The Wheel" with "Gimme Some Lovin'," and "I Need a Miracle" with "Dear Mr. Fantasy" followed by the coda from "Hey Jude."

3/16/88, Kaiser Convention Center (Oakland, California)—Unbelievable "Fire on the Mountain"; "Watchtower"; "Morning Dew."

3/27, Hampton Coliseum (Virginia)—"Sugar Mag" into "Scarlet-Fire"; first "To Lay Me Down" in four years; debut of "Ballad of a Thin Man." Best show of 1988?

4/13, Rosemont Horizon (Chicago)—"Sugar Mag" into "Bertha"; "space" into the "Playin' " reprise; "Morning Dew" into "Sunshine Daydream."

4/22, Irvine Meadows (Laguna Hills, California)—"Half-Step"–"Stranger"–"Franklin's" opener; soulful "Louie Louie."

6/28, Saratoga Performing Arts Center (New York)—"Foolish Heart" close for first set; scorching "Scarlet-Fire"; "Estimated" into "Crazy Fingers."

7/2, Oxford Plains Speedway (Oxford, Maine)—Long first set; "Uncle John's" into "Terrapin."

7/17, Greek Theater (Berkeley, California)—"Foolish Heart" opener; excellent "Box of Rain"; rare "Believe It or Not."

7/29, Laguna Seca Recreation Area (Monterey, California)— "China Cat"→"Crazy Fingers"→"I Know You Rider"; wildest "Playin' " of the Eighties.

9/24, Madison Square Garden (New York City)—Occasionally inspired rain forest benefit with the Dead joined by Suzanne Vega, Mick Taylor, Hall and Oates.

12/28, Oakland Coliseum (California)—"Jack Straw" close in first set; superb "I Need a Miracle" jam into a late-second-set "Foolish Heart."

1989

At the beginning of the year, three more songs from *Built to Last* are played for the first time: "Standing on the Moon," "Just a Little Light," and "We Can Run." "Picasso Moon" premieres in April. The real excitement in this generally hot musical year comes in the fall, when a slew of old tunes are revived: "Dark Star" (last played in 1984), "Help on Way" (1985), "Attics of My Life" (1972), and "Death Don't Have No Mercy" (1970). And during the summer tour, they break out "We Bid You Goodnight" for the first time in twelve years. Musically, the biggest change in the band's sound is Garcia's MIDI guitar, introduced in the late spring. All of a sudden songs we've heard a thousand times have entirely new textures: electronic trumpets, saxophones, you name it. The "space" jams also take on an exciting new dimension.

2/11/89, Great Western Forum (Inglewood, California)—The first great "Standing on the Moon"; Airto and Flora Purim join the Rhythm Devils; "Eyes of the World" out of "space."

4/6, Crisler Arena (Ann Arbor, Michigan)—"Bird Song"; "Scarlet-Fire"; long pairing of "Playin' " and "Built to Last."

6/19, Shoreline Amphitheater (Mountain View, California)— Very trippy "Bird Song"; superb versions of "I Know You Rider," "Watchtower," "Black Peter," "Not Fade Away."

8/4, Cal Expo Amphitheater (Sacramento, California)— "Truckin' " opens second set; combo of "Cumberland" and "Eyes of the World."

8/19, Greek Theater (Berkeley, California)—One of the best versions of "The Other One" in modern times; "Uncle John's," "Wharf Rat."

10/8, Hampton Coliseum (Virginia)—The return of "Help on the Way" after a five-year absence; "Morning Dew."

10/9, Hampton Coliseum—First "Dark Star" since 1984; "Playin' " as second-set opener; "Death Don't Have No Mercy"; first "Attics of My Life" since 1971.

10/16, Brendan Byrne Arena (New Jersey)—"Picasso Moon" opener; "Let It Grow" with MIDI "horns"; "Dark Star" to open second set; second verse of "Dark Star" into "Attics of My Life."

10/19, The Spectrum (Philadelphia)—Best 1989 "Help on the Way"; "Estimated"–"Eyes"; "Death Don't Have No Mercy."

10/26, Miami Arena (Florida)—Second set opens with "Estimated"; interplanetary "Dark Star."

1990

The spring tour is tremendous from beginning to end and yields most of the live album released in the fall of 1990, *Without a Net*. On that tour, Weir road-tests a new version of "Black-Throated Wind," missing in action since 1974. (Later in the year he goes back to the original words, for the most part.) Another tune from that period, "Loose Lucy," is revived in a perkier arrangement by Garcia. The most interesting new cover is "The Weight" (by the Band), with Jerry, Bob, Brent, and Phil each singing a verse à la the Band. Of course, the big event of 1990 is the death of Brent Mydland shortly after the end of a very strong summer tour. He's replaced by former Tubes and Todd Rundgren keyboardist Vince Welnick in time for a fall eastern swing. And the keyboard slot is further augmented by the addition of Bruce Hornsby on grand piano and (occasionally) accordion for shows at Madison Square Garden in New York and all but one of the concerts on the band's October European tour (first in six years.) The septet is going strong at year's end; the infusion of new blood clearly gives the group a burst of fresh creative energy.

3/29/90, Nassau Coliseum (Uniondale, New York)—A classic with Branford Marsalis on sax for "Bird Song," sequence of "Eyes"→"Estimated"→"Dark Star," and more.

3/30, Nassau Coliseum—"Help on the Way"–"Slipknot"–"Franklin's Tower" show opener; "China Doll"→"Uncle John's"→"Terrapin" sequence; "Attics" encore.

6/8, Cal Expo Amphitheater (Sacramento, California)—"High Time"; "Uncle John's" into "China Cat" opens second set; "Fire"-like jam after "Foolish Heart."

6/23, Autzen Stadium (Eugene, Oregon)—"Me and My Uncle" into "Cumberland"; fine "Eyes" to open second set; "Playin' " and "Playin' " reprise split by "Uncle John's"; "Morning Dew."

7/12, RFK Stadium (Washington, D.C.)—"Foolish Heart" into a very strong "Dark Star"; "Dear Mr. Fantasy" into "Touch of Grey."

9/19, Madison Square Garden (New York City)—Outstanding "Help on the Way"–"Slipknot"–"Franklin's Tower" to end the first set; "Uncle John's" into rare second-set "Let It Grow"; fine Garcia-Hornsby jam before "drums."

9/20, Madison Square Garden—Post-"drums" "Dark Star" split by "Playin' " reprise; "Touch of Grey" closer; "Lovelight" encore.

10/20, The ICC (Berlin, Germany)—Long "Dark Star" split by "drums" and "space"; "Black-Throated Wind"; second set opens with "Eyes" into great "Samson."

12/12, McNichols Arena (Denver, Colorado)—Sequence of "Iko," "Dark Star," "Terrapin"; "Mexicali"–"Maggie's Farm"; "The Weight."

12/31, Oakland Coliseum (California)—More jamming with Branford Marsalis on "Eyes," "Dark Star," "The Other One," etc.; Hamza El-Din and Mickey duet.

1991

Another strong year for the band, as Bruce Hornsby and Vince Welnick settle into their roles as the Dead's new keyboardists. (Hornsby misses occasional shows because of his busy schedule, but otherwise seems fairly committed to playing with the band whenever he can.) No new original songs are introduced, but a few beloved covers are revived, including "New Speedway Boogie," which hadn't been played since 1970, "Might as Well," "Attics of My Life," and "The Last Time" (the last two absent since Brent's death). Dylan's "It Takes a Lot to Laugh, It Takes a Train to Cry," sung by Garcia, turns up as part of a medley with "C. C. Rider." "Reuben and Cherise," long a staple of the Jerry Garcia Band, receives four playings by the Dead before it vanishes from the repertoire. The most interesting trend in 1991 is the "Dark Star" tease, in which the band toys with that song for a few seconds or even a couple of minutes at odd points in a show. There are also several full-blown versions of "Dark Star" in 1991. It's a good year for Dead-related bands, too: The Garcia Band mounts a successful East Coast and Midwest tour in support of their excellent live album; Mickey Hart's *Planet Drum* album, book, and concert tour are ecstatically received by both Deadheads and world music fans; and Bob Weir and Rob Wasserman make several forays into the heartland for shows in small theaters.

2/21/91, Oakland Coliseum (California)—Chinese New Year show with "Help on the Way"–"Slipknot"–"Franklin's Tower" opener, long "Playin' in the Band," "drums" with Airto, and post-"drums" "Eyes."

4/1, Greensboro Coliseum (North Carolina)—Extraordinary stretch linking "Dark Star," "drums," "space," more "Dark Star," and the "Playin' " reprise. Ultra-spacey.

4/7, Orlando Arena (Florida)—First set includes "Black-Throated Wind" and "Reuben and Cherise"; "Crazy Fingers"→"Playin' "→ "Uncle John's" sequence; "Box of Rain" out of "space."

6/17 Giants Stadium (East Rutherford, New Jersey)—Several short "Dark Star" jams/teases; first "Eyes of the World" opener ever; "New Speedway Boogie" into "Uncle John's."

6/22, Soldiers Field (Chicago)—Fantastic "Shakedown Street"; "Foolish Heart"; "Terrapin"; "Dark Star" jam out of "space."

6/25, Sandstone Amphitheater (Bonner Springs, Kansas)—"Scarlet-Fire"; rare "Comes a Time" into "Goin' Down the Road."

9/10, Madison Square Garden (New York City)—Branford Marsalis plays on entire show, including "Shakedown," "Help on the Way," "Dark Star," "Estimated." Incredibly powerful!

9/25, Boston Garden—Fine "Help on the Way" opener; "Crazy Fingers"→"Playing' "→"Terrapin"; only version of McCartney's "That Would Be Something."

9/26, Boston Garden—"Dark Star" into "Saint of Circumstance" opens second set; "The Other One" into reprise of "Dark Star"; "Attics of My Life."

10/31, Oakland Coliseum—"Dark Star" with Quicksilver's Gary Duncan on guitar and Ken Kesey's rap about Bill Graham's death; "The Last Time"; "Werewolves of London" encore (for Halloween).